OUT OF ATHENS

OUT OF ATHENS

The New Ancient Greeks

Page duBois

Harvard University Press
Cambridge, Massachusetts
London, England

Copyright © 2010 by the President and Fellows of Harvard College
All rights reserved
Printed in the United States of America

First Harvard University Press paperback edition, 2012

Library of Congress Cataloging-in-Publication Data
DuBois, Page.
Out of Athens : the new ancient Greeks / Page duBois.
p.   cm.
Includes bibliographical references and index.
ISBN 978-0-674-03558-4 (cloth: alk. paper)
ISBN 978-0-674-06407-2 (pbk.)
1. Greek literature—History and criticism.   2. Greek literature—Influence.
3. Greece—Civilization.   I. Title.
PA3052.D83   2010
880.9'001—dc22   2009017347

For John Daley

CONTENTS

	Acknowledgments	ix
1	Prologue	1
2	Spartacus	27
3	Sappho between Africa and Asia	40
4	The Tattoos of Epimenides	57
5	Slaves in the Tragic City	72
6	Alexandrias	91
7	Histories of the Impossible	114
8	Jesus and Other Jews	130
9	The Persistence of Oedipus	157
10	Twenty-first-Century High Theory and the Classics	173
	Notes	201
	Index	233

ACKNOWLEDGMENTS

This book is about webs and networks—proliferating, unpredictable connections. I find myself in such a web stretching between past and future, and across continents, neither a spider nor a fly, but a potato or an orchid in a vast system, owing much to many.

I thank my teachers William Darling, Ted Doyle, and Jean-Pierre Vernant.

I thank the doctors Sara Hurvitz and Helena Chang, and the practical and compassionate Heather Lewin. And Dr. Tai-Nan Wang, teacher, healer, and friend. And Antonia Meltzoff most of all.

I thank my friends Melvyn Freilicher and Joe Keenan, Lisa Lowe, Don Wayne, Helen Deutsch and Michael Meranze, Mary Kelly, Susan Smith and Sheldon Nodelman, Kate Harper and Harper Page Marshall. Thanks to Dean Michael Bernstein.

I am grateful to many colleagues who invited me to speak and write, at the University of Chicago; the University of Crete at Rethymnon; at Duke University; in Paris, Evanston, and New York: Anastasia Serghidou, Hollis Clayton, Ahuvia Kahane, Jonathan Hall, Shadi Bartsch and David Wray, Stephen Moore, Phiroze Vasunia and Srinivas Aravamudan, Tom Habinek, David Roselli. Thanks to Susanna Lee and Rita Felski. And to Julia Stern and Bonnie Honig.

No chapter of this book reprints verbatim entire articles or essays previously published. But I have drawn on sentences, paragraphs, and arguments from earlier work in writing *Out of Athens:* "The Coarsest Demand: Utopia and the Fear of Slaves," in *Peur de l'esclave—Peur de l'esclavage en Méditerranée ancienne,* ed. A. Serghidou (Besançon: Presses universitaires de Franche-Comté, 2007), 435–444; " 'The History of the Impossible': Ancient Utopia," *Classical Philology* 101 (2006), 1–14;

"Reading the Writing on the Wall," *Classical Philology* 102 (2007), 45–56; "Oedipus as Detective: Sophocles, Simenon, and Robbe-Grillet," *Yale French Studies* 108, 102–115; "Toppling the Hero: Polyphony in the Tragic City," *New Literary History* 35 (2004), 63–81.

Thanks to James Porter, for my title, and to my students at UC Irvine, especially Kourtney Murray, Jesse Weiner, and Debra Freas.

Thank you, Sharmila Sen, for being an inspiring and inspired editor.

Sappho says the most beautiful thing on the dark earth is what one loves; I love John Daley.

OUT OF ATHENS

1

PROLOGUE

The neighborhood Mexican restaurant where I dine in Los Angeles has on its wall a florid poster advertising the bullring in Barcelona, embellished with the figure of a torero flourishing a brilliant red cape. One of the fighters listed on the program is "Espartaco," named after, long after, the Thracian gladiator who led a rebellious army of slaves—up to 120,000 followers—against several Roman armies until he was defeated in 71 B.C.E. The name survives from an ancient colonized Thrace to a slave gladiators' school in Capua, through slave resistance to Roman empire, to an emblem of an ancient proletariat, through novels and film to a Catalonian corrida, to the one-time colony of Mexico and its incorporation into imperial and hybrid California and onto the Worldwide Web, where Espartaco's history of victories, bulls' ears and all, is listed on his Web site: www.portaltaurino.com/matadores/espartaco.

Disciplining Antiquity

In the current circumstances of globalization and postcoloniality, it seems ever more imperative to attend to the ways in which traditional disciplines in the humanities, based as they are on nationalisms or on élite culture, no longer reflect the state of scholarship in the human sciences or the state of the world of readers. Classics is a striking example of these difficulties: Much work in the field still centers on high classical Athens and Rome, urban capitals that exemplified antiquity for many centuries but represent only a tiny portion of the ancient world, let alone the contacts constantly made in practice between the Greeks and Romans and the rest of the ancient world. Our present, too, contains constant engagement with ancient thinking and ancient objects. In this book, I point to tendencies that have long been visible in classical studies, from the work of Gregory Nagy and others on connections between Greek and Vedic poetry, to Jean-Pierre Vernant and Jacques Gernet's comparative study of ancient Greece and ancient China.[1] I argue for a new definition of classical studies no longer confined to Athens, Rome, and their later "reception." This book has its affinities with the work of such scholars as M. L. West, who has insisted on Greek links with Southwestern Asian culture and with the "East"; with Walter Burkert, who has long drawn connections with the ancient Near East and the Greeks; with the ongoing comparativist studies of Marcel Detienne; and with the work of Dan Selden, Phiroze Vasunia, Mary Beard, and Simon Goldhill on ancient texts and monuments and their many historical vicissitudes and persistence in the present.[2] Burkert notes, in *Babylon Memphis Persepolis* (2004), that "Greek culture had the good fortune to find successors who established a heritage and took care of it continuously, while neighboring civilizations fell victim to the ravages of time and to the victory of either Christianity or Islam. This has created the mirage of a classical civilization in isolation."[3] I differ from some of these scholars in seeing great potential in the theoretical developments of the present, and agree with some in arguing for a consideration of our own position as readers of antiquity in a globalizing present.

Although there is some recognition of "other places," and even of "other times," much work in classics is still governed by empiricist or positivist principles derived from the scientific ambitions of the German university of the nineteenth century.[4] Theoretically, the field of structuralism, which dominated literary classical studies for some decades in the hands of such eminent scholars as Charles Segal and Vernant, may have contributed to seeing the culture of Greece, in particular, as a closed entity, to be analyzed in terms of its internal relations, without paying heed to geographical and temporal extension.[5] Especially in its importation into Anglo-Saxon contexts, the work of Vernant and the Parisian school has often been uprooted, detached from the political sources and motivations of engagement, and turned into a "tool" in a toolbox of depoliticized techniques for analysis.[6] Charles Segal, one of the most gifted of readers, highly influential in his attention to theoretical tendencies new to classical philology, in his presidential address to the American Philological Association in 1994, said, "Classical studies in the United States have some of the advantages of American cuisine. That is to say, if you get tired of French or Italian you can try Russian, German, or British."[7] The danger is that such an approach can produce a deracinated, decontextualized, depoliticized importation of European ideas, where their theoretical differences are never confronted.

The best recent work on "reception" moves beyond these boundaries and engages with the *politics* of reception.[8] For example, Miriam Leonard's study of postwar French intellectuals' engagement with the classics locates with great subtlety the issues at stake in debates about Oedipus, Antigone, and Socrates, of which more in Chapter 9, "The Persistence of Oedipus." Leonard concludes her study with this call to attention: "To some extent, whether they know it or not, classicists are all Hegelians (and Foucauldians, and Vernantians and . . .) and understanding that genealogy is essential to self-understanding."[9] I would add that, although we cannot always predict or control the aftermath, political and otherwise, of our methodological choices, these are choices. We are not simply picking dishes from a cosmopolitan menu but allying ourselves with tendencies that have consequences, in terms of a desire for change and for resistance to conventional or hegemonic ideas, or for a philology that is naturalized and conservative in its intentions.

Another exemplary work of "reception" is Barbara Goff and Michael Simpson's *Crossroads in the Black Aegean: Oedipus, Antigone, and Dramas of the African Diaspora*.[10] The authors explore in detail why the particular myths of their title have been taken up in postcolonial contexts:

> To adapt or transpose any of the plays of the Theban cycle is to reflect on one of the most charged themes within anti-colonialism or postcolonial literature and theatre: that theme is identity, and the difference and violence on which it may depend . . . The Theban cycle is disposed to represent the postcolonial moment because these particular Greek dramas oscillate around the very threshold of civilization, almost prior to culture, when those taboos that are the conditions and the beginnings of social being, as they are the conditions of possibility of law, language, and exchange, are first instituted and tested. (2)

Most important, in the authors' view, are the plays' "notions of how culture is transmitted from one generation to the next and from one location to another" (2–3). "These dramatic adaptations of African descent all suppose, in virtue of their investment in the Theban plays, that one of the chief models of cultural transmission within colonial culture is that of oedipal strife overcome" (3). This is in contrast to the post–Soviet bloc's investment in the *Oresteia* "as the script for Western liberal democracy" (25). Referring to earlier histories of colonization and occupation, the authors argue, "The substance of this postcolonial contest between *Oresteia* and *Oedipus* is that Europeans seek to present themselves as Athenians with the settlement of justice to their credit, but they are revealed as Thebans with no settlement, devoted to violence, and it is this very absence of a settlement that they forcibly export to other societies" (25). Lorna Hardwick, in *Reception Studies,* recalls that Nelson Mandela, during his twenty-seven years of imprisonment on Robben Island, played Sophocles' Creon in a performance of *Antigone* (99). And this event was later addressed in Athol Fugard, Winston Ntshona, and John Kani's play, *The Island,* first performed in 1973.[11]

Goff and Simpson offer a contrast between what they characterize as "cool" versus "warm" reception studies; a warm version acknowledges texts with plural antecedents, relayed into a "transected" tradition based on theories of the transmission of culture already contained in the tradition with a self-reflexive dimension. This is in contrast to a "cool" model of transmission, "in which even time and space are measured imperially on the basis of a common standard, and all parts of the world coexist in a single medium" (35). And "constraining, as well as empowering, reception studies is precisely the fact that it is always itself an act of reception" (36). So work in reception forms part of the relay, is itself therefore limited and situated, and should be self-conscious in this regard. And should not substitute, as it may in some cases, for engagement with the ancient world as *ancient,* that is, remote in time, distant, and different from the contemporary world. Some reception studies constitute studies of contemporary culture, a way for repentant classicists to turn themselves into historians of the present, focusing only on the ways that the classics have been used in recent history and letting go of analysis of ancient objects in their own cultural context. In these cases, we are in danger of throwing out the baby with the bath water.

Along with many others in a general trend to reorient classical studies, I want to work critically with new models, including those generated by globalization and postcolonial studies and questions of subalternity, migration, and diaspora, as well as Michel Foucault's description of heterotopias, and even the paradigms of Gilles Deleuze and Félix Guattari, which are appropriate to describe, for example, the survival and return of the name of Spartacus after almost two thousand years.[12] Rather than comparing the ancient Greeks with contemporary cultures that have been the objects of anthropological scrutiny, I would prefer to consider these issues in the context of a politics of globalization. We ourselves inhabit a world of postcoloniality and increasing globalizing, and our readings of antiquity are inevitably affected by our situation in the present. As we become more conscious and more attentive to other places in the world, our readings of antiquity are enriched and deepened by a recognition of the geographical extent, the diasporic nature of ancient civilizations, from east to west and back, and into the present. The reading of Sappho, for example, is profoundly transformed when she is seen not only as one of the great poets of Greek antiquity, but also as a devotee of the goddess Aphrodite, herself akin to Ishtar and Astarte, Sappho's lyrics akin to Vedic song, all part of an Eastern Mediterranean and Eurasian culture that included not just the eastern Aegean island of Lesbos, but stretched far east, and south to Egypt and Arabia, and then recurring in the material world of 2005. Sappho is not precisely a "European," not just a poet of antiquity.

Other Models

In *Provincializing Europe,* Dipesh Chakrabarty remarks, "I am aware that an entity called 'the European intellectual tradition' stretching back to the ancient Greeks is a fabrication of relatively recent European history. Martin Bernal, Samir Amin, and others have justly criticized the claim of European thinkers that such an unbroken tradition ever existed or that it could even properly be called 'European' " (5).[13] Yet the " 'first in Europe, then elsewhere' structure of global historical time was historicist; different non-Western nationalisms would later produce local versions of the same narrative, replacing 'Europe' by some locally constructed center" (7). "This move of historicism is what Johannes Fabian has called 'the denial of coevalness' " (8).

Chakrabarty is concerned with the double bind within which the postcolonial historian works, using the models worked out on European histories to describe non-European peoples:

> Insofar as the academic discipline of history—that is, "history" as a discourse produced at the institutional site of the university—is concerned, "Europe" remains the sovereign, theoretical subject of all histories, including the ones we call "Indian," "Chinese," "Kenyan," and so on. There is a peculiar way in which all these other histories tend to become variations on a master narrative that could be called "the history of Europe." (27)

Chakrabarty is a historian of India, yet he acknowledges that in his theoretical and methodological introduction

> "Europe" and "India" are treated here as hyperreal terms in that they refer to certain figures of imagination whose geographical referents remain somewhat indeterminate . . . For the moment I shall treat them as though they were given, reified categories, opposites paired in a structure of domination and subordination. (27)

He goes on to say, "Europe works as a silent referent in historical knowledge" (28).

And although Chakrabarty is discussing modernity here, this statement holds for histories that include Greece and Rome as points of origin for the West:

> Only "Europe," the argument would appear to be, is *theoretically* (that is, at the level of the fundamental categories that shape historical thinking) knowable; all other histories are matters of empirical research that fleshes out a theoretical skeleton that is substantially "Europe." There is one version of this argument in Husserl's Vienna lecture of 1935, where he proposed that the fundamental difference between "oriental philosophies" (more specifically, Indian and Chinese) and "Greek-European science" (or as he added, "universally speaking: philosophy") was the capacity of the latter to produce "absolute theoretical insights," that is "*theoria* (universal science)," whereas the former retained a "practical-universal," and hence 'mythical-religious" character. (29)

Further, Chakrabarty says, "The world presented itself as a 'thematic' to theoria" (29).

As a historian of India and one of the founders of subaltern studies, Chakrabarty argues that the "Indian people," as "a split subject, . . . speaks from within a metanarrative that celebrates the nation-state; and of this metanarrative the theoretical subject can only be a hyperreal 'Europe,' a 'Europe' constructed by the tales that both imperialism and nationalism have told the colonized" (40). And this Europe, though a fiction, has its roots in antiquity, in Greece and Rome as the origins of Europe and of the West. Michael Hardt and Antonio Negri, in *Multitude,* link the definition of Europe to their description of the present crisis: "Spatial elements are always present in Europe's own self-definition, at times in expansive terms and at others in conflictual, tragic, and obsessive ones, from Homer's Aegean to Columbus' Atlantic."[14] As Chakrabarty acknowledges, "This Europe, like the West, is demonstrably an imaginary entity, but the demonstration as such does not lessen its appeal or power" (43).

I accept Chakrabarty's insistence or recognition that this Europe he poses is imaginary; yet further to undermine its imaginary integrity, to destabilize its originary status, to dethrone it from its primacy, seems imperative. If the imaginary Europe that led to modernity began in Athens, with the *polis,* the proto-nation, the proto-state, then we are beginning to see through, behind, beyond this story to another, of networks, diaspora, hybridity, cosmopolitanism, and contact that gainsay the representations of a hermetically sealed, miraculously democratic and philosophical Athens of the sort beloved by some political theorists.[15]

Chakrabarty cites his disagreement with Richard Rorty, writing that the latter "follows the practice of many Europeanists who speak of the histories of these 'democratic societies' as if these were self-contained histories complete in themselves, as if the self-fashioning of the West were something that occurred only within its self-assigned geographical boundaries" (45). Again, although the subject under discussion is post-Enlightenment, modern democracy, these narratives extend back to the Greeks, seen as European, as founders of the democratic European tradition.

Each of the chapters of my book, as a kind of case history, seeks to develop the notion of "other spaces," of extension, geographical and temporal, of the classical, beyond the confinement of the classical to Europe, to a European Greece focused on Athens, fixed in antiquity, in particular. Following a roughly chronological trajectory, to illustrate the heterogeneity of the classical, chapters focus on the survival of Sappho's lyrics and the intimate space of women's religious culture on Lesbos; popular culture in modernity and the tattooed magicians in ancient Greece; the multitude that undermines the tragic hero and the appearance of subaltern, exile, slave women in Athenian tragedy; the representation of slaves in the polyglot, heterogeneous African city Alexandria and subsequent transfers of knowledge and imagery along trade routes leading east and west; histories of empire and resistance in slave rebellions in Western Asia; Jesus as an inhabitant of the ancient Greek and Roman world; the survival and reemergence of the myth of Oedipus in the twentieth century; and the work of contemporary theorists engaged in debates beginning in ancient Greek society, confronting democracy, the role of philosophy, gender, the sacred exception, sovereignty, and empire. I support an opening up of the idea of the classical not only to enrich the readings we make of ancient texts, but also to bring classics more fully into engagement with the concerns of the present, for scholars as well as general readers who might see the classics not as something preserved under glass in museums, but as elements of a living present.

Resistance and "Western Civilization"

There are certainly strenuous and vocal arguments against such an extension of classical studies, against the embrace of contemporary theory or the broadening of the geographical to include other ancient civilizations in our definitions of antiquity. Many institutions in contemporary society still advocate the teaching of Western civilization to the exclusion of world civilizations, and such an advocacy often has a political dimension. In their book *Hubris: The Inside Story of Spin, Scandal, and the Selling of the Iraq War,* Michael Isikoff and David Corn describe the early planning for the Bush administration's ill-fated invasion of Iraq, a program of covert infiltration code-named, rather ominously, "Anabasis," recalling the name given to the ancient author Xenophon's account of a Greek mercenary adventure through lands now claimed by the nation-states of Turkey and Iraq and back.[16] They also recall a meeting organized by Dick Cheney that included classicist Victor Davis Hanson: "Cheney had . . . bought copies of one of Hanson's books for members of his staff, and he had assigned one of his aides to consult with Hanson regularly. Hanson was, as *New York Times* columnist Maureen Dowd acerbically dubbed him, Cheney's 'war guru'" (159). At the meeting, the group discussed Hanson's *The Soul of Battle,* profiling George Patton, General William Tecumseh Sherman, and Epaminondas of Thebes: "All three, in Hanson's study, were misunderstood figures. Each had been maligned during their day for employing ruthless tactics. But Hanson contended that their willingness to crush completely the armies of their enemies . . . had been effective" (159). "Cheney was especially interested in the 'bum rap' that Patton, Sherman, and Epaminondas had gotten in their respective day—and how each would later be vindicated by history" (159).

Victor Hanson argues for the return of the Greeks, and a purely Western tradition of civilization, to public discourse.[17] Lee Pearcy's *Grammar of Our Civility,* another text engaging in this debate, advocates a curriculum in which classics would be central again.¹⁸ His work contains a valuable account of the history of classical scholarship in America and the acute analysis of problems the discipline faces today. But I disagree with his prescription for the future, in relation both to classical studies as an academic discipline within the university, and to its place in American education. Pearcy argues, "American Classics can become the type of intellectual praxis, a best way to think about the self in action and to educate American citizens in the negotiations of culture" (144). I find persuasive arguments for the perpetuation of Greek and Roman studies in the situation of Greece and Rome at the beginnings of Western civilization, and in the fascinating study of centuries of accreted commentary on them. But we need to be less hermetic and insular, more conscious of debates about citizenship, sex and gender identity, colonization, empire, and questions of perspective, the unnamable, and indeterminacy, in the contemporary work of Judith Butler, Giorgio Agamben, Etienne Balibar, Jacques Rancière, Slavoj Žižek, Alain Badiou, Eric Santner, that can help bring classical studies into the larger debates in the humanities and social sciences. Pearcy ventriloquizes Nietzsche's *We Philologists:* "Philology as knowledge of the ancient world cannot, of course, last forever; its material is exhaustible. What cannot be exhausted is the always new adjustment every age makes to the classical world . . . This is the antinomy of philology. *The ancient world* has in fact always been understood only *in terms of the present*" (110).

Classicists sometimes rely on the argument that Greek and Latin are difficult languages, their mastery requiring extraordinary effort and years of devotion that limit the possibilities of following debates in other areas of the human sciences. But a colleague of mine once remarked on how convenient it is for Hellenists to find all ancient Greek texts on one CD-Rom of the *Thesaurus Linguae Graecae,* while he, who works in English literature, has an almost infinite set of literary materials to contend with, not to mention newspapers, and many other sorts of textual and material culture produced all over the world.

Furthermore, with respect to the place of classical studies in undergraduate education, those who work in the intellectual centers of the founding fathers, at schools and universities where the ecclesiastical foundations of the eighteenth century or earlier once focused on training Protestant ministers, using the Hebrew Bible and Cicero as their basis for formation of citizen-leaders of an enlightened republic, have a particular history in relation to ancient Greece and Rome. Yet all our students now come from families with mixed legacies, from Africa, from Asia, from Southeast Asia and South Asia, from the Pacific Islands, from Latin America, Central America, Mexico, and indigenous American societies, as well as from Europe. They all have heritages of civility and civilization.

I teach in a two-year course that surveys the history of world civilizations, from prehistory to the present. In the quarter on ancient civilizations, I teach not only ancient Greece and ancient Israel, but also Mesoamerica, Mesopotamia, Egypt, ancient India, and ancient China. Part of what interests me most about this course is the pleasure of comparison. These cultures invented forms of architecture, government, law, writing, and worship that shaped the world around them for millennia to come, that carry the authority of the "classical," the superior past. They left behind "classic" texts—texts that are regarded as canonical: the Hebrew Bible in ancient Israel, providing the foundations of Jewish and Christian and Islamic religious traditions; Homer, Herodotus, and Thucydides, the tragedians, Plato's dialogues, inventing philosophy as a discipline; the Bhagavad Gita, setting out Hindu forms of polytheist devotion; the writings of Confucius, preserving principles of social order for millennia of Chinese culture.[19]

Teaching these texts, coming from the perspective of a multiplicity of ancient civilizations, one sees Greek and Roman civilization, the "West," not as inevitable, but as one particular permutation in a series of developments across the world, in relation to specialization of labor; growing densities of population; expansions of sovereignty, urbanization, monumental architecture; the invention and transmission of writing systems; ideologies of rule, along with the concomitant resistances to civilization, as it brings stratification and gender oppression.[20] The specificity of Western European institutions, as well as their descent from Mesopotamian and Near Eastern developments, emerge with greater clarity when set against the evolution of institutions in other places in the same ancient period.

Comparison

In *The Ambitions of Curiosity: Understanding the World in Ancient Greece and China*, G. E. R. Lloyd focuses on forms of knowledge, among them versions of history in the West and in China:

> Herodotus and Thucydides share with Sima Qian not just a commemorative but also didactic and advisory ambitions. The beginnings of historiography

in both cultures are political. But the ways they negotiate those functions vary, reflecting differences both in their own positions and in the political realities they faced. Both ancient Greece and ancient China (among other ancient societies) came to use the active study of the past as a resource for understanding the present and anticipating the future... However, the routes Greece and China took to develop those potentials were different, and so too were their end-results. Call one the official, the other the unofficial, route.[21]

The freedom of Herodotus and Thucydides from imperial oversight meant that they had neither bureaucratic security nor the archival resources of a great state. "The early Greek historians had neither the advantages nor the drawbacks of an Emperor in the wings, none of the support an official position could offer, but none of the constraints either." "Historiography, in China, was an affair of state" (19). Although Sima Qian had the resources of the state, along with the economic security of belonging to an imperial apparatus, he could not tell just any story he liked. And, through the intimate voice in the letter to Ren An, written probably in 93 or 91 B.C.E., we learn of the terrible price he paid for his proximity to and dependence on the imperial court. Having displeased the emperor for speaking of a friend's merits, he was "thrown into the 'silkworm chamber' [where castrations are performed]."[22] Choosing not to commit suicide, the honorable path, he lived as a eunuch, suffering great humiliation in order to complete his historical work:

> I have gathered up and brought together all the old traditions of the world that were scattered and lost... Before I had finished my rough manuscript, I met with this calamity. It is because I regretted that it had not been completed that I submitted to the extreme penalty without rancor. When I have truly completed this work, I will deposit it in the Famous Mountain archives. If it may be handed down to those who will appreciate it and penetrate to the villages and great cities, then though I should suffer a thousand mutilations, what regret would I have? (236)

The extraordinary voice of this historian survives through the centuries; literacy in both ancient Greece and China provides the possibility of contact between these ancient thinkers and our present, and also allows for a perspective on the specificities of culture in both.

There are various models for comparative study. François Jullien, in *Detour and Access: Strategies of Meaning in China and Greece,* retains the shape of two reified, radically different entities in his analysis of "strategies of meaning" in Greece and in China.[23] His project is to enable a critique of Western philosophy "from the outside" (371). "As seen from China, the articulation of myth and discourse *(muthos/logos)*, such as it was conceived in Greece, *again becomes* surprising" (372). In the West, he argues, here relying on the work of Marcel Detienne in *Masters of Truth, logos* emerges from the *muthos* of the ancient "poets, sages, and soothsayers" (372): "As soon as logos ... can no longer give an account, as soon as it falters or weakens in the face of mystery, then myth takes over ... In Plato, when the work of dialectics is exhausted, myth relieves it; on a larger scale, when the discourse of knowledge, whether scientific or philosophical, admits its limitations, the discourse of belief replaces it" (372). He analyzes various texts, including treatises on military strategy, poetic writings, the works attributed to Confucius and Plato, the Taoist Wang Bi and Plotinus, observing that "indirect expression in China is of the order of rhetoric" (33). He concludes that, in contrast to "the Western confidence, which has existed since Antiquity, in the power of speaking and explaining" (372), "in China, skepticism about the word's power to explain led to a belief in the word's subtlety; the unsaid moves onto the same level as discourse as it becomes *allusive*" (373). He continues: "For the Greeks, discourse has an object, which one attempts to surround as closely as possible, whereas the Chinese recommend that the word be slackened because the proposition is all the more subtle if it only *lets* one have a glimpse. This is the essential point: through its evasiveness, the proposition plays into the hands of immanence" (375). He makes broader claims about the cultural difference between Greece and China based on his rhetorical analysis: "The Greeks favored the mimetic relationship (particularly between the perceptible and the idea) and were scarcely interested in the correlation of things ... The opposite is true for the Chinese" (375–376). "Chinese thought is relational" (376). "One thing cannot be conceived of without the other because the one is already the other; that is, it is latently present in it and necessarily refers back to it ... The world, for the Chinese, is a permanent exchange between the latent and the manifest" (376). "Detour *in itself* gives access" (377). "Isolation in principle and essence ... seems characteristic of Greek thought (377). Jullien further reduces this cultural difference to a contrast between a "detour" and a "split," "where everything refers to itself but on another plane, which it imitates and which informs it and from which it derives its reality" (378). Alluding to Heidegger, he points to the loss involved in the Western "split": "This super-world of theory has devalued the Western world; this transcendent outside has cut us off from phenomena" (378). Nonetheless, this split has allowed the West to conceive of "the ideal," the soul, and God, and, he argues, freedom (378). He ends with a very Western acknowledgment: "If there is fecundity in the evasive and the implicit . . . there is also a fascination in wishing to speak from the *closest point.* Alongside the subtlety of detour, there is the jubilation of being explicit" (379).

The problem of relying almost exclusively on Western scholars' comparative work is engaged in Marcel Detienne's practice of editing collective volumes, where the particularities of state foundation or Athenian legal practice, for example, emerge in sharp relief when compared with ideas on murder, judgment, and punishment as reported by anthropologists in diverse societies. In *Tracés de fondation,* the Indologist Charles Malamoud illuminatingly discusses the practices of Vedic culture, which are tellingly different from those of ancient Greece, in relation to the question of foundation. There are contributions in this volume concerning Japan, Taoist Chinese practices, the Hittites and the temple of Jerusalem of Judaism, the Bobo and Gourmantché and Kasena in Africa; concerning ancient Rome, the absence of foundation in Vedic India, other essays on temple and village foundation in India; two essays on South America, and several on ancient Greece, including one by Detienne himself on Apollo.[24] As noted above, Malamoud's essay concerns the *absence* of foundation in Vedic India:

> Different from the India of the classical periods, and from the traditional India we can grasp today, the India of the Vedas is silent on the question of foundations. In this vast massif of hymns and prayers, instruction on rites, of speculation and delirium on the correspondence between rites and the world, words and humankind, which are the Vedic text, we would seek in vain for any account of foundation, or even the mention of a site concerning which we might think that it is there because it was founded, and that invites men to recall and to celebrate the moment and the *raison d'être* of this beginning.[25]

Scholars find names of mountains and rivers, of regions, but the names of "localités" are very rare, obscure, and mentioned only in passing. This is not, according to Malamoud, because of a nomadic character of Vedic society, which was in fact sedentary, with a landscape of villages, cultivated fields, towns, and fortresses. Yet the texts offer a "glorification" of life in movement.

And there is no foundation of temples; "the India of the Veda rejects also the idea that the encounter of men with the gods must take place permanently in fixed locations" (184). The requirements of ritual concern orientation, nature of the ground, vegetation, proximity to water, and so forth, but these are abstract characteristics, not the specification of a particular locality. What matters is a field of connections rather than a concrete place, and there is no tradition of pilgrimage to holy sites, as in post-Vedic Hinduism. In Vedic ritual, the sacredness is coextensive with the rite but does not survive as "foundation." Even funerary rituals, based on cremation, favor the complete elimination of the dead person's remains, and when, in rare cases, a funerary tumulus is erected, it exists on the other side of an impassable barrier; these are, as Malamoud puts it, "monuments construits pour l'oubli" (monuments constructed for oblivion) (187), and in fact sites of *non*-foundation. There is also a denial of beginning, of commencement; even the so-called primal sacrifice requires the preexistence of a sacrificer. Rituals are not invented, not founded, but discovered, revealed, rituals that were always already there. Malamoud makes a firm distinction between founding and beginning a ritual; there is some danger associated with the human undertaking to perform a rite, which the author connects with the necessity to escape from the singularity of places and moments (191). The contrast with Greek practices is revealing, demonstrating the extraordinary nature of ceremonies and provisions for foundation that are taken for granted by the Greeks and the tradition they found.[26]

There are problematic issues of periodization in some of the comparanda adduced by Detienne's assembly of data, and often a reliance on Western scholarship to the exclusion of the indigenous. One notes early ventures like Jean-Pierre Vernant and Jacques Gernet's comparative work on ancient Greece and ancient China: in an exchange with Gernet, Vernant recalls the comparative work of André Haudricourt, which compared the "mentalities" of the Greeks, herders and sailors, and the Chinese:

> The domestication of animals led the herding peoples to conceive the action of a man upon his fellows—in particular the power of a king over his subjects—on the model of the relationship of the shepherd to his flocks, that is to say, as a form of direct and compelling interventions. In contrast, gardening peoples take "indirect and negative action" as their model for

human relations. For them, the best authority—that is, that which conforms most closely with the natural order—is that which, being immanent in all things, never needs to intervene.[27]

Such generalizations might cause shudders in scholars of today, but they are of bracing clarity. Typically for a French essay of this period, there is no footnote to this work, exemplifying the more casual, and more Gallocentric character of French scholarship in contrast to the "mastery" model of Anglo-Teutonic tradition. Yet such scholarship nonetheless draws attention to the varieties of human ingenuity and the differences at the beginnings of civilizations that in the present need to negotiate with each other, and are producing new and compelling hybrid forms of technology and art.

If there are various models for comparison among civilizations, few acknowledge hybridity and contact and the impure beginnings of Greece—not really European, not really Western. Even the most enlightened of classicists, such as Vernant, accepted the structural integrity of "Greek civilization" and urged comparison with other such integral societies; in his introduction to Louis Gernet's *Anthropologie de la Grèce antique,* first published in 1968, Vernant wrote:

> Despoiled of its pretension to incarnate absolute Spirit/eternal Reason, the Greek experience recovers its colour and full shape. It finds its full meaning only when confronted with great civilizations as different as those of the Near East, India, China, Africa, and pre-Columbian America; it appears as only one way among others in which human history has developed.[28]

These remarks have the great virtue of dethroning the Greeks from their pedestal as the point of origin of human civilization *tout court,* but also the limitations of a Western perspective that sees the Greeks as autonomous and isolated from the Near East, Africa, and India, a perspective now eroded by our situation within globalization, which opens up new possibilities of contact, hybridity, nomadism, transgression, and traveling in general.

Mondialisation

As Kristin Ross pointed out in discussing the invention of a program in "world literature," it is "important to rid oneself of the representation model, or the 'part for the whole' model of the globe."²⁹ "What we meant by world was merely a relational way of thinking about global culture and literature, such that students could not henceforth think about Europe or America in isolation from other global spaces."³⁰ Thinking differently about a discipline, about its historical development, rethinking protocols of inclusion and judgment, means calling into question unexamined assumptions and disciplinary practices—that is, practices of the discipline, but also the system of rewards and punishment and evaluation that defines a field. Ross insists that the word "world" in the title of the program she helped found implies "the refusal to allow our object of knowledge to be naturalized in advance, defined or delimited as either a unit of area studies or a particular historical period" (671).

Such embrace of the "world," moving beyond traditional disciplinary training, raises the problem of the impossibility of "mastering the bibliography," a traditional requirement of the address to any question or problem in the field of classics. If one desires thus to "enslave" a bibliography, to have read and consulted all possible previous writing and thinking on a particular subject, then the attempt to look beyond a rigorously always already delimited object is always already lost. Fear of venturing outside the limits, of discussing something new, unknown, unmastered, in languages unknown, can inhibit forever any attempt to look outside, beyond the familiar. So one must accept a position of humility and modesty, rely on the work of others, deplore the fact that most comparative work is now accessible only in the languages and scholarly work of the West, and nonetheless try to open up the boundaries of a rigidly defined disciplinary field.

Considering the Greeks within a global perspective, temporally and geographically extended, might entail looking at various nodal points, new kinds of spaces, contacts rather than boundaries, heterotopias inside, too, using a language of "deterritorialization" of classical studies that here justifies not only my choice of chapters, but also allows for comparative details, a focusing on similarities. This is the productive analysis of difference, looking also at contact and influence and exchange. The ways in which the specificities of different cultural situations express themselves make more visible the one Hellenists know best.

The Greek medical model, for example, entails an emphasis on structure, perhaps inherited or derived from Egyptian interest in mummification, and a knowledge of anatomy leading to surgery, in contrast to Chinese ideas of process, the sacredness of the human body as a microcosm of the whole, not to be cut into, so that process, the hydraulic model, obtains. In *The Expressiveness of the Body and the Divergence of Greek and Chinese Medicine,* Shigeshisa Kuriyama compares understandings of the human body, both objective and subjective, in these two cultures:

> We encounter a well-developed theory of the muscular body already in the works of the Greek doctor Galen (130–200 C.E.); and by the end of the Latter Han dynasty (25–220 C.E.), which produced such canonical classics as the *Huangdi neijing* and *Nanjing,* the essential outlines of classical acupuncture would be securely in place.[31]
>
> Greek pulse takers ignored the local variations that their counterparts in China found so richly telling; Chinese doctors saw nothing of muscular anatomy. (272)

The comparison between these early histories of interpreting and inhabiting the body are mutually illuminating; neither history conceived in isolation tells us so much about the inevitable naturalization of received ideas of the body.

Making the study of ancient Greece and Rome the centerpiece of education ignores the opportunities of the present. Such proposals look backward, to a time when classical studies were used as a gatekeeper for a ruling class that no longer exists in the same form. Looking forward requires that we accept our place among a great *range* of civilities and civilizations, and that we no longer assume that we have privileged access to value, truth, and a superior form of civilization, or even, as Lee Pearcy names it, a "best way" of achieving a "negotiated self." Our students need to know their neighbors, to be cosmopolites, to read the books of the Maccabees as well as *The Iliad,* the poetry of Li Po as well as Sappho, to recognize that other traditions have their beauty and importance in the new circumstances of the twenty-first century. Like many others, I am no longer willing to argue or to teach students that the West is best, that the perceived ideals of Western civilization should trump all else; this is ultimately a deeply conservative argument.[32] Should we insist on training our students to celebrate, for example, Athenian democracy, which excluded women, slaves, and metics, even if we recognize these defects, while ignoring Ashoka's reign of tolerance in Buddhist India? Or take for granted the Western emphasis on the self, on individualism? Why not encourage students to compare, to explore the rich literature and cultural evidence of other societies, ones that give more place to ecological questions, for example, like Taoism, or stress compassion, or familial identity, or definitions of existence that extend to collectivities rather than ending with the individual?

Students of the West and its cultural and political traditions have sometimes tended consciously or not to adopt the ethnocentric position that what we know is best, the culmination of human culture, in a Hegelian arrogance that disregards the great variety of human solutions to questions of the organization of society. I am not suggesting that we all set ourselves to learning Chinese and attempting to master the history of the world. But we could be more conversant in contemporary theory, in the human sciences, participate in comparative projects, learn from colleagues in other fields of ancient history, and be more open to perspectives outside of the Western and Western European and American, which have always been porous and become ever more so. Much as I continue to be fascinated by ancient Greece, and to find endless satisfaction in writing, teaching, and thinking about the Greeks, I see no compelling reason that our students should privilege the Greeks and Romans above all others. We should accept that the ancient Greek and Roman civilizations are part of *global* history, that they have had great influence on the development of Western civilization and on its sometimes imperial ambitions elsewhere.

Part of what is most interesting about current developments in classical studies is work on the contact between what were once seen as miraculous and insular cultures and the rest of the world; here I study the Hellenistic world, the complex negotiations among Pharaonic Egypt, the rest of Africa, the Maccabees, western Asia Minor, and Macedon, the societies of Asia Minor stretching to the Indus and beyond, the silk routes, all that connects worlds once seen as separate, and therefore disciplinarily discrete in the university. I do not suggest that *classicists* should stop studying and teaching Greek and Latin, the Greeks and the Romans, especially through questions of eros, gender, class, colonization, slavery, ethnicity, and empire, but only that we see the Greeks and Romans as part of a world, a part that *we* treasure and know, but that has no magical power to civilize barbarians.

Theories

Some recent work on empire, colonialism and postcolonialism, and globalization, has great value for ancient studies. To say this is not to urge the denial of the specificity of ancient culture and anachronistically to apply postmodern theory to ancient societies, but rather to argue for the urgent need for expansion of the definition of the classical in the twenty-first century. A redefinition of the classical could include other spaces in ancient Greece, especially, but also move beyond to Hellenistic, North African geographies, beyond the Mediterranean to Asia Minor and eastward as the ancient Greek and Hellenistic world came into contact with so-called Hindu and Buddhist cultures. I argue here for a classical studies that includes self-conscious consideration of the classical scholar in a twenty-first-century landscape of globalization and postcoloniality. I propose not a simplistic application of contemporary postcolonial theory to ancient history, nor an exclusive focus on reception, but rather a consideration of what, for example, work on diasporas can offer to those who study the traveling of culture over vast temporal and geographical distance.

The theoretical orientations of the present that seem to offer most to the student of classical antiquity include the works of Michel Foucault, of Gilles Deleuze and Félix Guattari, of Sigmund Freud and Jacques Lacan, of postmodern feminists, and of postcolonial and globalization theory. I will briefly discuss these sometimes fruitful and often contradictory tendencies in the current theoretical landscape, suggest ways they enable new readings of ancient texts and objects, and elaborate on some of them more fully in the chapters that follow. The chapters lie within a (Bermuda) triangle of contradiction, influenced most profoundly by postcolonial theory, especially of a Marxizing bent; by psychoanalysis; and contradictorily, by a tradition that derives from the work of Gilles Deleuze and Félix Guattari, who wrote the groundbreaking, some might say "raving," text of the twentieth century *Anti-Oedipus: Capitalism and Schizophrenia,* an attack on traditional psychoanalysis and a critique of or hymn to capitalism. In the second volume of this work, *A Thousand Plateaus,* Deleuze and Guattari set out an opposition between what they conceived as symmetrical, "arboreal" structure, and an alternate they pose, which they identify as the "rhizomic," alluding to the endlessly proliferating root system of the humble potato, for example, in contrast to an oak:

> unlike trees or their roots, the rhizome connects any point to any other point, and its traits are not necessarily linked to traits of the same nature; . . . The rhizome is reducible neither to the One nor the multiple . . . It has neither beginning nor end, but always a middle *(milieu)* from which it grows

and which it overspills. It constitutes linear multiplicities with *n* dimensions having neither subject nor object . . . Unlike a structure, which is defined by a set of points and positions, . . . the rhizome is made only of lines: lines of segmentarity in its dimensions, and the line of flight or deterritorialization as the maximum dimension after which the multiplicity undergoes metamorphosis, changes in nature.[33]

The field of classics might be defined as an especially arboreal discipline, one that values, in a sort of apostolic succession, descent from such great men as Ugo von Wilamowitz-Moellendorff. In a hilarious essay on the classical footnote, entitled "Fussnoten: Das Fundament der Wissenschaft," Steve Nimis points to the intimidating force of the Germans in the American branch of the disciplinary tree: "There is nothing which strikes greater awe in the heart of the typical American classicist than the prospect of a vast tome of German scholarship. Indeed, historically the professionalization of classical studies was largely a nineteenth-century German affair"[34] In his analysis of "the Wilamowitz pile"—the obligatory footnote to the great man and to a whole arboreal genealogy, sometimes hundreds of scholars who discuss the same minute point—and of the struggle between Wilamowitz and Nietzsche, Nimis points out that classical philology is an ideology, that "Wilamowitz's call for disinterested scholarship is neither less nor more ideological than Nietzsche's call for an all-out appropriation of the past," (132) neither of which I recommend, by the way. Wilamowitz was one of the classical scholars who expressed a most vehement, detailed, and scornful contempt for the work of the classicist Friedrich Nietzsche when Nietzsche ventured to connect his speculations on Greek tragedy with the operas of Richard Wagner.[35]

In the great intellectual ferment that followed the failed revolution in France in May 1968, in the wake of disillusionment both with existentialism and communism, Deleuze and Guattari offered a critique of traditional disciplines, classics among them, inspired in part by the example of Nietzsche. They characterized classical scholarship in *A Thousand Plateaus* when they described "the first type of book [as] . . . the rootbook. The tree is already the image of the world, or the root the image of the world-tree. This is the classical book" (5). "All of tree logic is a logic of tracing and reproduction . . . Its goal is to describe a de facto state, to maintain balance in intersubjective relations . . . It consists of tracing, on the basis of an overcoding structure or support axis, something that comes ready-made" (12).

Classical studies has long privileged, for example in the study of the history of texts, the *stemma,* a tree-like mapping of the relationship among various manuscripts as a crucial tool for discerning which of them is older, which depend on one another, in an attempt to establish a more perfect text; such practices emphasize filiation, descent, a metaphorical arborealism, rather than the proliferation and reappearance, the multiplicity and resurgence of a plant that has survived underground. Recent work in the field of textual scholarship has begun to erode these assumptions, moving toward a sense of the haunting of classical texts by a long series of editors and privileging "textual plurality" rather than a perfected and restored original.[36]

Although it may seem perverse to return to psychoanalytic theory, after citing the work of Deleuze and Guattari, whose *Anti-Oedipus* is a determined assault on the colonizing of psyche and state by the Oedipal triangle, mummy-daddy-me, of psychoanalysis, in fact one could argue that their critique of Freudian and Lacanian theory is a symptom of the significance of this body of work, a cry against their own Oedipalization by psychoanalysis. Yet their overt hostility to Freudian and Lacanian theory has its analogy in some current theoretical work, especially in Foucauldian and new historicist thinking. Greg Forter and Paul Allen Miller offer a cogent analysis of the resistance to psychoanalysis in some recent theory in their *Desire of the Analysts* (although to my mind they neglect important feminist and queer theory critiques of psychoanalysis, such as that of Judith Butler in *Gender Trouble*). They write, after tracing the sources of disillusionment with psychoanalysis exemplified by Stuart Hall and cultural studies, and by Michel Foucault's version of critical historicism:

> The hostility to the psyche among intellectuals risks, in this context, lending authority to an amnesiac culture of depthlessness whose disavowed condition is the machiadora [*sic*] and the literally "projected" sweatshops of the third world . . . It appears to us worth trying to reclaim the critical power of a mode of thought that honors the materiality of psychic suffering in the name of enriching our expressive projects and our material analyses of culture.[37]

As it turns out, the only essay in this volume that discusses cultures before the early modern is the classicist Paul Allen Miller's, which includes mention of a work by Juvenal, along with others by Mallarmé, Leyner, and

Sartre (35–56), perhaps illustrating the difficulties of extending psychoanalytic readings back into Greek antiquity.[38] I am interested less in allegorical readings of societies, using psychoanalytic categories, like that of Deleuze and Guattari in *Anti-Oedipus*, or even in the brilliant and illuminating work of Victoria Wohl on the Athenians, *Love among the Ruins*. I have been marked forever by the work of Jean-Pierre Vernant in "Oedipus without the Complex," in which he presents what seems to me a devastating critique of the anachronism of imagining the Greeks, individual or collective, as possessing a psyche just like our own and thus amenable to psychoanalytic interpretation.[39] One might better deploy psychoanalysis as a discourse for thinking about reading and listening, as in Shoshana Felman's volume, *Literature and Psychoanalysis*, and in the work of Ellen Oliensis, although they are both principally concerned with literary texts, while I would like to extend such techniques of reading to discourses, including the discourse of classical studies.[40] Oliensis writes, "I would prefer . . . to retain the dream with all its noncommunicative figural density, as my model of textual dynamics . . . I would propose detaching the text from the author's psyche and treating it, provisionally at least, as a dream without a dreamer."[41] I'm not convinced that it makes sense to term ancient texts as "literature" at all.[42] Rather than treating our culture, or a text, or the Greeks as an analysand, oneself as analyst who then interprets the object, it seems to me more fruitful to deploy the work of Freud and Lacan as a technique for an attentive listening.[43] This is an attitude I associate with a reader encountering a surface troubled by unmanageable forces.[44] Psychoanalytic categories can illuminate the practices of historical scholarship. Disavowal, like the themes of the unconscious—projection, transference, and counter-transference—adduced to account for the operations of the human mind, acknowledges the difficulties, even impossibility, of a pure, immediate access to our objects of inquiry. Psychoanalysis tries to recognize and name, but never fully to master, all that inevitably interferes with a perfect, true, and objective knowledge of one's self, of others, of texts, of all that one encounters in life. Psychoanalysis, with its rich vocabulary for describing the troubling, noisy, interfering investments we bring to any object, opens up new kinds of reading. To the confidence of the positivist working toward a clear, unblemished account of the ancient past, I prefer the self-conscious, self-critical, self-reflexive mode of knowing recorded in Freud's accounts. As Freud and Nietzsche insist, every perspective is particular, internally troubled, marked by conscious or unconscious investments. One can never know or understand all the determinants of one's inquiry, never fully represent the object. There is no single, true, whole picture of the past. It is impossible to get it right, to see clearly a distant past, to bracket successfully our own desires and needs vis-à-vis the objects of scholarly work. It seems to me better to acknowledge and meditate upon them rather than to pretend they can be overcome, or mastered.

Postcolonial theory produces another story, one reliant on diaspora, one that emphasizes cosmopolitanism, multiplicity, deterritorialization, rupture, disconnection, and heterogeneity and could influence a classical studies that includes "Espartaco" as well as the stemmata of textual criticism, along with George Fitzhugh, the North American antebellum proslavery writer who used the model of ancient Greece to argue for the enslavement of the weak, black and white, in his critique of impoverishing capitalism. I do not think we can uncritically apply postcolonial theory to antiquity, overriding the immense differences between the cultures of the ancient Mediterranean and those of post-Enlightenment, capitalist new worlds.[45] As James Clifford points out in relation to the term *cosmopolitan:* "separated from its [European] (sic) universalist moorings, [it] quickly becomes a traveling signifier, a term always in danger of breaking up into partial equivalences: exile, immigration, migrancy, diaspora, border crossing, pilgrimage, tourism."[46] My point is not that we can apply these theories indiscriminately and ahistorically to ancient Greece.[47] Rather, it seems to me that given the move away from structuralism, from confined objects hermetically sealed and symmetrically balanced, the current state of the world leads us to see not only reactive nationalisms and ethnocentrism, but also hybridity, fusion, and diaspora. If we look at the city of Athens in a traditional way, following a century of political theory and literary scholarship, we can continue to study a closed entity, one concerned with self-fashioning, self-definition, xenophobia; even if we allow for an anthropological curiosity in such authors as Herodotus, the focus has been on the ways the Athenians defined themselves.[48] If, however, one looks for heterogeneity and heterotopias, for dynamism, flow, hybridity, fusion, contact, and diaspora, the ancient world looks very different. Some ways in which this might be the case is the subject of this book.

Method

In Latin, *contamino* can mean to render (a sacred object, etc.) ritually unclean, profane; to pollute, desecrate. Who we are "contaminates" what we write. I mean *contamination* in this etymological sense: that contact that produces mingling, impurity, hybridity, not necessarily a negative infection or pollution. It is better to acknowledge a fusion of temporalities than to claim a pure, unmediated access to the past. I attend to vestiges, the almost invisible traces of resistance, the other utopias of Greek antiquity, for example, those that we barely glimpse, that never achieved the textual monumentality of Plato's *Republic,* and connections and events that emerge in the rips and crevices of history, that in retrospect express the impossibility of certain kinds of alliance, contact, and transformation. These are sometimes wild, eccentric events, like the conversation between the Buddhist arhat Nagasena and Menander, the Greek king of Bactria, inassimilable in the smooth narration of universal history. My writing may seem like free association to some readers, less governed by a rigid logic of explication and more attentive to drifts and flows than to contained objects and causal relations. I seek not to impose my will on readers, to make them see it all my way, but rather to provoke, to be conscious of my own intentions as much as possible and to allow for my unconscious, my fascinations with Sappho and Antigone, for example, to guide some of the choices made here.

New historicism, and the whole great tradition of historical work in English influenced by Michel Foucault, has a tendency to refuse the poetic, the playful, the unheard and meaningful in texts, to read works literally and prescriptively. Foucault, for example, in his *Use of Pleasure,* extracts passages from ancient Greek texts to derive a prescriptive message about *askesis,* when the works themselves, especially those of literary artists like Plato, allow for a much more complex and ambiguous interpretation. In this book I have tried to be attentive to the vast geographical range of "the Greeks"; to their astonishing historical survival into the present; and also to silenced events, voices, acts of resistance to monarchy, domination, hierarchy, and empire and to remember gestures of defiance that barely survive.

These are what I see as other currents in this text, themes that leave their mark without being central to the issues of geographical and temporal extension yet have their affinities with a project aimed at opening up the discipline of the classics. There is the possibly scandalous minor motif of tattooing, which recurs in several chapters concerned with the marking of the body, its meanings as signifier of domination and liberation. There are several *ekphrases,* that is, rhetorical descriptions, descriptions in words, of works of visual art, including tattoos, of course, and an intermittent emphasis on rhetoric and its history. There is a utopianism, acknowledged or submerged, repressed and resuscitated, that haunts this text, as well as a belief in the possibility of difference, of abrupt change, evental disjunction, moments that change the world, rather than continuity and glacial change. Slaves appear and reappear. The theme of multitudes, of anonymous collective agents, recurs in several chapters, often in contrast to readings that concentrate on the great man, the great woman recognizable as a distorted modern self across centuries. I touch on the Gramscian definition of hegemony, so useful for the discussion of cultural artifacts that produce and reinforce social order, difference, and hierarchy, along with the forms of coercion used by ancient rulers. Another issue is the critique of a purely philological classical studies, one that relies exclusively on microanalysis, on linguistic evidence, that is perhaps derived more from the most orthodox German traditions of scholarship, and the English, than from some radical tendencies of the French, especially the Parisian school of Gernet and Vernant, that in some ways is most indebted to the renegade German classicist Friedrich Nietzsche. These latter strains I find more congenial as they trace a scholarly genealogy not only from material culture but also from a philosophical, sociological, or anthropological past.[49]

The discipline of classics itself can often seem closed off both to the present, to tracings of its survival and resurgence, and to its connections with a very early global network. "There is no discipline," Moses Finley used to say, "whose borders are more heavily patrolled than those of Classics."[50] As I said earlier in this introduction, the chapters that follow proceed in a roughly chronological order and seek to exemplify the sorts of geographical and temporal extensions that open up the field of classical studies beyond the hermetic and confined spaces of fifth- and fourth-century Athens. They may seem disconnected, intermittent, arbitrary, but they are nodes in a vast web that stretches in space and time, fruits in the rhizome. Chapter 3, "Sappho between Africa and Asia," considers the heterotopic, the other, utopian space potential in Lesbian lyric poetry and, in a vast temporal and geographical extension, the twenty-first-century discovery of an almost new Sappho poem in a German library, and its connections with Africa and Asia, including Indo-European verse forms. The fourth chapter, entitled "The Tattoos of Epimenides," discusses nineteenth-century freak shows, draws on research on Asian shamanism and on Vedic and Mesopotamian traditions of the wise man. It contemplates ancient Greek bodily space; magic and magicians and the reverence in which they were held by the nonélite classes of antiquity; and Epimenides, whose tattooed body was displayed in Sparta after his 300-year life. "Slaves in the Tragic City," Chapter 5, seeks to counter versions of theory on tragedy that focus on the hero and turns to the spaces occupied by tragic choruses of women, often captive slaves brought to Greece from remote lands, from India with Dionysus, for example, unsettling catharsis in the space of the theater. The sixth chapter, "Alexandrias," begins with the foundation of this African city by Alexander the Great and moves on to ancient mime, always considered a "low" genre, dwelling especially on its representation of slaves. In Alexandria, Macedonians, Greeks, Egyptians, Nubians, Jewish Judaeans, and others forged a hybrid culture after Alexander's imperial adventures. The chapter goes on to consider how that city's foundation eventually affected and was affected by the cultures of what are now called the Middle East and South and Central Asia, including the iconography and sacred texts of Buddhism. "Histories of the Impossible," Chapter 7, uses Michel-Rolph Trouillot's *Silencing the Past,* on the Haitian Revolution, to examine a failed slave revolt in ancient Asia Minor almost obliterated in the triumphalist historical record of Roman imperial conquest. "Jesus and Other Jews," Chapter 8, considers religious studies and their separation from classical studies, and looks at Hellenistic Jewish martyrdom; connections among Jesus, Dionysus, and Socrates; Jesus as magician; and the homophobia of the Christian tradition. Chapter 9, "The Persistence of Oedipus," reads psychoanalytic interpretations of the Oedipus myth and their deployment in analyzing detective fiction and looks at two twentieth-century novels that give new life to this Oedipus. The concluding chapter, "Twenty-first-Century High Theory and the Classics," also considers the persistence of the classics into the present, examining work by Alain Badiou, Jacques Rancière, Giorgio Agamben, Judith Butler, and Antonio Negri and Michael Hardt, all of whom both look back to the classical and speak to the future. To call their engagement with antiquity "reception" is to use too pallid a term; they engage directly with ancient thinkers on questions of democracy, sacredness, gender, empire, and the conditions for philosophy today, for transformation tomorrow.

2

SPARTACUS

To illustrate what I have in mind as an expansion, an extension geographical and temporal, of the classics, take the example of Spartacus, mentioned in the prologue. Especially in the history of cinema, Spartacus has been the subject of much scholarship in recent years.[1] He has great geographical and temporal range; he moves intermittently through the world and into the present. What is the power of Spartacus, that he has had such a long life, from before the Common Era into globalizing, postmodern, postcolonial California?[2] The image of the bullfighter strikes classicists strongly; bullfighting has echoes of Minoan Crete, of the bull dancing performed by a Cretan acrobat, the bull itself the creature of Çatal Hüyük in Neolithic Anatolia, his horns emblematic of the potency of the animals subject to an ancient goddess. The seals of the ancient Indus Valley civilization also portray horned bulls. The bullfighter of contemporary Spain, brought into the taqueria, visited on the Internet, summons up ancient figures of combat with wild nature—dangerous and violent beasts—and their taming and subjection to human and animal fertility. Espartaco the bullfighter may have experiential resonance with Mexican culture and may also echo the films made of the life of Spartacus, films in several languages that celebrate the warrior and his efforts to lead his armies out of slavery, back to their homelands, or to Rome to defeat the official Roman armies assembled against them.

One of the important accounts of Spartacus' struggle against the Romans comes in Plutarch's *Life of Crassus*. Plutarch's *Lives* are the site of some of the earliest versions of biography, each focusing on the trajectory of a single human life rather than an account of a city or empire's history.[3] Crassus, paired in Plutarch's account with Nikias, the Athenian general of the Peloponnesian War, died at the hands of the Parthians in what is for now northern Iran, just south and east of the Caspian Sea, fighting against an army famous for shooting darts as it retreated and, back in Rome, for a sexual position named after this practice. In a hideous enactment of Euripides' *Bacchae,* the head of Crassus was deployed as a theatrical prop:

> Crassus was killed by a Parthian, called Pomaxathres; . . . Surena sent the head and hand of Crassus to Hyrodes the king, into Armenia. When the head of Crassus was brought to the door, the tables for dining had just been taken away, and one Jason, a tragic actor of the town of Tralles, was singing the scene in the *Bacchae* of Euripides concerning Agave. He was receiving much applause, when Sillaces, coming to the room, and having made obeisance to the king, threw down the head of Crassus into the midst of the company. The Parthians receiving it with joy and acclamations, Sillaces was made to sit down, while Jason handed over the costume of Pentheus to one of the dancers in the chorus, and taking up the head of Crassus, and acting the part of a bacchante in her frenzy, in a rapturous impassioned manner, sang the lyric passages—
>
> "We've hunted down a mighty chase to-day,
> And from the mountain bring the noble prey. . . ."[4]

Crassus, who had ordered the crucifixion of all of Spartacus' remaining troops after their defeat in Southern Italy, here received his fate at the hands of Rome's enemies deep in Asia, in this scene that stresses the reach of Greek culture, from Athens to Macedon, the site of Euripides' exile and composition of the *Bacchae,* into Armenia. This is Athenian tragedy given a weird afterlife in the Hellenized, anti-Roman world of post-Alexandrian Asia.[5]

Plutarch had, previous to this scene set in Asia, described the revolt of Spartacus, a gladiator of Thracian nomadic origin, from the gladiators' training camp in Capua. Spartacus was characterized by Plutarch as "a man not only of high spirit and valiant, but in understanding, also, and in gentleness superior to his condition, and more of a Greek than the people of his country usually are" (730). In a trope typical of the leaders of slave revolts, including Eunus and others in Sicily, predecessors of Spartacus, he is marked by supernatural signs:

> When he first came to be sold at Rome, they say a snake coiled itself upon his face as he lay asleep, and his wife, who at the latter time also accompanied

him in his flight, his countrywoman, a kind of prophetess, and one of those possessed with the bacchanal frenzy, declared that it was a sign portending great and formidable power to him with no happy event.[6]

The association of slave revolts with Dionysiac phenomena goes back at least to Bacchanalian conspiracies of the second century B.C.E., recounted by Livy: for example, "The praetor Lucius Postumius, to whom the province of Tarentum was assigned by lot, savagely repressed large-scale conspiracies of herdsmen and diligently completed the judicial inquiries into the last elements of the Bacchanalian conspiracies" (39.41.6–39.41.7).[7] The Bacchanalia had been consistently associated with slave revolts in the south, perhaps because they threatened to erase distinctions between slaves and free persons. Salvius, leader of the second slave war in Sicily, had been a mantic flute player at women's religious festivals, according to Diodorus Siculus, as preserved in Photius' *Library*.[8] Therefore, it is particularly intriguing that the general who destroyed Spartacus' rebellion was himself finally appropriated, his head used for the scene in which the mother of Pentheus, a bacchante herself, claims to have killed him. Dionysus is present here in these moments of rebellion and vengeance.

Drawing on the work of Frantz Fanon, Homi Bhabha sees the colonialized persons he discusses as parodic, ironic mimics of their masters, the colonized imitating their masters with a difference, a supplement of recalcitrance: "The discourse of mimicry is constructed around an ambivalence; in order to be effective, mimicry must continually produce its slippage, its excess."[9] Difference, ambivalence, and recalcitrance may come into play in Aristophanes' representations of slaves in his comedies. In ancient Greek comedy, the actors playing slaves were not themselves slaves, yet the texts seem to call for ironic, mocking, parodic playing of the subjected subaltern in relation to the master. In literary representation, and in drama especially, subjection to the master is a performance, one that can contain many layers of reservation, "hidden agendas" in James Scott's term, shades of irony and parody that preserve the integrity and dignity of the subjected and provide a kind of subversion of the superficial obedience required in these situations of domination.[10]

The Parthians, not slaves themselves, but threatened with assimilation into the Roman Empire, were seen in the text of Plutarch to use the head of Crassus in a complicated enactment of subjection. Highly literate in the forms of Greek culture, they saw the head of Crassus as a prop, standing for the head of Pentheus, the Greek king—that is, like the general, the person nominally in command. But in Euripides' play, Pentheus is subjected to Dionysus, drawn by his own desire into an invasion of the Bacchantes' celebration of their god, and then even further subjected to the women's power as they dismember and devour him. The inversion of power stands at the heart of the play, and of Dionysus' domain, and the Parthian camp enacts a brutal and decisive dethroning of Roman power with Crassus' head. In a deferred and displaced vengeance for the crucifixion of Spartacus' warriors, the Parthians are the empire's foes striking back, the edges of the Roman world, from which Spartacus might be said to have come, recoiling on the emissary from Rome, the center.

Other accounts of Spartacus' revolt in large measure conform to Plutarch's account. They connect the gladiator's sustained rebellion with other such uprisings, those in Sicily that had preceded his, including one by the Syrian ex-slave Eunus, who declared himself king and even minted coins in the name of Antiochus.[11] According to Diodorus Siculus, as preserved in Photius, "Eunus killed his own masters, Antigenes and Pytho. Crowning his head with a diadem and adorning himself with all of the other accoutrements and symbols of kingship, he declared his partner to be his queen" (83–84). According to Diodorus Siculus, as preserved in Constantine Porphyrogennetos' *Excerpts,* Eunus "staged dramatic mime performances for the people inside the city [Akragas] on the theme of the slave rebellion—dramas in which the slaves themselves acted out the events of the rebellion against their masters. In these dramatic skits, the slaves poured contempt on the arrogance and outrageous insolence that had led to the slave owners' self-destruction" (92–93). In the second slave war, in Sicily, the rebellious slaves chose a certain Salvius as king: "He had a reputation of being skilled at foretelling the future, and he had also been a mantic flute player at women's religious festivals" (113). This man began calling himself King Tryphon; also, according to reports concerning the writings of Diodorus Siculus, "Whenever King Tryphon conducted official business, he donned a purple Roman toga and a wide-bordered Greek cloak. He also had lectors holding the symbolic axes to precede him, as well as all of the other accoutrements that are suitable to the embellishment of royal power" (118). Such display leads Keith Bradley to conclude that these leaders had in mind not freedom from slavery for their followers, but rather the instituting of Easternizing monarchies, like the Syrian, from which they had come, in their new land of Sicily.[12]

Spartacus differed interestingly from these Sicilian leaders in that he persisted in a nomadic style of rebellion, moving with his bands, then army, across the whole terrain of Roman Italy, and also in planning to escape from Italy and return his soldiers and their companions to their homelands. He did not establish a fortress or a palace, nor did he institute royal accoutrements or forms of deference. His was a strategy of movement and intermittent confrontation, a guerrilla warfare before the fact. He never established a stronghold, even having his soldiers, early in their struggle, climb down from Mount Vesuvius on vines so they would not be trapped in the simulacrum of a fortress. He also dispersed his army at times, in a move that may have brought about their defeat, since he sent out one large group under another general, which weakened his own defenses; when they were defeated, he was vulnerable to Crassus' forces, which hurried to defeat him before others could arrive and take credit for victory over the slaves.

The reader might think of analogies with the American civil rights movement of the 1960s. In his *Logics of Worlds,* the contemporary philosopher Alain Badiou uses Spartacus as an exemplary figure in his explication of the "event," a crucial element of his philosophical position.[13] For Badiou, using a difficult and idiosyncratic philosophical vocabulary, there is, in a significant configuration resulting from some crucial occurrence, the "trace" of the event, and a body *(corps)*. In his account of these relationships, the subject is "subjectivation of a link between the physics of the body and the name (or trace) of the event" (51). After the revolt of a handful of gladiators around Spartacus, in 73 B.C.E., some slaves *fassent corps,* "form a body, instead of being dispersed into packs." Badiou says the "trace" of the event-revolt is the statement "We, slaves, we want to return home" (51). He gives a detailed and elaborate analysis of the Spartacus episode, asking whether what he calls the "form subject" is the operation by which the new "body" of the slaves, their army and its dependents, is joined with the trace of the event. It is this conjunction that commands the strategies Spartacus pursues: He looks for a passage toward the north, toward a frontier of the Roman Republic, and then toward the south, to find boats and leave Italy. However, Badiou argues, in another sense this is not the "form subject," because the subjective identity that is fashioned in and by these military movements is not identical with them; operations of another nature constitute subjective deliberation, division, and production. The slaves, he says, as a body, an army, move themselves in a new present, because they are no longer slaves (51). *Pace* the doubts of ancient historians such as Bradley, Badiou argues, "And thus they show (to the other slaves) that it is possible, for a slave, no longer to be a slave, and to do so *in the present*" (51). And from this comes the growth, soon perilous, of the body. "This institution of the possible as present is typically a subjective production. Its materiality is constituted by the consequences drawn day after day from the event's course, that is, from a principle indexed to the possible: 'We, slaves, we want to *and can* return home'" (51). There are connections here with my discussion of Aristonicus in chapter 7 and with Michel-Rolph Trouillot's discussion of the impossible and its irrepresentability. For Badiou, the event makes for possibility, just as Aristonikos' revolt seems to have introduced the possibility of a city of slaves, which would be a city of persons no longer slaves, the Doulopolis.

In the case of Spartacus, Badiou maintains, the result of the Spartacus revolt is that a subject exists, as the localization of a truth, and it is in its acts that we see the "becoming true" of the subject. For example, we see the military detachments becoming specialists in confronting the Roman cavalry. Badiou uses the example of an escaped slave who is joining an army; subjectively, this is the realization in the present of a "hitherto unknown possibility" (52) (*un possible anterieurement inconnu*). And it is into this present that the escaped slave is "incorporated," becomes corporeally part. The more slaves who join the body, the army of Spartacus, the more the "Spartacus-subject" (52) (*sujet-Spartacus*) is amplified and changes its nature.

Badiou actually reduces these features of the Spartacus narrative to an almost algebraic formula: $\varepsilon/\cent \to \pi$; this is "the matheme of the faithful subject" (53). Epsilon is the trace, $\cent$ the body, and pi the present; an arrow stands for the consequence and the bar, subordination. He sees the disciplined body of the detachment confronting the cavalry as one thing, as opposed to the general disorder of the rest of Spartacus' band, with its multiplicity of peoples and languages, women, rivalry of various heads, which draws the whole toward "the termination or impracticability of the new possible" (53). "Nevertheless, in different circumstances—for instance, the organization in the encampment of a new form of civic life—this order-less multiplicity without order, this unheard of and improvised cosmopolitanism, will be an inestimable resource, offset by the arrogance of well-trained detachments of gladiators" (53).

The "body" described by Badiou is always divided; so his c is barred, divided. The escaped slave is described in the matheme above as a pure subjective form; there is a body crossed out (the army on the way to formation but still without unity), subordinated to the trace, but only in view of an incorporation into the present, which is always a consequence. These consequences found in the present a new truth: "that the fate of the wretched of the earth is never a law of nature, and that it can, if only for the duration of a few battles, be revoked" (53).

The faithful subject is not, as such, in any one letter of Badiou's matheme, but is the formula as a whole. The new and divided body, like the active unconscious of a trace of the event, engenders the enlargement of the present and exposes "fragment by fragment" a truth. Such a subject accomplishes himself in the production of consequences, and that is why he is called "faithful," that is, faithful to epsilon, and thus to the vanished event of which epsilon is the trace. The work of this faith, this fidelity, is the new present that gathers, point by point, the new truth. The division of the body falls under the bar, until the present, when he will rise up in his own light.

Badiou considers the great mass of slaves not called up by Spartacus and his armies. The current interpretation is that they maintained in themselves the laws of the old world: "You're a slave—resign yourself or seek a legal redress" (54). But Badiou resists this interpretation, citing what he calls "reactionary novelties" (54) (*les nouveautés réactionnaires*), forged to respond to and resist the new, arguments of resistance adjusted to the new. So the reactionary is contemporary with the present to which it reacts. It is not the pure permanence of the old. (He cites the *nouveaux philosophes*' response to "the red sequence" (54) [*la séquence rouge*] of China's cultural revolution, the United States' refusal of the Vietnam War, and France's May 1968. They set up, against an opposition of revolution versus imperialist order, an enduring and ideologically useful opposition between democracy and dictatorship or totalitarianism.) There is not only a faithful subject but also a reactive subject who says no to the event but also is productive in his present, "an extinguished present" (55) (*un présent éteint*). That is, a slave who will benefit from the fear produced in his master by Spartacus' revolt to receive a tiny amelioration of his situation.

Karl Marx discussed the career of Spartacus in an 1861 letter to Engels, here translated by Brent Shaw: "Spartacus emerges as one of the best characters in the whole of ancient history. A great general (unlike Garibaldi), a noble character, a genuine representative of the ancient proletariat."[14] Karl Liebknecht and Rosa Luxemburg, inspired by the ancient slave revolt, signed letters against intervention in World War I with the name of Spartacus and later founded the ill-fated group called the Spartacist League, in 1918.[15] Helmut Trotnow, in his biography of Karl Liebknecht, wrote, "As these letters were illegal, they were signed with the pseudonym of the famous Roman slave leader 'Spartakus' and first appeared in duplicated form on 27 January 1916."[16] As W. Z. Rubinsohn recalls in a monograph on Spartacus and on the discipline of ancient history as practiced in the Soviet Union, workers' sports clubs in Czechoslovakia, Germany, and the USSR were in the 1920s named after Spartacus. "When the All-Soviet Games took place for the first time in 1928, they were called Spartaciads. These games were conceived as something specifically proletarian, an answer to the national Olympics . . . Spartacus . . . became a part of the revolutionary mythology and martyrology of the Soviet Union."[17] Rubinsohn details how Soviet historians in this period may have preferred the field of ancient history as a less treacherous realm of study than that of more recent times as they negotiated the rapids of the Stalinist period, even though Stalin's own theory of history anachronistically and inaccurately attributed the fall of Rome to the slave uprisings of the Roman Republic, and this question in particular had to be addressed very carefully; those who deviated from Stalin's own line suffered (6).

The Soviet composer Aram Khachaturian, whose Armenian name indicates his relationship to neighbors of the ancient people who watched the head of Crassus used as a prop in a performance of the *Bacchae,* wrote music for a ballet called *Spartacus,* which had an uneven history. The ballet was first produced in the Soviet Union, in what was then called Leningrad, at the Kirov Ballet, in 1957. The composer explained his motives and his research for this composition:

> The image of Spartacus had always appealed to me. Some were surprised at my choice of the topic and reproached me for delving deep back into history. But I feel that the theme of Spartacus and the slave revolt in Ancient Rome has huge significance even for our times and a big public resonance today, when all the nations are fighting for their freedom, when colonialism is finally due to collapse, the people need to know and remember the names of those who at the dawn of human history bravely rose against the enslavers to struggle for their liberty and independence.[18]

Khachaturian recalled his research and his travel to Rome with a group of Soviet musicians, artists, and writers:

I studied ancient pictures and sculptures, saw buildings from the times of Ancient Rome, the magnificent Arches of Triumph made by the hands of the slaves, the barracks of the gladiators and the Colosseum . . . I often walked in the places where many centuries ago the gladiators proceeded, led by Spartacus, a hero who has gone down in history as the popular, intrepid leader of the slaves. (22)

The libretto of the ballet was based on the novel *Spartaco,* published in Italy in 1874 by Raffaello Giovagnoli, and on Plutarch's *Lives.* Later productions of the ballet altered various aspects of the original production but, as Grigorovich and Vanslov report: "Since then [1958], Khachaturian's ballet *Spartacus* has never left the stage in the Soviet Union."[19] In the hands of Grigorovich, as choreographer, the ballet reached its definitive form, moving from Crassus' camp to Spartacus' in alternating scenes. Betrayal and tragedy come, in this version of the story, through the treacherous hetaera Aegina, Crassus' concubine, who uses "wine and vice" to weaken and distract Spartacus and his troops; through her treachery they are easily taken prisoner by the Romans (32). "Dozens of enemy spears pierce the body of Spartacus" (89), and he resembles a martyred Jesus or Saint Sebastian at the climax of the ballet. Thomas Wiedemann points out, "As late as the 1960's Soviet school books portrayed the dying Spartacus as a substitute for Christ crucified."[20] The class struggle read by Marx is overdetermined by the Jesus story and by conventional misogyny, the rebels' betrayal by a wicked woman.

Arthur Koestler's novel on the Spartacus revolt, *The Gladiators,* took a more pessimistic and cynical position toward the ancient rebellion. His version of the story is a sort of allegory concerning the possibility of revolution. Written by this dedicated anticommunist—the author of 1949's *The God That Failed,* required reading in my high school in the McCarthyist era—*The Gladiators* traces what is made to seem an inevitable decline in the fates of the rebels, from bloody early insurrection through a communalist phase to Spartacus "Imperator," the former gladiator become the executioner of his former comrades in the name of the revolution. The references to the likes of Lenin and Stalin are difficult to ignore, as are such pronouncements from the omniscient narrator as this:

> No, one could neither guide it from outside nor from above, not with the pride of the lonely seer, nor with the cunning of detours, nor with the cruel kindness of the prophet. The century of abortive revolutions had been completed; others

will come, receive the word and pass it on in a great wrathful relay-race through the ages; and from the bloody birth-pangs of revolution again and again a new tyrant will be born—until at last the groaning human clod would itself begin to think with its thousand heads; until knowledge was no longer foisted on it from outside, but was born in laboured torment out of its own body, thus gaining from within power over the happening.[21]

Koestler describes what he saw as the inevitability of internal dissension in revolution, the struggle for power among revolutionaries, "those people . . . so obliging as to quarrel among themselves just at the decisive moment; a phenomenon apparently in character with all revolutions, which thus furnish their own safeguarding antidote," as one character says (314). For Koestler, Spartacus becomes a paradigmatic Stalinist tyrant.

There are many Spartacuses on film, and Maria Wyke brilliantly shows how various Italian and American versions differ one from another.[22] These cinematic versions of Spartacus' story reveal changing currents of ideology, in which novels and films respond to differing versions of collectivity and individualism—in which the leader of the slave armies is enlisted as a romantic hero or as merely the voice of the will of his people. One of the compelling questions of the various deployments of the name and narrative of Spartacus is the role of the individual versus the group in the telling of his story. William Fitzgerald, in his essay on the toga films of the 1950s, points to the many ambiguities that govern the representations of the Roman Empire in the genre: where the private represents a haven from the cynicism and exhaustion of the public sphere, which is nonetheless presented as full of spectacle and pleasure; where homoeroticism and heterosexuality coexist uneasily; where the male body is invulnerable and yet crucified; where sons battle for authority to replace their fathers and redeem the corrupt public sphere.[23]

In *Spartacus*, the American film of 1960, Kirk Douglas seemed especially interested in presenting a heroic, romantic story of a rebel leader. The film distorts dramatically the novel *Spartacus* written by Howard Fast after his short imprisonment for failing to name names in the great cold war attempt by the U.S. government to rid the United States of communists and their sympathizers. The movie has been much written about. I would point to three features. One is the haunting presence of the holocaust of Europe's Jews in the film. Martin Winkler in his very useful book about the film emphasizes the ways it also presents a narrative focused on American freedoms and in fact parallels the contemporary civil rights movement, especially with the solidarity between Spartacus and his black fellow gladiator Draba. "In its presentation of Spartacus as a messianic protagonist, the film expresses a dual emphasis on freedom and religion that is more important than any of the political analogies that it contains and more revealing about how Americans see themselves."[24] Yet as important as this allusion to the civil rights struggle is a constant echo of the sufferings of the past, especially of Europe's Jews at the hands of the Nazis. The very opening scene of the film, with Spartacus laboring in the mines of Africa, recalls the perhaps mythic episode of the Israelite enslavement by the Pharaohs recorded in the Hebrew Bible and in such contemporary U.S. films as *The Ten Commandments*. In his autobiography, Kirk Douglas suggests the connection between Roman ruins and the pyramids of Egypt: "I see thousands and thousands of slaves carrying rocks, beaten, starved, crushed, dying. I identify with them."[25] One might also interpret one of the final scenes of the film, in which Crassus demands that the defeated slaves surrender Spartacus, promising leniency if they do so, in light of the holocaust. One slave begins, "I am Spartacus," and other voices follow his lead. This moment seems to point to the possibly apocryphal story of the Scandinavian king who, when the Jews of his realm were ordered by the Nazis to wear the Star of David, appeared on his balcony the next morning himself wearing the yellow star.

Howard Fast's novel betrays the homophobia of the Communist Party in its representation of ancient homoeroticism and the decadence of upper-class Romans. Caius Crassus, the young friend of Crassus, exhibits incestuous feelings toward his sister Claudia, as well as homosexual desires. After he rejects the unwelcome advances of his host's wife, who says, "We're all rotten, we're all sick, diseased, full of death, bags of death—we're in love with death" (48), Crassus enters the young man's room; then, after a discreet change of chapters, we find Caius "tired and satiated and sensual as a stretching cat" (49). In the film, Crassus, played by Laurence Olivier, notoriously tried to seduce Antoninus (Tony Curtis), with his talk of oysters and snails, in a scene censored from the film's first release. In the next scene, Antoninus has lit out for the rebels' territory.[26]

The name and story of Spartacus persist beyond antiquity and beyond the boundaries of the Roman Empire, Europe, and the Americas, beyond the Asia of Spartacus' origin. In a novel called *Le Devoir de Violence,* published in Paris in 1968 by Yambo Ouologuem, the ghost of Spartacus haunts the central character.[27] As the sweep of his epic novel approaches the historical period of the Malian author himself, we encounter Raymond-Spartacus Kassoumi, his father's first born:

> The life that Raymond lived . . . was the life of his whole generation—the first generation of native administrators maintained by the notables in a state of gilded prostitution—rare merchandise, dark genius maneuvered behind the scenes and hurled into the tempests of colonial politics amidst the hot smell of festivities and machinations—ambiguous balancing acts in which the master turned the slave into the first of the slaves and the arrogant equal of the white master, and in which the slave thought himself master of the master, who himself had fallen to the level of the first of the slaves. (136)

Raymond-Spartacus goes to Paris, and, from a prostitute he learns is his sister, he hears the news that his fiancée is dead, his father has been sold, and his two brothers were drugged and went mad; his sister dies in the brothel, cut by a razor blade left in her soap by a sadistic customer. When he finds a male lover, his memory goes back to his homeland: "His search was not so much for ecstasy as for the profound meaning of his own destruction, the stain on his face suddenly splattered by his name: Spartacus!" (156). After Raymond-Spartacus returns home, Ouologuem writes, "He himself was a problematic existence, a living conflict. In this alienation, to be sure, Raymond-Spartacus Kassoumi found an open door to revolt: for him and his Africa it was in a sense a duty to be revolutionary. But how . . . ?" (168). The name Spartacus obliges him to violence, to revolutionary action like his imaginary ancestor's, but the contradictions and ironies of the relationship between Africa and France, and within Africa itself, lead him to an endless round of alienation.

In the tradition of the toga movies discussed by Wyke, but with a dramatically different emphasis in a new atmosphere of global empire, appeared the 2007 film *300,* a celebration of the Spartans at Thermopylae as they resisted the invading Persian empire, led by Xerxes, in 480 B.C.E. The film is an unabashed hymn to the U.S. president George W. Bush and to the isolation of the United States in invading Iraq. In the film, the other Greeks leave before the end of the battle at Thermopylae, and the Spartans stand alone. The right-to-life issue is obliquely engaged, as Ephialtes, the traitor who leads to the Spartans' defeat, is presented as a deformed Spartan whose parents took him away from Sparta so he wouldn't be "discarded," in a subtle allusion to the ancient Greek practice of exposing unwanted children to the elements, here linked to an anti-abortion position.

Although Ephialtes grows up to be a traitor, his bitterness derives from the cruelty of the Spartans toward the unwanted child. Xerxes offers him women and a uniform, and he gladly gives away the goat path the Persians take to surround the Spartan 300.

In the film, the Persians appear as a mongrel, multicultural mass, all slaves to their emperor. All heralds appear to be Arabian, and the emperor Xerxes is marked as effeminate and decadent, sporting a shaved head, highly plucked eyebrows, and cosmetics and covered in chains and silver bracelets and piercings. His emissaries are black, and some warriors wear armor that resembles Arab women's veils. He travels with elephants, a rhino, a giant with bad teeth, and a creature with saws for arms whom the emperor uses to punish his useless generals. The Persians travel with transvestites, highly made-up men, and various scantily clad women who writhe about and pleasure Ephialtes. There is much slow motion and balletic slaughter, much swirling of the Spartan red cloaks as the beautiful young son of the Spartan second-in-command is beheaded and his father's heart is filled with hatred and a just thirst for vengeance. The Spartans sport very tight, tiny, bathing suit–like undergarments, red cloaks, and helmets and overdeveloped abdominal muscles. As all the Spartans are killed, after an interval the camera looks down on the battlefield; Leonidas, leader of the Spartan band, lies below with arms outstretched like Jesus on the cross, his body penetrated by arrows like that of Saint Sebastian, with his men dead all around him.[28] This is the toga film at the service of U.S. militarism, imperial expansion, and self-congratulatory pathos, the classics deployed in the name of reaction.

Spartacus and his kind have a long reach and are available to multiple meanings as the classical persists and survives into the present. This first toga movie of the twenty-first century rejoices in a sort of anti-*Spartacus*, a Sparta centered not on a slave rebellion, or even a helot struggle, but rather on white European slave-holding soldiers who, even as they lose the battle to the Asiatic hordes, crush the slavish Asian enemy ideologically in their heroism, integrity, and beautiful deaths.

3

SAPPHO BETWEEN AFRICA AND ASIA

Like other narratives in the tradition of historical novels, ballet, films set in antiquity, the story of Spartacus sometimes shares utopian aspects with other slave revolts from antiquity, as he and his comrades yearn to return to the lands from which they were stolen, in Asia and in Africa, and Spartacus survives to haunt postmodernity. This chapter is about extending our idea of Sappho as well, beyond the island of Lesbos, beyond her possible travels to Sicily and Asia Minor, to include other parts of the ancient world and the traveling of her poetry into the twenty-first century. Even as the poetry has a utopian quality, a yearning, a nostalgia for what has been lost, it persists into the present, defying the mood of failed utopic memory.

The myth of the eternally aging Tithonus, who appears in Sappho's most recently recovered papyrus, as well as in Homer, in the *Homeric Hymn to Aphrodite,* in other lyrics, and in a fragment of Hellanikos (140 Jacoby), represents connections with Africa and Asia, as well as the avoidance of ultimate ruin, even as it accepts fragmentation into a multitude, the nameless horde of anonymous cicadas, worshippers of the muses. The ruination of the classical world might here be embraced, not lamented, since it entails not just a breaking up, and a yearning for restoration and wholeness, but also a recognition of human fragility, our bodies in pieces as infants and in aging, and thus diaspora, dissemination, fragmentation, anonymity and passing, as strategies of persistence.

Sappho's world includes heterotopic space within archaic antiquity, and also stretches far beyond such locations in time and space. Lesbian poetry, from the island of Lesbos, not only has affinities with ancient India and the Vedic, but is also entwined with the world of ancient Egypt and its survival. M. L. West, in his work on Indo-European poetics, indicates the connections between Greek and Vedic poetry:

> The governing principles of prosody and versification are essentially identical in Vedic and early Greek. (46)
>
> The sum of correspondences, not only in the structure of individual lines but also in their relationship to one another and in the patterns in which they are combined, is sufficient to show the persistence both in the Rigveda and in Greek poetry of forms already established at any rate by the Graeco-Aryan period. (50)[1]

In an earlier book, *The East Face of Helicon,* West also compares the antiphonal fragment 137 with "the so-called divine love lyrics of Sumer, which include erotic dialogue songs between Inanna and Dumuzi. . . . Among the love songs and excerpts which make up the Song of Solomon, too, we find fragments of he-she dialogues. The form is also found in Egyptian love poetry of the New Kingdom." He notes that although there is an abundance of Near Eastern elements in Sappho's verse, her Lesbian contemporary Alcaeus "offers little material for comment" (531).[2]

The Egyptian collection of erotic poetry called "Poems of Love and Devotion," from the New Kingdom (1570–1090 B.C.E.), much earlier than Sappho's lyrics, has strong affinities with Sappho's themes. For example, the catalogue that turns the lover's head:

> Distracting is the [foliage] of my [pasture];
> [the mouth] of my girl is a lotus bud,
> her breasts are mandrake apples. . . .[3]

These lines recall Mesopotamian hymns to Inanna, and the erotic verses of the Hebrew Bible's "Song of Songs": "She is a garden enclosed, my sister, my bride; / a garden enclosed, a sealed fountain. / Your shoots form an orchard of pomegranate trees, / the rarest essences are yours: / nard and saffron, / calamus and cinnamon . . ." (4.195–200).[4] As in these African and West Asian erotic images of the garden and the body of the beloved, there is a utopian, spatially allusive aspect to Sappho's work; she recalls beautiful female bodies: "as the sweetapple reddens on a high branch / high on the highest branch and the applepickers forgot—no, not forgot; were unable to reach. . . ."[5]

Michel Foucault, in his essay on "other spaces,"[6] argues that "our time," the present, is one of space, not time, and he discusses, in contrast to the unreality of utopias, based on analogy, various forms of what he calls heterotopologies, listing heterotopias of biological crisis, like the spaces set aside for birth or menstruation in some cultures, being replaced by spaces like the prison; the refunctioning of spaces, as when the cemetery, for example, moves from the center of the city to its outside; the juxtaposition of spaces, as in the Persian garden, or by means of the flying carpet; other spaces linked to "heterochronies," like the museum, linked to other times; the heterotopia of illusion, that exposes other spaces as illusory or compensatory:

> Either the heterotopias have the role of creating a space of illusion that denounces all real space, all real emplacements within which human life is partitioned off, as being even more illusory. . . . Or, on the contrary, creating a different space, a different real space as perfect, as meticulous, as well-arranged as ours is disorganized, badly arranged, and muddled. This would be the heterotopia not of illusion but of compensation. . . . (184)

This essay triggers the imagination, even though Foucault assumes a closed, homogeneous space, France, say, with a brief detour to the ship of fools, the colony, and the American motel room. What I am interested in is something quite different, spaces inside and outside that are mixed, hybrid, heterogeneous, like the shrines of slaves from Thrace and elsewhere in the Piraeus, the port city of ancient Athens, or the Piraeus in general, or Bactria—the mixture of Buddhist and Greek philosophy in the questions of King Menander (Milinda in Pali), or Alexandria, of which more later.

Although Foucault is discussing material space, it seems to me his concepts can be extended to such spaces as those imagined by Sappho, who in some of her poems creates illusory, heterochronic and utopian space: women's space, erotic, lost space, recreated with longing and offering an implicit critique of Homeric and archaic warrior cultural spaces. As Louis Marin wrote about Sir Thomas More's *Utopia,* published in the sixteenth century: "Historically, utopia functions as a twofold discursive practice—poetic and projective. . . . The play of spaces utopic practice produces (in both senses of the word 'play') constitutes its particular historical mode of being, the 'aesthetic' mode of its historicity. And thus we note the remarkable relationship utopic practice maintains with ideology. It is an ideological critique of the dominant ideology."[7] One might adapt these words, written about a text that rides the transition from feudalism to capitalism and foresees the invention of the social sciences as a consequence of utopian speculation, to archaic Lesbos, and to the world of women's worship and eros, so different in many ways, so like in others, from the aristocratic men's societies of the preclassical period. Sappho's world includes utopian spaces within archaic antiquity, and also stretches far beyond such locations in time and space. Some of Sappho's poems can be read as oases, and I think of her as an almost tragic utopian or heterotopian writer, as someone who creates imaginary worlds in her poems, places that are no-where, but the no-wheres of which color the subsequent history of ancient poetry.

Let me begin by citing the two poems most evocative of heterotopologies; then I will turn to the startling and unpredictable survival of Sappho into the twentieth and twenty-first centuries.[8] Poem 94 is the most utopian of all:

> I simply want to be dead.
> Weeping she left me
>
> with many tears and said this:
> Oh how badly things have turned out for us.
> Sappho, I swear, against my will I leave you.
>
> And I answered her:
> Rejoice, go and
> remember me. For you know how we cherished you.
>
> But if not, I want
> to remind you
>   ] and beautiful times we had.
>
> For many crowns of violets
> and roses
>   ] at my side you put on
>
> and many woven garlands
> made of flowers
> around your soft throat.
>
> And with sweet oil
> costly
> you anointed yourself
>
> and on a soft bed
> delicate
> you would let loose your longing
>
> and neither any [ ] nor any
> holy place nor
> was there from which we were absent

no grove [ ] no dance
>] no sound
[

*(trans. Anne Carson)*⁹

This poem calls up nostalgia for a lost, other, "different" space. Utopia is an early modern invention, that place imagined by More, both no-where and a good place, *ou* being the Greek negative, *eu* being the adverb "well," so that the space is perhaps imagined by More to be "good," but also acknowledged to be nowhere. In this poem there is a good space, but it is gone, not spatially displaced but temporally irretrievable. The poem emphasizes this aspect, the longing, or *pothos,* for what is not: no sound, no grove. And when set against the lyric poetry of Sappho's contemporary and fellow Lesbian, Alcaeus, who writes in praise of warriors, describes a fabulous armory full of archaic weaponry, and denigrates Helen of Troy, whom Sappho presents as an exemplum not of treachery but of erotic compulsion, the Sapphic text presents perhaps an illusory, but also compensatory, other space.

The other relevant poem is fragment two, this one found on a potsherd from the third century B.C.E., with another sacred grove:

here to me from Krete to this holy temple
where is your graceful grove
of apple trees and altars smoking
>   with frankincense.

And in it cold water makes a clear sound through
apple branches and with roses the whole place
is shadowed and down from radiant-shaking leaves
>   sleep comes dropping.

And in it a horse meadow has come into bloom
with spring flowers and breezes
like honey are blowing
>   [   ]

In this place you Kypris taking up
in gold cups delicately
nectar mingled with festivities:
>   pour.¹⁰

The mythic, incantatorily summoned space contains the goddess and her celebrants. Of course, this is not all there is to the corpus of work heuristically attributed to a poet named Sappho. There is the lover whipped by eros, like an oak tree tossed by a violent storm in fragment 147. There is the predatory love of the first poem, asking Aphrodite to tame the object of her desire. The poet mocks the crudity of her rival in fragment 55. Many moods, different generic strains, varying audiences, perhaps, and kinds of address, characterize the tiny corpus of Sappho's poems that remains. But these two poems create a utopian time and space that are like little else in lyric poetry of this period, and that can perhaps be linked to nostalgia—for a lost past, the pain of exile, and even to the yearning for a return home of such displaced slaves as Spartacus and his comrades.

There is an erotics here, of course, of the Sapphic sort, yearning for a lost union of women, but also a poetics of the utopia of the poem itself, the lines producing an elsewhere, a nowhere, a good where, that one can inhabit as long as one reads and dwells inside the lines of the broken, fragmentary, but still legible verse. The utopian, heterotopic texts, in a further distancing of that imagined other space, make up part of the ruin that is what remains of the material world of Greek antiquity, into which the contemporary reader is drawn through the poetics of longing, nostalgia, and a desire for return.

How do Sappho's fragments, among the ruins of antiquity, papyri, as well as sculpture and architecture, painting and inscriptions, speak to us? Lennard Davis begins a chapter in his *Enforcing Normalcy*:

> She has no arms or hands, although the stump of her upper right arm extends just to her breast. Her left foot has been severed, and her face is badly scarred, with her nose torn at the tip, and her lower lip gouged out. Fortunately, her facial mutilations have been treated and are barely visible, except for minor scarring visible up close. The big toe of her right foot has been cut off, and her torso is covered with scars, including a particularly large one between her shoulder blades, one that covers her shoulder, and one covering the tip of her breast where her left nipple was torn out.[11]

After this *ekphrasis* of the Venus de Milo stressing mutilation and ruin, Davis insists on what he interprets as a psychic necessity to refuse and to repress a recognition in the present of the loss and mutilation and ruin of ancient works of art, citing such art historians as Kenneth Clark, in *The Nude*:[12]

> The amnesia of art historians to the subject of mutilation and decapitation (the Esquiline Venus has no head) is not accidental. . . . This amnesia, this looking away from incompleteness, an averting of the attention, a sigh, is

the tip of a defensive mechanism that allows the art historian still to see the statue as an object of desire. So the critic's aim is to restore the damage, bring back the limbs, through an act of imagination. (135)

Mutilation and dismemberment are the rule, not the exception, in the study of the ancient world, in our gaze at statues, buildings, vases, papyri. And one of the driving impulses of classical scholarship has been to make whole what is broken, to restore what is absent, to find the missing pieces and see the monuments and objects of antiquity as totalities, as ancient people did. This is as true of the works of Aristotle—remember *The Name of the Rose,* and the search for the missing half, on comedy, of Aristotle's *Poetics*—as it is of the Parthenon and its frieze, dispersed now among London, Paris, Copenhagen, and Athens. The experience of the Parthenon frieze can now only be "virtual."

An exhibit in Paris in 2007 at the ethnographic museum on the Quai Branly, on Africa, showed the meticulous effort performed by those who use them in sewing back together, mending, and healing broken and damaged sacred ritual vessels. As the curators noted, there is no attempt to conceal the wound, the scar, the mending; the healer-craftsman-artist treats the sacred object like a human body in need of surgery and prosthetics and requiring gentle and expert stitching, suturing, welding, or replacement of lost parts. In the care and tending of the Greek and Roman classics, there has sometimes been a desire to efface the marks of suture, to disguise the labor of the mender, and to restore the object—be it temple or text—to an imagined pristine form. Is this part of the *attraction* of the field of ancient studies? It is not just a denial that antiquity lies in ruins, not just a wish that the ancient be made whole again, but also that the brokenness of the past has its own pathos, a call to the scholar to attend to it in its damaged state.

Davis himself is less inclined to recognize the fascination of the ruined body, the ways in which it speaks to us, although he makes a powerful argument for every viewer's capture by the mutilated Venuses of antiquity. Relying himself on Lacanian ideas of the body in pieces, and the defensive imagination of the whole body, the whole self, after passage through the mirror stage, he leads the reader to see how each spectator of these ruins is potentially disabled, through the retrospective fantasy of dismemberment, through the potential for disability in aging. In the work of Jacques Lacan, and his description of the state of the developed self, inhabiting an ego that is only an illusory part of the psyche, troubled by imaginary identifications and an unruly, expressive unconscious, we see how we might find echoes of our sense of self in the ruins, in the fragmentation of ancient objects. Along with a melancholy associated with the remnants of the past—some sense not only our reflection in these broken things, but also a reminder of the passing of empires as well as the inevitability of aging and death, and therefore of our joining the multitude of the dead whom we acknowledge through the study of their history, available only through the scattered fragments they have left behind—there is also a pleasure and fascination associated with these bodies in pieces.[13]

Among these ancient ruins are the mummies and their wrappings, the papyri in their broken and fragmentary state, from which many ancient texts, such as the love poems cited earlier, as well as information about everyday life in ancient Egypt, have been retrieved. These ancient remnants, surviving into the present, have their own fascination and erotic power. In an enactment of the reappearance of these ruins in modernity, we see how a mixture of revulsion and fascination characterized reactions to these remains.

Dominic Montserrat discusses the strangely stimulating erotic legacy of these Egyptian fragments:

> In the 21st Dynasty (c. 1000 BCE) the breasts and thighs of women, desiccated by the mummification process, were rounded out with subcutaneous packing to restore a lifelike fullness. The result gives the bodies an almost doll-like appearance. In later periods, women's nipples were gilded and vaginas covered with gold plates, or the entire body might be covered with gold leaf so that the dead person was reborn with the golden flesh of a divinity. The erotic foci of men's bodies were also highlighted, with the penis being gilded or sometimes an artificial one included in the mummy wrappings, to act as a substitute should the original be lost or damaged.[14]

The beauty of these remains ensures their potency in the afterlife. One moment in the trajectory of these ancient bodies and the papyri included in their wrapping involved "displays of the unrolling of actual mummified bodies . . . a vogue as a fashionable pastime for the English élite in the 1830s and 1840s" (182).

Montserrat cites the amateur archaeologist David Hogarth, in *Accidents of an Antiquary's Life* (1910), on the ambiguous, sometimes repulsive quality of these remains when discovered *in situ* in Africa: "Crawling on all fours in the dark, one often found the passage barred by a heap of dim swaddled mummies turned out of the coffins by some earlier snatcher of bodies; and over these one had to go, feeling their breast-bones crack under one's knees and their swathed heads shift horribly this way or that under one's hands" (186). The frisson of the dark source of these ancient bodies is part of their allure.

Colette and her lover, the Marquise de Belbeuf, gave an early performance piece, *Rêve d'Egypte,* at the Moulin Rouge in January of 1907, in which the marquise, "in drag as a male archaeologist, encountered the mummy of Colette, swathed in gauzy bandages. Colette arose and performed an erotic dance enacting her loves of old, meanwhile gradually shedding her wrappings until, almost nude, she and 'Yssim' [Missy, nickname of the marquise, Marie de Morny, spelled backwards] closed the scene in a passionate embrace" (193–194). In a deterritorialized reading of Sappho's work, all this is part of the context of our encounter, embracing a twenty-first-century understanding of queer erotics, postcoloniality, a critique of the seizure of precious ancient objects from colonialized territory, and the encompassing rejection by militant anticolonial movements of a classical and pre-Alexandrian Pharaonic past even as other strands of postcolonial postmodernity celebrate and commodify the touristic potential of ancient artifacts.

What are we to make of the ruined, partial, yet fuller survival of another version of Sappho's fragment 58, which centers on the ruin of the body in aging? A new Sappho fragment was discovered in 2004, when two scholars, Michael Gronewald and Robert Daniel, identified a papyrus acquired by the University of Cologne as belonging to a roll containing some poems of Sappho. The roll of reed paper, which came from Egyptian mummy wrapping, is the earliest of the manuscripts of the Lesbian poet's poem, copied in the early third century B.C.E. It is especially appropriate that this poem was found in the cartonnage, the wrapping around a mummy, holding the dead, since it touches on questions of aging and survival, perhaps even after death. The dry, brittle, friable papyrus onto which Sappho's lines were once copied, like a corpse, a mummy itself, is now brought to light and re-embodied by contemporary readers.

The poem was partially known before in a fragment from another roll dating from 600 years later, the third century C.E.; when scholars combined the two fragments, they were able to reconstruct a poem that is almost complete.[15] The earlier fragment consisted mostly of line endings, which ran into other line endings from other poems; the beginnings of lines were completely absent. Now the break between this poem and others seems reasonably clear, and scholars are able to establish a fairly stable version of a poem of six two-line stanzas, although some argue for the continuation of this fragmentary portion by lines from the older papyrus (P. Oxy. Fr. 1. 4–25, fr. 2.1+fr. Nov. [Lobel S. m. p. 26]).

This is M. L. West's translation:[16]

> [You for] the fragrant-bosomed [Muses'] lovely gift
> [be zealous,] girls, [and the] clear melodious lyre:
>
> [but my tender] body old age now
> [has seized;] my hairs turned [white] instead of dark;
>
> my heart's grown heavy, my knees will not support me,
> that once on a time were fleet for the dance as fawns.
>
> This state I oft bemoan; but what's to do?
> Not to grow old, being human, there's no way.
>
> Tithonus once, the tale was, rose-armed Dawn,
> love-smitten, carried off to the world's end,
>
> handsome and young then, yet in time grey age
> o'ertook him, husband of immortal wife.

Much of the debate has focused on whether the poem ends here or continues, as did the previously published fragment, with "But I love elegance *(habrosune)*" and something broken up, about eros and the sun. I will just hold this question in suspension, let both fragmentary endings be, and go on to suggest some ways in which a reoriented reading of this poem might supplement more traditional, and essential, valuable classicist textual scholarship—acknowledging first the survival of this poem, unread until 2004, into the twenty-first century—and links with other ancient places and their presence in our global reality. This poem conjures up not the *polis,* but a heterotopia—women's intimate, ritual space. It enacts a "becoming-animal," through lines of flight into other species; it alludes to other other spaces—the East of Eos, the Sanskrit Vedas, Amazonia, Ethiopia, land of the sun, Arabia, land of aromatics, of the harvest of cinnamon and frankincense; and the theme of aging leads to Tithonus, to cicadas, to Plato and the sounding of the poem in new bodies.

The poem is addressed to the young, Sappho's companions who now must dance in her place and honor the gift of the Muses and the lyre, made from a tortoise's shell, a musical instrument that once was part of an animal, its making recounted in the *Homeric Hymn to Hermes.* The animal is dead, but it has been incorporated into worship, the music and dance for the Muses, as it sounds beautifully in ceremony. The voice in the poet is that of someone whose tender body has been cruelly seized by old age, and the language here suggests a violent capture. Her hair has turned white, her heart heavy, her knees weak. The knees were a crucial feature of the architecture of the ancient body, as the late R. B. Onians argued long ago, pointing to their sanctity: "the fluid or liquefiable content of the joint, its true function not being known, was classed with the cerebro-spinal fluid or liquefiable substance, the fluid of life."[17]

The voice in the poem expresses regret about white hair, a lack of strength, and she recalls a different time, in a "line of flight," as Deleuze and Guattari would call it, writing of metamorphoses in Kafka: "To become animal is to participate in movement, to stake out the path of escape in all its positivity, to cross a threshold, to reach a continuum of pure intensities where all forms come undone, as do all the significations, signifiers, and signifieds, to the benefit of an unformed matter of deterritorialized flux, or non-signifying signs."[18] Sappho's utopian recollection suggests another sort of "becoming-animal," not the dead stasis of the tortoise's shell that expresses music, but movement in the dance and an escape backward, into the past and the atemporality of animal existence, away from the ruin of human aging and the consciousness of individual death.

The imagery of this poem condenses themes of predation and vulnerability, capture and escape. The fleet animal is the target of the hunter, who kills and skins the prey. The poet remembers the grace, the flight of young animals imitated in the dance, perhaps a Bacchic dance in which maenads donned the skins of fawns, as represented in tragedy and on vase paintings, in honor of the three gods of Lesbos—Zeus, Hera, and Dionysus, "who consumes raw flesh," in Alkaios' words (fr. 129).

Other lyric poets lament their own loss of erotic potency as they age and their bodies approach a state of ruin. Archilochus condemns an aging woman in fragment 188:

> Your tender skin has lost its former bloom,
> Dries out in furrows; ugly age
> Makes you its prey. Sweet charm from your fair face
> Has hopped it. . . .
>
> *(M. L. West translation)*[19]

Semonides describes being overtaken by old age (fr. 1) and urges the listener not to dwell on woes. Tyrtaeus describes the disgraceful fall of an elderly man in the front line of battle when the young hold back (fr. 10), a shameful and scandalous sight compared with the beautiful sight of the lovely fallen young man. (Tyrtaeus also mentions Tithonus' beauty (fr. 12), and the happiness in growing old, in the celebrity of a successful warrior.) Mimnermus complains that "when painful age / comes on, that makes a man loathsome and vile. . . . / He is abhorred by boys, by women scorned; so hard a thing the god made old age to be" (fr. 1, trans. West). Much of the regret about aging is associated with Eros, as in this fragment from Anacreon (fr. 379, trans. West): "Love, seeing me with graying beard, flies past; / I feel the draught of his gold-gleaming wings."

Sappho does not insist on a loss of erotic powers. She conceives her aging as a diminution in her power to dance, even as she acknowledges, as do the other lyricists, that human beings must age. In a characteristic move, Sappho goes on to prove her point that the most beautiful thing is what one loves with the example of Helen in fragment 16. Here in a paradoxical formulation, perhaps in an attempt to ward off what seems to be an inevitable association, a progression of thought from aging to death, Sappho reminds us of a mortal man who aged but did not die, Tithonus, the once mortal lover of the goddess Eos, Dawn.[20]

Dawn became enamored of Tithonus, a son of Laomedon, king of Troy, and begged Zeus to make her mortal lover immortal, and he did. But Eos failed to ask Zeus for agelessness for her lover. As the Sappho poem concludes, we see succinctly and compactly recorded the fate of Tithonus. The myth, truncated here, deftly alludes to the terrible ironies of this union, which are drawn out in greater detail by other poets, the most poignant telling of the Tithonus-Eos story coming in the *Homeric Hymn to Aphrodite*. After seducing the mortal Anchises, the goddess tells him the monitory tale of the dawn goddess:

> So . . . , golden-throned Eos abducted Tithonos,
> One of your own race, who resembled the immortals.
> She went to ask Kronion, lord of dark clouds,
> That he should be immortal and live forever.
> And Zeus nodded assent to her and fulfilled her wish.
> Mighty Eos was too foolish to think of asking
> Youth for him and to strip him of baneful old age.
> Indeed, so long as much-coveted youth was his,
> He took his delight in early-born, golden-haired Eos,
> And dwelt by the stream of Okeanos at the ends of the earth.
> But when the first gray hairs began to flow down
> From his comely head and noble chin,

> Mighty Eos did refrain from his bed,
> Though she kept him in her house and pampered him
> With food and ambrosia and gifts of fine clothing.
> But when detested old age weighed heavy on him
>
> And he could move or lift none of his limbs,
> This is the counsel that to her seemed best in her heart:
> She placed him in a chamber and shut its shining doors.
> His voice flows endlessly and there is no strength,
> Such as there was before, in his crooked limbs.[21]

Sappho's poem refers only obliquely to the whole of this tragic narrative.

Eos can be associated with possible Indo-European sources, and with Vedic hymns to the goddess, or goddesses, of the dawn. Homer refers to Dawn as "rose-fingered." According to West, "The spread hand as an image of the sun's rays may be inherited from older poetic tradition. The Vedic *suanguri-*, 'with good fingers' is a complimentary epithet of goddesses, but when it is applied to the solar god Savitr (RV 4.54.4) it is surely to be understood in terms of rays."[22] West finds further parallels between Eos and the Vedic dawn goddess:

> Usas is not associated with a specific mortal lover. But there seems to be a suggestion that she might be tarrying with one in 1.30.20:
>
> Who is there for you, O whose-friend Dawn,
> to enjoy, (which) mortal, immortal one?
> Whom are you visiting, radiant one?
>
> If there is no Indian Tithonos, growing ever older in the house of his perpetually young consort, there is at least an awareness of the tragic contrast between her and us. "Bringing old age, thou has come, O unageing Dawn. . . . Unageing, thou dost make to age all else." [TS 4.3.11.5; cf. RV 1.124.2][23]

Eos and her Vedic counterpart share an immortality that causes pain to mortals, even though, as Nagy points out, "The Rig-Vedic Usas is an overtly beneficent goddess, well known for her function of dispelling the darkness (1.92.5, 2.34.12, etc.). Yet her epithet *diva(s) duhitar-/duhitar-divas* is ambivalent."[24]

The Greek goddess embraces and carries away her lover to the ends of the earth, in a phrase that associates Tithonus with the eastern limits from which the dawn arises, where Eos had her *khoroi*, her dancing places (Od. 12.4). "Eos' house (*oikia*, neuter plural) may be put beside the mythical eastern mountain of the Avesta called Usidam-, 'Dawn-house' (Yt. 1.28, 31; 19.2, 66)."[25] The pair's sons are Memnon, who traveled south to become king of Ethiopia and brought the Amazons from the far northeast to Troy, and his brother, the Arabian Emathion. Memnon died at Troy and was either made immortal at his mother's request or commemorated by the metamorphosis of his funeral pyre's smoke into birds who fought each other, then fell into the fire as offerings to the dead; according to the poets, birds gather every year at the tomb (Ovid *Met* 13.576–622).

Later versions of the myth of Tithonus report that his thin, tiny, tinny voice finally metamorphosed into the tribe of cicadas, this in Hellanicus, a fifth-century B.C.E. mythographer and writer of chronicles; he, like Sappho, was a Lesbian.[26] Cicadas constitute an anonymous, collective multitude, singing ceaselessly in a light voice, and they are associated with the aged very early, with legends of long life, like the trees and their dryads and nymphs, and with immortality, as they are on the Shang bronzes of ancient China. One of the most beautiful and evocative explorations of the voice of the cicada is in Plato's *Phaedrus*, where he recalls another version of their origins that also touches on the theme of immortality through solar imagery and song that Sappho leaves us with in this poem. Socrates and young Phaedrus go on a walk outside the wall of Athens and stroll alongside the river Ilissos. They come to a plane tree and a nymphaeum, a shrine to the nymphs. There the character Socrates recounts the myth of the origins of the cicadas:

> The story is that once upon a time these creatures were men—men of an age before there were any Muses—and that when the latter came into the world, and music made its appearance, some of the people of those days were so thrilled with pleasure that they went on singing, and quite forgot to eat and drink until they actually died without noticing it. From them in due course sprang the race of cicadas, to which the Muses have granted the boon of needing no sustenance right from their birth, but of singing from the very first, without food or drink, until the day of their death, after which they go and report to the Muses how they severally are paid honor among mankind, and by whom.[27]

This alternate version of the origin of the cicadas preserves the notion of the persistence of the voice in a body that gradually disappears from around it.[28]

This is a compelling figure for the survival of poetry, especially lyric poetry, the voice overheard, the voice brought back to life, sounded, especially through the ancient practice of reading aloud. As Jesper Svenbro puts it in *Phrasikleia:* "The reader is . . . the sonorous instrument of what is written."[29] The poet immortalizes the hero, as Homer does; he becomes immortal as the one who praises the hero, and then the hero disappears, and the poet herself is immortalized, like Horace and Ovid, whose monuments survive the fall of empire. In the case of Sappho fragment 58, the poem itself is re-embodied, reanimated for us, in the mummy *cartonnage* of Cologne.

How does the presence of the aging animal, human body, connect with other sorts of ruins, ancient papyri and the ruins of ancient monuments? Tekmessa, in Sophocles' *Ajax,* refers to slaughtered animals as *ereipia nekron*—"broken bodies" (308), "ruins of corpses," brought to death by the hero's violence. Tekmessa, as messenger, describes his madness, and his recovery: "And when he saw his dwelling full of Ruin [*Ate*] / He beat his head and bellowed. There he sat, / Wreckage himself among the wreck of corpses" (trans. J. Moore).[30] This terrible moment, conveyed through the voice of a witness, compels the English translator to use the word *Ruin,* capitalized in the translation, a personified deity, Ate, the monster that is Ruin.

Other bodies, as they near death, approach a ruinous state. In the case of the ruined bodies created by Ajax's mad slaughter, violence creates ruin. What of the body that ages and dries out naturally? In *Parva Naturalia,* Aristotle makes a distinction between death from violence and natural death, which occurs through the gradual lessening of warmth in the body, which dries as it ages and cannot continue to sustain sufficient heat to preserve life. Aging is a drying up of the body's sap but also a fettering of what once was mobile, free, and limber.[31] The *keres,* powers of evil and death, bind their victims; old age is seen as a bond that fetters or a veil, a skin over the body. This is "confirmed by *Homeric Hymn to Aphrodite,* 224, according to which Eos forgot to ask for youth for Tithonus and to 'scrape away baleful *geras* [old age].' "[32]

It is possible to liken, as Aristotle does in *Rhetoric* 3.11.13, "a ruin to the rag of a house"; he himself links the trope of metaphor with aging, when he says, "It is metaphor, above all, that produces the effect [of pleasant, easy learning]; for when he [Homer] calls old age stubble, he teaches and informs us through the genus; for both have lost their bloom" (*Rhetoric* 3.10.2). The ruin of the living body, and especially its "falling away" in aging, casts light on the question of ancient ruins in general. In metaphor, a catalyst of wonder and new understanding, the ruin of the aging human body stands among the others we encounter as we engage classical antiquity in broken, mutilated marble figures, the crumbled outlines of ancient temples, and the friable, eroding sheets of plant material that survive and surrender up the texts of ancient poets. All recall a lost whole, a fleeting, ephemeral totality, a perfect and inaccessible whole that excites a drive for restoration to perfection.

As mentioned earlier, one of the sons of Eos and Tithonus—not the Arabian Emathion, but Memnon, king of Ethiopia, who ruled in Africa and brought the Amazons to Troy—was killed in battle by Achilles, like Penthesilea, after Zeus weighed the rival warriors' souls, a scene represented on vases, in a practice that resembled the judgment of Osiris in ancient Egypt.[33] I want here to recall another representation of Memnon, however, one linked to the themes of Egypt and the ruined body, the remains of antiquity that haunt the present. One of two colossal statues of the Egyptian pharaoh Amenophis III of the mid-second millennium B.C.E., this one depicting the seated pharaoh, was apparently damaged in an earthquake in 27 B.C.E. and lost its top portion. The loss, the ruining of the sculpture, produced a strange acoustical phenomenon until it was repaired by Septimius Severus in the early third century C.E. This statue was associated with Memnon, perhaps because of the similarity of his name with that of Amenophis III. It was visited by Juvenal and marked by numerous inscriptions left behind by other visitors. According to the Paradoxographus Vaticanus of the second century C.E., this statue was heard by many visitors to sing to the rising sun, and was revered as a monument to a lost hero, son of Dawn and Tithonus, the ruined and broken Memnon crying out to his mother Eos (PV 23).[34]

Although the other archaic lyric poets tended to associate aging with a diminished power to seduce boys and women, with a loss of their erotic potency, Sappho connects it with a diminished power to worship and celebrate the Muses with her own body. Yet the myth of Tithonus allows us to read beyond and remap this story. Just as the embodied readers of antiquity reread this poem or sang it to one another, sounding it in the shells of their bodies, like the tortoise shell that becomes an instrument of the celebration of the Muses, so the song of Sappho persists uncannily, reembodied, like the song of the cicadas, those nameless, anonymous, collective, immortal singers descended from the disembodied voice of the aged but immortal Tithonus. If her body begins to betray her, to age, her voice, her song, like the cicadas', survives even into our twenty-first century. If the complex of allusions in the poem is indeed, as Gregory Nagy suggested before the discovery of the new fragment, entwined with Indo-European ideas about the sun, dawn, and sunset and the rebirth and rebeautification of goddess and lover, the survival of the poem touches on these very themes.

How does all this make for a borderless classical studies, a deterritorialized, diasporic, and unpredictably branching discipline, extended in time and space? We have Sappho, the Lesbian lesbian, on an island close to the edge of Asia, looking toward the Asian city of Sardis, a lover of women distinct from the other lyric poets with their emphatically phallic presence. Her poems establish a heterotopia, an other space, distinct from the classical *polis* that has long been the focus of much work on the ancient Greek world. And the poem invokes worlds beyond the Greek mainland, the eastern world of the dawn invoked in the Rig Veda, the Ethiopian and Arabian domains of the sons of Tithonus and Eos, and the land of the Amazons, around the Black Sea. The poem itself, in its ruined, broken state, with an ambiguous ending, having traveled from Lesbos to Alexandria and Greek Egypt, wrapped in the covered coffin of an ancient Egyptian, preserved on papyrus as a trophy in a collector's hoard, remains for now in a library in Cologne. Every time we read Sappho's lines, the human voice re-embodies the dead poet and brings her voice unexpectedly into the twenty-first century. All of the elements associated with this survival are part of a new imagining of the current presence of an ancient world. And if the planet falls into the possession, finally, of the sturdy cockroaches, as some predict, or if human culture survives only in computers that will launch themselves into outer space, as Jean-François Lyotard foresaw, then let us hope they will be resounding the songs of Sappho.

4

THE TATTOOS OF EPIMENIDES

The poetry of Sappho is rhizomically connected to Vedic hymns to the goddess of the dawn, and to the verse forms of the earliest Indian epics. As we have seen in the last chapter, her fragmentary and broken corpus of poems has many links with Egypt: Sappho's brother was said to have traveled to Egypt, and her poetry was copied and buried with the mummies of ancient Egypt, reborn in the nineteenth- and twentieth-century discoveries of tombs, mummies, and papyrus, which animated an intense erotic cathexis, as in the performance art of Colette.[1] The utopian aspects of Sappho's lyrics, her setting aside of a lyric world defined by female intimacies, the presence of Aphrodite, song and worship, created a heterotopia within the intensely engaged political struggles of archaic Lesbos. There is a magical, incantatory aspect to some of Sappho's poems that connects it as well with the powerful figures of the archaic world who, through a special wisdom, could move between the world of the living and that of the dead, who had special access to knowledge of the past and future, and who were enlisted into the service of the city of the archaic age.[2] These characters, among them Epimenides of Crete, who may have seemed freakish even to ancient people, shared attributes with wise men of other civilizations, especially Mesopotamia and India.

I am especially interested in this chapter in the stranger, in the slippage between the abnormal and the unnatural, and in people who deliberately set themselves outside the norm, choose to be abnormal, in order to become unnatural, especially in the case of the magician or sage or shaman, to be unnatural in their conquest of death, who travel, for example, outside of the norms of human existence, living outside the world, visiting the land of the dead, living immense life spans, returning themselves from death.[3] This chapter concerns not just the norm and the abnorm, but rather characters of legend, shamans or magicians, who stand as freaks of nature in the stories told of them.

In the nineteenth century, freaks were usually corporeal anomalies of the conjoined twin sort, but Rosemarie Garland-Thomson provides a list of the corporeal wonders characteristic of the American freak show of the last century, revealing the geographical range of strangeness, the ways the early American empire recruited exotic characters from distant places in a newly accessible world: "from wild men of Borneo to fat ladies, living skeletons, Fiji princes, albinos, bearded women, Siamese twins, tattooed Circassians, armless and legless wonders, Chinese giants, cannibals, midget triplets, hermaphrodites, spotted boys, and much more."[4] Some of these extraordinary bodies figure in the disturbing classic film *Freaks,* released in 1932. Of all Garland-Thomson's freaks, only the tattooed Circassian has, perhaps, made himself a freak; the others are born anomalous in color, shape, or body, extraordinary to look upon, or are seen as freakish only because they come from foreign lands. In the traveling freak shows, human beings were viewed with both fascination and disgust, wonder and horror; they were not admired for their special powers nor emulated by the possessors of ordinary bodies. And in some ways their bodies map a new imperial cartography, allowing access to once remote parts of an already globalizing modernity.

Leonard Cassuto provides a convincing historical argument concerning the role of these spectacles of pathos and difference from the 1840s to the 1940s:

> Freak shows filled a gap that they did not create. This space, between the desire for absolute racial difference and the fact that none exists, was wide and deep in a culture that relied on such difference for its very organizing principles. The gap was occupied by fetishing practices like blackface minstrelsy . . . and also by freak shows . . . Freak shows were a performance of one kind of imaginary difference in an effort to assert another.[5]

In the scientistic atmosphere of the nineteenth century, when power and knowledge converged to produce the object of medicalized psychopathology and psychoanalysis, the abnormal dialectically produced a notion of the norm, which is deployed still in social science, even as postmodern theory—and queer theory in the hands of such thinkers as Judith Butler—have sought to call it into question.

In a series of lectures delivered at the College de France in 1974 and 1975, published under the title *Abnormal,* Michel Foucault discussed the genealogy of our current conception of the norm.[6] He traced a development over several centuries, from the early modern period to the present:

> The "abnormal" individual that so many institutions, discourses and knowledges have been concerned with since the end of the nineteenth century derives from the juridico-natural exception of the monster, the multitude of incorrigible individuals caught in the apparatus of reification, and the universal secret of childhood sexuality. In fact, the three figures of the monster, the incorrigible, and the onanist do not merge. Each is inscribed within autonomous systems of scientific reference: the monster in a teratology and embryology . . . ; the incorrigible in a psychophysiology of sensations, motor functions, and abilities; the onanist in a theory of sexuality that is developed slowly starting from Kaan's *Psychopathia sexualis*. (328)

Foucault's category of the monster most closely resembles the strange power of the stranger, of the uncanny shamans of classical antiquity, although he is referring to individuals who are caught up in a developing legal system. The idea of the monster, he argues, is a juridical notion, since it "concerns the laws of nature as well as the laws of society" (323). Antiquity presents myriad monstrous creatures such as the centaur or the Amazon, some inherited from hybrid creations of Egypt or the ancient Near East and exemplifying not a juridical anomaly, but rather a fascination with borders, with those who live beyond the known limits of civilization, or who cross species border lines.

Our interest in the ab-normal may emerge dialectically from our position in the norm, in the regime of knowledge and power where we are trapped by ideas of norm, normalcy, normality. Foucault himself sees monsters, the abnormal, from this perspective, the monster as an individual who produces anxiety, who is a problem for the law, for bio-juridical power, who is an object of governmentality. What interests me most about such beings is not the horror associated with the abnormal, the unnatural, but rather the great power of the abnormal, the freakish, an aura of sacredness that inheres in the strangeness of the unnatural in antiquity. Jack Winkler, much concerned throughout his seminal book *The Constraints of Desire* with the category of the "unnatural," analyzed the possibility that *unnatural* can be a term of praise.[7] He wrote, "The word 'unnatural' in contexts of human behavior quite regularly means 'seriously unconventional' and is used like a Thin Ice to mark off territory where it is dangerous to venture" (17). He attributes the contrast between nature and convention, *phusis* and *nomos*, to the sophists of the fifth century B.C.E. and points to "isolated bits of moralizing texts" (18), of the sort Foucault relied on for his *Use of Pleasures,* the second volume of the *History of Sexuality,* as "unrepresentative" (18), giving a false idea of "Greek" ideas about pederasty, for example. In his anthropological enterprise, Winkler points to other sources, including Thucydides' account of the women of Corcyra, who supported their husbands by tossing roof tiles onto the heads of enemy oligarchs: Their participation in the battle is called "unnatural," *para phusin* (3.74). "In this case," Winkler argues, " 'unnatural' is a term of praise, as the wives transcend their socialized reticence and engage in open violence in support of their families' interests" (20). Nature means convention, that is, culture.

Freak might be translated into Greek as *teras,* "monster," or as *thauma,* "wonder" (related to *theaomai,* "gaze at with a sense of wonder"), the wonder that Aristotle in the *Metaphysics* says is the beginning of philosophy (1.2, 982b10–982b18).[8] The pseudo-Aristotelian treatise "On Marvellous Things Heard" *(peri thaumasion akousmaton),* probably written by a later Peripatetic, sets out a wide spectrum of wonders, including a wild Paeonian beast called a *bolinthus,* which had a hide that when skinned covered the space of eight couches and which defended itself by "kicking and voiding excrement over a distance of forty feet . . . excrement which scorches so fiercely that it will scrape off a dog's hair" (830a). In two accounts, or anecdotes, that connect the Aristotelian treatise with the magician and sage Epimenides, the text recounts the marvelous story of Demaratus, who fell ill, became dumb for ten days, and when recovered said that he had had the happiest time of his life (847a). The treatise contains another wondrous tale, of a man who fell asleep in a cave on the Aeolian island Lipara after drinking heavily, was found on the fourth day and taken for dead to his own tomb, but "after receiving all the usual rites he suddenly arose and told all that had happened to him" (839a).[9]

Two strands, delight in the unnatural, and the inhibiting conventionality of the natural, come together in this chapter on the magical freaks of antiquity, one of whom I propose to look at in some detail: Epimenides the "magician," who breaches the boundary between the living and the dead, in an even wider extension of the ancient Greek world. We must first, however, acknowledge the problematic move of calling anyone a magician. In antiquity, and perhaps in the present as well, for many people magic is other people's religion; magic can have the virtue of exoticism, the fascination of a distant thing, but sometimes the term *magic* is a semantic trap that colonizes, diminishes, trivializes the rituals of other, often "primitive" people. In the present, there is often an implicit condescension from location in a western monotheism that disavows its own magical aspects. Some of the most interesting recent scholarship in classics focuses on the popular culture, archaeology, and rituals of so-called magic.[10] From some perspectives, abnormally developed individuals of the human species, *thaumata,* are divine, masters of truth, or shamans rather than magicians. Yet to call them magicians is to set them in the ancient context, as *magoi*—that is, from the perspective of high culture, charlatans or sorcerers; from another perspective, persons of extraordinary gifts and powers.

Many features of the life of Epimenides, sometimes listed as one of the seven sages of archaic Greek antiquity, call attention to him as unnatural, abnormal, an adept at what were later identified as magical practices. He probably lived in the seventh century B.C.E., a Cretan of Knossos, with the unusual feature that he had Pythagorean long hair—"differing by the letting down of his hair . . . he did not look like a Cretan."[11] In a biographical account relying on Theopompus, Phlegon of Tralles in *On Longevity,* and Xenophon of Colophon, Diogenes Laërtius sets out his strange career, a career that calls up not so much questions of the abnormal, although he certainly was that from the statistical perspective of modernity, but especially questions of the unnatural, in that Epimenides violated many of the natural rules governing human existence, defying death by returning after his long life to visit the mortal, decaying, human world again.

Diogenes tells the story of Epimenides' youth: His father sent him into the countryside to search for a sheep. At noon he turned aside *(tes hodou ekklinas)* and went to sleep in a cave, where he slept for fifty-seven years (D.L. 1.109). Then he got up and went looking again for the sheep, which were not to be found, but Epimenides did not yet know that he had been asleep. This is, as E. R. Dodds notes in *The Greeks and the Irrational,* a common feature of folktales, but he adds that the Long Sleep at the beginning of the story of Epimenides "suggests that the Greeks had heard of the long 'retreat' which is the shaman's novitiate and is sometimes largely spent in a condition of sleep or trance."[12] According to another source, Epimenides, a master of truth, while in the cave on Mount Dikte conversed in a dream state with the gods and met *Aletheia* and *Dike,* "Truth" and "Justice" (Diels FVS7, 1, 32 17 ff).[13]

Epimenides, not finding the sheep, went back to his father's farm and found someone else in possession of it. He found both country and city utterly changed; going to the *astu,* the city, entering the house, he discovered people there who wanted to know who he was. Finally, he came upon his younger brother, who had become an old man, and learned *pasan ten aletheian,* "the whole truth." He was thereafter known by the Greeks as *theophilestatos,* "most dear to the gods." This epithet has several aspects. First of all, there is the weird and freakish fact of Epimenides, while preserving his own youth, sleeping just long enough to catch the end of his brother's life, therefore being out of sync with his own generation, his own natural life span, but still able to learn the truth from someone who was living a normal, natural life. Such a *décalage,* a time lag, is a standard feature of science fiction, in which people who engage in space travel or experience time warps come back to their previous reality and find everything changed. Then there is the fact that Epimenides, having fallen asleep and then reawakened, is seen as favored by the gods; this is in remarkable contrast with the account in Herodotus of the lives of young Biton and Cleobis, who, in answer to their mother's prayer, fell asleep in the temple of Hera, to which they had transported their mother, never to wake again. The anecdote, told in the context of Solon's visit to Croesus, reinforces the notion that those whom the gods love die young. Solon says, "The god used them to show that it is better for a person to be dead than to be alive." The goddess had given them "whatever it is best for a human being to have."[14] Solon went on to stress the negative consequences of long life, even though he himself lived a long albeit natural life span: "Anyone who lives for a long time is bound to see and endure many things he would rather avoid" (1.32). Croesus notoriously failed to learn this important lesson. And Epimenides, freakishly, is said to be most beloved by the gods, even though his career so clearly defies the principles adduced by Solon. This is another strain then, contradicting the pessimism of the classical period, or perhaps an optimism surviving from an earlier age, or even a strand of the ideology of another class, the same populace that will later embrace the practices of magic flourishing beneath the surface of more official cult.

Because of his fame, the Athenians called on Epimenides when they were subdued by a plague and were advised by the Pythia at the Delphic oracle to purify the city. Nicias, son of Niceratus, went to Crete to request Epimenides' aid. Epimenides arrived in the forty-sixth Olympiad, that is, between 595 and 592 B.C.E., cleansed or purified *(ekatheren)* the city, and stopped the disease. His method curiously echoed the earlier story of his long sleep. He took sheep, the very beasts he had sought as a boy near Knossos on Crete. This time there were many sheep, both black and white, the pure and the impure, the pure white animal the one ritually chosen for sacrifice. He brought the animals to the Areopagus, and let the animals wander where they pleased, "instructing those who followed them to mark the spot where each sheep lay down *(kataklinoi)* and offer a sacrifice to the local divinity" (1. 110). (*Kataklinoi* echoes *tes hodou ekklinas:* "He turned aside out of the way" of his earlier adventure in the cave [1. 109].) In this case a sacrifice was offered to the *prosekonti theo,* the "local divinity," the god belonging to the spot, perhaps Ares. This is intriguing in part because Epimenides himself, after lying down in his spot, the cave, perhaps the very Idaean or Dikteian cave in which the god Zeus was raised, was precisely not sacrificed, did not die, but spent his fifty-seven years asleep, in a pseudo-death, only to awaken and carry on as if nothing had happened.[15]

Epimenides' powers allowed him to work out the proper method of catharsis for Athens. If it was in fact Ares to whom the sacrifices were made, it seems appropriate for the sort of feud being carried out between rival aristocratic families in Athens.[16] Epimenides, whose nature it was, according to Robert Parker, "to be wrapped in swathes of the fabulous,"[17] put an end to the plague, caused by pollution following the murder of the followers of Cylon. the Athenian aristocrat and an Olympic victor, who had married the daughter of the tyrant of Megara and seemed to have schemed for the tyranny of Athens himself, when with others he seized the Acropolis in the Olympic year 632. Besieged, he escaped, but his friends, who surrendered and sought sanctuary at an altar or, according to Herodotus, at the base of the statue of Athena, were persuaded to quit the statue with assurances that they would be spared, were killed. A curse thereafter fell on the archon of the city, Megakles, and his family, the Alcmaeonids (for Megakles' son Alcmaeon; Alcibiades, favorite of Socrates, had an Alcmaeonid mother) (Herodotus 5.71, Thucydides 1.126). Perhaps the slaughter of both black and white sheep refers to a compensatory killing of two opposing sides in a struggle; the sacrifice of both sorts evens the score and mediates the difference that had produced the pestilence.

Diogenes Laërtius reported that Epimenides was said to have founded the temple in Athens dedicated to the Eumenides, which is suggestive given their transformation from vengeful furies to benign presences, and also to have been the first man ever to found temples. He was said to have purified houses and fields *(oikias kai agrous).* In his life of Epimenides,

Diogenes Laërtius said that altars were still to be found in Attica in his day (probably the first half of the third century C.E.) without names inscribed on them, "memorials of this atonement" *(exilaseos)*. In the first version of the story, it is suggested that sheep, the most common sacrificial animals, were killed to avert the plague. But Diogenes goes on to report that Epimenides said directly that the Cylonian pollution was the cause of the plague; that he showed them how to remove it; and that two youths, Kratinos and Ktesibios, were killed in a human sacrifice to release the city from the disaster. This is a more violent and archaic version of the story concerning the lying down of sheep on the Areopagus. Epimenides was also said to have had prophetic powers and to have predicted that Mounichia, a hill and harbor near the Athenian port of Piraeus, would bring evils on the Athenians and, if they knew the dangers, "they would destroy it even if they had to do so with their teeth" (D.L. 114). (This prophesy contradicts Aristotle's claim about Epimenides in the *Rhetoric* that he "did not praise divination about the future; only about the obscurities of the past" [1418a21].) But according to Diogenes, Epimenides called himself Aiakos, after a judge in the underworld, made other prophecies, and suddenly became old "in as many days as he had slept years" (115).

Plutarch, in his *Life of Solon,* recalls that the Athenians

> sent for Epimenides the Phaestian from Crete, who is counted the seventh wise man by those who will not admit Periander into the number. He seems to have been thought a favourite of heaven, possessed of knowledge in all the supernatural and ritual parts of religion; and, therefore, the men of his age called him a new Curies, and son of a nymph named Balte. When he came to Athens, and grew acquainted with Solon, he served him in many instances, and prepared the way for his legislation. He made them moderate in their forms of worship, and abated their mourning by ordering some sacrifices presently after the funeral, and taking off those severe and barbarous ceremonies which the women usually practiced; but the greatest benefit was his purifying and sanctifying the city, by certain propitiatory and expiatory lustrations, and foundations of sacred buildings, by that means making them more submissive to justice, and more inclined to harmony.[18]

Plato's Clinias, in his conversation with "the Athenian" and the Spartan Megillus, as they walked from Knossos to the cave of Zeus, also recalled the visit of Epimenides to Athens, in the context of lawmaking, where Epimenides was seen as a precursor to the great lawgiver Solon:

Clinias: You have presumably heard of Epimenides, an inspired person born in this city [Knossos] and connected with my own family, who visited Athens ten years before the Persian Wars at the bidding of the oracle, and offered certain sacrifices enjoined by the god, besides telling the citizens, who were alarmed by the Persian preparations, that the enemy would not come within ten years, and when they did, would depart again with their purpose unaffected, after receiving more damage than they inflicted. That was when my family contracted their friendship with your countrymen, and my ancestors and myself have had a kindness for them ever since.[19]

This recollection of alliance serves as an invitation to the Athenian to expound on what was seen as the superiority of the Athenian laws, beginning with true education. Elsewhere Diogenes discusses the peculiar eating habits of Epimenides, which mark his kinship with other sages of the ancient world, with other civilizations; he was reported to receive special food from the nymphs, which he kept in a cow's hoof; he consumed this food, which was never excreted *(medemia kenousthai apokrisei),* and he was never seen to eat (114).

Thomas McEvilley, in his voluminous study of relationships between ancient India and ancient Greece, considers fully the possibility of "diffusion channels in the pre-Alexandrian period": "I will make a measured attempt to establish significant intrusions first from India to Greece in the pre-Socratic period, then from Greece back to India in the Hellenistic period."[20] He argues that "around 1500 to 1300 B.C. full East-West transport of goods—almost from one end of Eurasia to the other—was achieved. The final link was the appearance of the caravan emporia of Bactria ... linking India, China, and Central Asia at one end with the Near East and the Mediterranean at the other" (4). Richard Martin, in an anthropological, cross-cultural essay on the myths associated with the Greeks' seven sages, points out in ancient India "an exact parallel in the ascetic activities attributed to the Seven Rsis, who fast and abstain."[21]

Evidence concerning the seven sages of the ancient Greeks, among whom Epimenides was sometimes though not always included, came to light in an important site of the late Hellenistic world:

It was only in October 1966 that French archaeologists discovered at Ai-Khanum in Afghanistan, site of an ancient Greco-Bactrian city, an important missing piece of the sages puzzle: a poetic inscription on a stele base which confirms that a list of 147 sayings of the Seven Sages, a list known up until then only from very late literary sources such as the Byzantine scholar Stobaeus, was extant in the third century B.C.E. and purported to be an exact copy, by the Peripatetic Klearchos of Soli, of a list inscribed in Apollo's temple at Delphi.[22]

Martin, disagreeing with Fehling, who argues that Plato made up the idea of the seven sages,[23] sees what he calls "features" that wise men in various cultures share—they are poets, are involved in politics, and are performers (113)—forming a "scatter pattern" (115).[24] He adduces anthropological material from New Mexico, Panama, and Cameroon, as well as ancient examples, possibly demonstrating the "Near Eastern origins of the idea of seven wise men" (121). "In Babylonian tradition there are Seven Sages," and in the *Epic of Gilgamesh,* containing "elements as early as 2000 B.C.E. and as late as 1200 B.C.E.," we learn that the walls of the great city of Uruk were said to have been built by seven wise men.

> Ancient India offers us a closer parallel to the Greek tradition of the Seven Sages. In Sanskrit texts from the Vedas on, one can [find] fairly frequent mention of a group called the Seven Rsis. The texts portray these men as both seers and poets, but also as creators, mystics, makers of sacrifice, and, in what seem to us stranger associations, stars—the Pleiades—and life breaths. As in Greek tradition, the later literature inflates the number of sages from seven to dozens . . . The rsis are said to be rulers or to be the gurus of kings, in many texts. Again, they are associated with the composition of hymns to the gods and with foreseeing future events or having seer-like knowledge . . . [and are] associated regularly with the performance of sacrifice. (121)

As noted earlier, the Cretan wise man, sage, magician Epimenides

> sustained himself without appearing to eat (Diog. Laert. 1.114). This sort of behavior has an exact parallel in the ascetic activities attributed to the Seven Rsis, who fast and abstain. They even have rivalry matches, each trying to outdo the other in performing ascetic practices. In a description of one of these contests we learn that the sage Vasistha controlled a river, and that furthermore he owned a cow that granted his every wish. Can we detect traces of the same activities in Thales' diverting the river Halys and Epimenides' cow hoof? I suspect that further work in Sanskrit will yield more. (122)[25]

"I wonder," writes Martin, "do we have to do here, in Greek on the one hand and Vedic Sanskrit on the other, with a tradition not as young as

Plato but rather as old as Indo-European antiquity?" (122). Of course, such figures, as Martin himself acknowledges in his cross-cultural exploration of the wise man, exist in many sites in the ancient worlds. His emphasis on more local origins suggests a bounded, hermetic aspect of Indo-European scholarship that echoes that of some classical studies, yet it also points to the ever-increasing expansion of the borders of the classical.

The Greek tradition also associated Epimenides with writing. He was a poet as well as a purifier and cleanser of pollution. Diogenes lists several long poems, including one on the birth of the Curetes and the Corybantes, and another, a theogony, of five thousand verses. All these divinities suggest ecstatic or orgiastic dimensions to Epimenides' interests. He also wrote a poem about *Argo,* the first ship, and about Jason's voyage to Colchis, home of Medea, surrounded by the Caucasus Mountains. This might be taken to support E. R. Dodds' claim of Epimenides' associations with shamanism, brought to Greece in the seventh century through the opening of the Black Sea to trade and colonization (142). Epimenides' poetic topics and adventures ally him with the East and, as noted above, with the sages and wise men of ancient Mesopotamia and Vedic India.

Diogenes also lists prose works by Epimenides titled "Sacrifices and the Cretan Constitution" and "On Minos and Rhadamanthys" (the latter, Cretan rulers and brothers who served as judges of the dead). The poetic works figure elsewhere in his story.[26] Not long after purifying Athens of the Cylonian pollution, Epimenides is said to have died back in Crete—according to Phlegon, having lived 157 years; according to the Cretans, 299. Xenophon of Colophon said he heard that Epimenides lived 154 years; in any case, Epimenides' would have been an abnormal, unnatural life span.

What became of Epimenides after his death remains in some ways the strangest aspect of his long career. Diogenes reports that, according to Sosibius of Sparta, "The Lacedaemonians guard his body in their own keeping in obedience to a certain oracle" (D.L. Epimenides 115). This rather cryptic remark is elaborated upon in the *Suda*. Jesper Svenbro considers this feature of Epimenides' afterlife in *Phrasikleia,* his anthropology of reading in ancient Greece. The Spartans were beholden to Epimenides because he had prophesied the victory of the Arcadians over Sparta, so they were appropriate keepers of his body, or rather, perhaps, of his skin *(derma),* which was discovered after his death to be tattooed with letters *(grammasi katastikon)* (*Suda,* under "Epimenides").

The possibility of the separation of the tattooed skin from Epimenides' body is an intriguing one. The most famous occasion of the skinning of a living being came with the defeat of the satyr Marsyas to Apollo in a kithara-playing contest, after which he was flayed alive, allegedly to be used as a wine skin. (According to Xenophon, the *askos*, the skin, could be visited in a cave at the source of a tributary of the Maeander River in Phrygia [*Anabasis* 1.2.8].) Svenbro insists that the word *derma* is used in the *Suda* merely because the word *soma* [body] has just been employed, thus for variation's sake: "Epimenides' *soma* would hardly have been stripped of its skin and thereby separated from it" (137, n. 76). But why should the skin, the surface of the body peeled from the corpse, not be exhibited detached from the body? Like parchment, the skin of animals on which texts were recorded, a more costly alternative than papyrus, the skin might be removed from the corruptible body and preserved, like the skin of Marsyas, or the skin Michelangelo painted as a self-portrait in the Sistine Chapel.[27] The Scythians, according to Herodotus, skinned their enemies killed in war: "Human skin, apparently, is thick and shiny-white—shinier, in fact, than any other kind of skin. They . . . often skin the whole of a corpse and stretch the skin on a wooden frame which they then carry around on their horses" (4.64). Epimenides' skin is especially portentous: the skin as the border between inside and outside, the garment in which the body is concealed, that part of the body that others see. Much of the strangeness of Epimenides resides in this tattooed skin, which connects him with the nineteenth-century freak show and its "tattooed Circassians," who came from the Caucasus Mountains at the eastern edge of the Black Sea.

Svenbro suggests that Epimenides—the sage, the wise man, the shaman, the magician—bore his own verses tattooed on his skin, like a scar, the record of a wound: "An ancient proverb alludes to his tattooed skin; according to the *Suda*, *epimenidein derma* 'Epimenidean skin,' was an expression used 'for secret things' *(epi ton apotheton)* . . . It is perfectly possible that Epimenides' *apotheta* are of a poetic nature, especially since this Cretan was himself a hexametric poet in the Hesiodic tradition" (137). It is as if—for those who encountered first the living body of Epimenides and then his skin, his pelt, after his death—the poems themselves, the verses themselves, emerged from inside the body to take up residence on the outside. The man was an embodiment of his poetry, his writing, marked from inside out, as if the words, turned into marks, emanated from him, through the skin, to remain on its surface. Svenbro's great interest in this feature of Epimenides' story concerns the anthropology of reading, the fact that Epimenides was inseparable from his writing, his *grammata,* in "the fusion of writer with inscription" (140). After death, "his tattoos change his *soma* into a *sema,* in both senses of the latter word" (141); that is, it is both a sign and a tomb. For Svenbro, when a ancient reader, reading aloud, voices the signs of Epimenides' body, he brings back the *psukhe,* the breath of Epimenides; just as when he was alive, the shaman could leave his body, taking his *psukhe* with him, and return to it at will. Epimenides' corpse "resembles a stele that is inscribed" (143). Interestingly, Clearchus of Soli (in "On Sleep," third century B.C.E.) reported that Epimenides was said to have rejoined the living after death. He added, laconically, "There is no need to go into detail" (F8 Wehrli).

Svenbro brilliantly shows how the letters inscribed on Epimenides' body allow him life after death, many breaths, many *psukhai* reanimating his writing as they read his letters. This tattooing makes the free Epimenides abnormal in relation to other free men, since tattoos in antiquity were later usually associated with barbarians and slaves. Thracians wore tattoos; Athenian vases show Thracian women and the maenads who killed Orpheus with tattoos. Elsewhere in the *Anabasis,* Xenophon describes the Euxine tribe called the Mossynoeci and

> some boys belonging to the wealthy class of people, who had been specially fattened up by being fed on boiled chestnuts. Their flesh was soft and very pale, and they were practically as broad as they were tall. Front and back were brightly coloured all over, tattooed with designs of flowers. These people wanted to have sexual intercourse in public with their mistresses, this being actually the normal thing in their country. Both men and women were pale skinned. Those who were on the expedition used to say that these people were the most barbarous and the furthest removed from Greek ways of all those with whom they came in contact. (5.4.32)[28]

In the fifth century, captive Thebans were tattooed by their Persian enemies, and the Greeks may thereafter have associated tattooing with barbarism, as Xenophon does here, and with punishment. Barbarians were not always allies, as in this passage, but were often captured and enslaved, their bodies covered with tattoos; other slaves were tattooed or branded with marks of possession or as punishment for disobedience or for attempting to run away from their masters.[29] In a description that suggests that inferior status, barbarity, or even slavery may be traced to a genealogical repetition, Aristotle reports a strange occurrence in his *Generation of Animals:*

> Children are born which resemble their parents in respect not only of congenital characteristics but also of acquired ones; for instance, there have been cases of children which have had the outline of a scar in the same places where their parents had scars, and there was a case at Chalcedon of a man who was branded on his arm, and the same letter, though somewhat confused and indistinct, appeared marked on his child.[30]

One of the most intriguing accounts of tattooing, related to Aristotle's suggestion that tattooing could be passed from one generation to the next, even among slaves by nature, is recounted by Diogenes in his life of Bion of Borysthenes (third century B.C.E.). When asked who he was, Bion replied, "My father was a freedman, who wiped his nothing on his sleeve"—meaning that he was a dealer in salt fish—"a native of Borysthenes, with no face to show, but only the writing on his face [*suggraphen epi tou prosopou*], a token of his master's severity" (4.46). Bion's father married a woman from a brothel, and such tattoos were associated with barbarism, slavery, and criminality.

Although tattoos may not yet have had such associations in the archaic age, for later readers Epimenides' tattoos marked him as abnormal, even monstrous. He assumed the degraded condition of the marked man, the criminal, the slave, the temple possession; yet he stood not below other free men, but above them with his wisdom, his prophetic powers, his extraordinary long life and capacity to return among the living after death. Like that of other magicians, who became more prominent in later ages, his knowledge was written on his body. He was a freak, abnormal, unnatural, freakish in his powers and longevity and immortality, not normal, not natural, especially in his ability to escape death. A strong current in the stories told of the wise men who lived long lives—and, in the case of Epimenides and, later, Apollonius of Tyana, were revered as great magicians—is the drive for that most seductive of utopian possibilities, the quest for the unnatural status of immortality.

If we are in postmodernity concerned with "norms," fretting under them and obsessed with statistics, the average, the conventional, perhaps our interest in the abnormal, the superhero with superpowers, represents an emancipatory impulse, a desire to embrace abnormality. And if so, we must recognize the utopian dimension of the abnormal, of the queer, bizarre, transgressive, and subversive, often arriving from distant lands—in Epimenides' case, coming from Crete to Athens—but also having affinities with ancient sages from an earlier Indo-European age, from a Vedic or a Mesopotamian prehistory. Rather than the abnormal to be institutionalized, pathologized, medicalized, psychoanalyzed, or euthanized, or the freak show as a racist performance piece, we find in the ancient figures of Epimenides and other shamans divinely marked persons whose abnormal, unnatural capacities freed them from constraints to which all other mortal beings are subject, who had extraordinary powers to move through time and space, echoed in the tattooed Circassians of the nineteenth-century freak show, and to survive through generations like the texts that record their histories.

5

SLAVES IN THE TRAGIC CITY

In this chapter, I return to the theme of multitudes, of the many who populate ancient texts, and to strangeness, the strangers, the others, persons from distant lands who inhabit the spaces of classical Greece and who link it with the rest of the ancient world. In particular, the city of Athens, locus in the fifth century B.C.E. of the composition and performances of tragedy, has served as a focus of much scholarly interest, in the fields of both literary study and political theory, a focus that can result in a hermeticism, a closure on the limits of the Athenian *polis* and the citizens of the city, that disregards the polyphonic, hybrid, multiple participants in this seemingly most Athenian and classical of all ancient institutions. I am interested especially in erasures in accounts of tragedy, in the ways the many heirs of the classical tradition, not only popular media, but also literary and philosophical intellectuals, when they think about Greek tragedy, see only the great man and his fall and then adjudicate the value, the "usability" of Greek tragedy in the present on the basis of what I see as a partial and reductive account of ancient drama. I want here to consider the history of this issue and to suggest that reflection on the relevance of Greek tragedy today should not be confined to the pathos of the great man, or even that of the everyman who comes to replace him.[1] The focus on the individual, in even the most sophisticated allegories using tragedy, remains a political choice that ignores the dialectic between part and whole, between individual and collective, and often erases, polemically, context and history, as we see also in contemporary calls to dethrone individual demonized tyrants such as Saddam Hussein and in newspaper stories that rely entirely on anecdotes and portraits of individuals to analyze the present.

Greek tragedy is not just about the great man, or even the little man; part of the problem is the "transecting," to use Goff and Simpson's term, the filtering and reduction of the rich and polymorphous heritage of Greek antiquity through centuries of interested readings.[2] And I include one of the earliest readers of tragedy, Aristotle, as a thinker who interpreted the legacy of tragedy in a partial and historically situated way. I here consider Aristotle's role as an early interpreter of tragedy and discuss various modern readers' roles in focusing attention on the great man as well. Then I want to look at other ways of seeing tragedy, of opening it to a more heterogeneous, unstable, or polymorphous kind of reading that might well speak to postmodernity, or a globalizing world of increasingly polarized power and powerlessness. My hypothesis is that just as Greek tragedy bore testimony to the beginnings of the formation of the Western subject in the fifth century B.C.E., in a troubled birth, so now readers nostalgic for the sovereign subject that developed from this formation see only that subject as they read or watch tragedy. But at a moment when that subject has been called into question by a variety of kinds of fragmentation, dislocation, and difference, we can see in tragedy a much richer and more diverse set of bodies and questions than Aristotle and modernity bequeath to us. If I take a historicist line here, it is meant to return us to a less partial and reductive view of Greek tragedy, in the name of discovering other kinds of relevance to the present, at a moment before the constituting of the closure of the individual subject, that might speak to its dissolution now. The foreign, the strange, the collective, the ecstatic, the enslaved are always there, from tragedy's beginnings, disrupting efforts to isolate the solitary, masterly self attempting heroically to grapple with fate.

In January 1997, at the height of the O. J. Simpson frenzy, I was invited to participate in the local Los Angeles NPR radio show *Which Way L.A.?* hosted by Warren Olney. In my capacity as a classicist working on Greek tragedy, the moderator asked me to be poised to comment on Simpson's trial, then being covered gavel to gavel and beyond on local and national television channels. Waiting tensely for my moment, I listened through almost an hour of remarks from criminal defense lawyers, district attorneys, academic legal experts, and participants from the School of Criminology at UC Berkeley. When at last Warren Olney came to me for a sort of epilogue, he asked: "Isn't O. J. like the hero of a Greek tragedy, a great man brought low by a tragic flaw?" I knew that he wanted me to expound on the pathos of the spectacle, the tragic dimensions of a man elevated to divine status by the masses and then dragged through the mud as a consequence of his own hubristic overreaching. Instead, I nervously blurted out that the situation did indeed resemble that of Greek tragedy, but in the sense that the ancient city staged its political and ritual life in public tragic performances. As ancient Athens made itself into a theater, it engaged in political reflection and political education through its worship of Dionysus. The parallel I made with the O. J. Simpson trial focused not on the great man fallen, but rather on the consequences, especially for African American defendants, in criminal trials all over America. If this particular jury with African American members acquitted Simpson, other juries would react to make sure that other defendants, especially African Americans, would not be acquitted, get off lightly, be saved from life imprisonment or death by lenient jurors. O. J. Simpson, who could pay for the best criminal defense possible, would be cited as an example by countless prosecutors, who would point to the injustice of the verdict. Poor African American defendants would suffer and be convicted and imprisoned to compensate for a general sense of outrage that O. J. had gotten away with murder.[3] In this sense, the trial did resemble a Greek tragedy; it was a political spectacle with political consequences. I wish I had talked too about the instability, weirdness, and multiplicity of persons on display in the trial, and how such features, to be found also in Greek tragedy, made it strange and wonderful and tended to undermine the triumphalist neoconservative account of the original stability, superiority, and homogeneity of Western civilization, celebrating eternal systems of justice, aesthetics, and philosophical coherence.[4] Such complexities proved, unfortunately, impossible in the sound-bite world of NPR. Yet, just as an analysis of the O. J. Simpson trial would be partial and distorting if it focused exclusively on the tragic hero, his fatal flaw and fall, ignoring the jury, the history of the police and African Americans in the city of Los Angeles, the history of racism and the past of slavery in the United States, so our readings of ancient tragedy must include more than Antigone and Oedipus if they are to illuminate our present and our future.

In popular culture, and in much literary theory as well, tragedy has become something like a dead signifier, connoting only these salient features: the great man or woman, the tragic flaw, the fall. How can such a model come to terms with Greek tragedy, with a lyric ode such as this in Euripides' *Bacchae*, in which a chorus of possessed, maddened, ecstatic women, men costumed as bacchantes, dance and sing of their devotion to their god Dionysus?

> Out of the land of Asia
> Down from holy Tmolus,
> Speeding the service of god,

For Bromius we come!
Hard are the labors of god;
Hard, but his service is sweet.
Sweet to serve, sweet to cry:
    Bacchus! Evohe![5]

Such moments, the chorus of male actors dressed as maenads, dancing and singing in ecstasy, with its collective voice and its insistence on another place from which the tragedy addresses its audience, have an unnerving, unfamiliar, untranslatable, and disturbing quality. This is not the familiar hero, faced with an ethical choice, acting with hubris and brought low by a character flaw, as so many undergraduates would have it. Athenian tragedy contains a Phrygian slave, choruses of Phoenician women, a tragedy set entirely in the Persian palace at Susa, with Persians lamenting their dead, soldiers from Egypt and Babylon. The Danaids, who seek refuge in their flight from Egypt, recount the flight of their ancestor Io:

Passing many races,
Cutting in two the land,
The raging strait defined;—

Through lands of Asia fast she went,
And across Phrygia grazing sheep;
And the city of Teuthras passing,
And Lydian vales,
Cilician hills,
Race Pamphylian hurried
Through ever-flowing streams,
And land of Aphrodite.[6]

This is not the familiar territory of ancient Greece, the city of Athens and its territory, Attica. Sophocles' Heracles, mortal hero and god, returns to his wife, having spent time in Lydia in Asia Minor, a bought slave to the foreign queen Omphale (*Trachiniae* 248–256).[7] The hero who becomes a god has been an Asian slave. When coming to terms with the legacy of ancient Athenian tragedy, a contemporary audience must acknowledge an almost uncanny unfamiliarity, a strangeness, a quality recognized by the maverick Friedrich Nietzsche, often repugned by classicists: "The chariot of Dionysus is covered with flowers and garlands; panthers and tigers walk under its yoke."[8]

The most influential reader of Greek tragedy is the philosopher Aristotle. Yet Aristotle is remote from the richest and most productive moment of Greek tragic production, his interests in the phenomenon of tragedy very different from those of the fifth-century citizens of Athens who created the genre, and readers of Aristotle have often misread him. John Jones points out that the probable date of the *Poetics,* Aristotle's principal text on tragedy, is 335 B.C.E., that is, "when Aeschylus has been dead for rather more than a century, and Sophocles and Euripides . . . for about seventy years."[9] Although for nonclassicists this may not seem significant, given the principle that the more remote things are from us, the closer they seem to each other—"It's all Greek to me"—in fact, the passage of time between Aeschylus' career and Aristotle's formulations matters a great deal in a historicist account of the theorization of Greek tragedy.

Much had happened during the 150 years between Aeschylus' birth in the sixth century B.C.E.; his first production of tragedy in 499 B.C.E.; his last work produced in Athens, the *Oresteia* of 458 B.C.E.; and Aristotle's treatise. Even if we consider the death of Sophocles in 406 B.C.E. as an end point to the great age of Greek tragedy, Aristotle, born in 384 B.C.E., was distant from it. Events, and structural changes, intervened. Athens had fought its rival, the league of states led by Sparta, through the last third of the fifth century and been defeated. The city had become a subject-ally of Sparta; and in 404, when the thirty tyrants sponsored by Sparta took power over the city, it became an oligarchy. Although democracy was eventually restored, reforms diminished its radical character, transferring legislation from the assembly of all citizens to a panel of six thousand. Struggles for hegemony over the Greek city-states continued in the fourth century, with Athens challenging Sparta in the company of other members of coalition forces, then allying with the Spartans against the rise of Thebes. When Athens sought to restore its empire, its allies rebelled. As Perry Anderson writes:

> Thereafter there was no chance of the Hellenic cities generating a unified imperial state from within their midst, despite their relatively rapid economic recovery from the effects of the long Peloponnesian war: the very parity and multiplicity of urban centres in Greece neutralized them collectively for external expansion. The Greek cities of the 4th century sank into exhaustion, as the classical polis experienced increasing difficulties of finance and conscription, symptoms of impending anachronism.[10]

To the north, Phillip II of Macedon continued to gain power, finally provoking Athenian fears and eventually defeating Athens at the battle of

Chaeronea in 338 B.C.E. Although the *polis* of Athens survived, it continued in a crucially changed form, no longer a radically experimental and imperially dominant democracy. Athens had begun its transformation into the center of education and culture that it became in the Hellenistic age, after the conquests of Aristotle's pupil Alexander.

Jean-Pierre Vernant argues for the historically specific "moment of tragedy," pointing to Aristotle's temporal distance from this moment: "Within a hundred years the tragic seam had already been exhausted and when Aristotle in the fourth century set out, in his *Poetics,* to establish the theory of tragedy, he no longer understood tragic man, who had, so to speak, become a stranger. Tragedy succeeded epic and lyric and faded away as philosophy experienced its moment of triumph."[11] In this account of the sequence of genres, Vernant sees tragedy as possible only in the conditions peculiar to the fifth century B.C.E., in a "gap" that is "wide enough for the opposition between legal and political thought on the one hand and the mythical and heroic traditions on the other to stand out quite clearly. Yet it is narrow enough for the conflict in values still to be a painful one."[12]

Not only did all the intervening events, the defeat and changes for democracy, the new leagues, the defeat by the Macedonians and the subordination of Athens to Macedon affect the position of Aristotle with respect to tragedy. His was not the attitude of a democratic citizen of Athens to the ritual and political institution of democracy.[13] Although he was a student of Plato and sometime resident in Athens, Aristotle inhabited Athens as an alien, leaving twice when the political mood of the city seemed dangerous for a philosopher and a Macedonian. His father had been court physician to a Macedonian monarch, and Aristotle may have spent part of his childhood in the court at Pella. As the anecdote has it, he left Athens to prevent the Athenians from sinning twice against philosophy—from executing him as they had Socrates—and his antidemocratic attitudes are typical of élite thinkers of antiquity. Aristotle tutored the future conqueror and founder of the Hellenistic empire, Alexander, and consistently in his political writings offered positions critical of democracy.

Aristotle's attitudes toward Athenian tragedy, therefore, must be located within a belated and antidemocratic situation.[14] Mostly apparent in his *Poetics,* a manual for writing, or "making," poems, his prescriptions reflect an administrative attitude remote from the highly charged political engagement of Athenian citizens in the new and radical democracy of the fifth century B.C.E. Whether his use of the term *katharsis* draws primarily on ritual contexts and connotes "purification" or "cleansing" or on medical concepts, connoting "purging," is not for me here the crucial issue.¹⁵ Rather, I want to point to the focus on management of a population, an attitude very distant in its prosaic and encyclopedic setting from the fervent participation of citizens in the tragic celebrations of Dionysus that were the ancient drama festivals. Simon Goldhill has described the civic and ritual aspects of those festivals, showing how far removed they were from a post-Romantic "literariness" and even from the perspective of the polymath Aristotle. Goldhill reminds us that the Great Dionysia, the principal drama festival celebrating Dionysus, included in the days preceding the performances the procession of a statue of Dionysus to a nearby village and back and another procession, with participants carrying ritual loaves and phalluses, followed by bull sacrifices. In the theater of Dionysus on the day of the performances, the city's generals poured a libation; the names of exceptional citizens crowned for benefiting the city were announced; tribute from the Athenian empire subject states was displayed; young men, the ephebes whose fathers had been killed in battle, paraded; and, according to some authorities, the names of freed slaves were proclaimed.¹⁶ Goldhill concludes, "The theatre was a space in which all the citizens were actors—as the city itself and its leading citizens were put on display" (57).

Aristotle's encyclopedic work on plants and animals, on the histories of philosophy and politics, and his manuals on rhetoric and the writing of plays and poems belong to a different regime of truth from that of the theater of Dionysus in the fifth century and the intense engagement of the city in its invention of itself as a radical democracy. Aristotle notoriously does not even mention Dionysus in his account of tragedy. As Vernant says, "The city . . . turned itself into a theater,"¹⁷ and Aristotle stands apart from this experiment. His views on catharsis, for example, refer to a disciplining of the social body, directing the reader's attention from the collective toward the individual member of the audience who experiences a catharsis of pity and fear. The philosopher offers a view of tragedy from the perspective of power, administration, and management of a population. He assumes a view from above and outside the city, concerned with identifying systems that prevent social disruption and disorder, where tragedy is useful, *contra* the view of Plato, precisely because it displaces unruly emotion into the realm of art in order to maintain order in the state. Tragedy becomes a site of mastery for the philosopher, who is a manager, analyst, and theoretician of the state.

The focus on the individual within tragedy, the great man, who in time becomes everyman, probably begins with a productive misreading of

Aristotle. John Jones discusses the importation of the tragic hero into the *Poetics,* "where the concept has no place."[18] In the *Poetics,* Aristotle says that tragedy is the representation of an *action (praxis)* that is "heroic and complete and of a certain magnitude."[19] There is no mention here of a "tragic hero" or a "fatal flaw." He further says, "Tragedy is not a representation of men but of a piece of action, of life, of happiness and unhappiness, which come under the head of action, and the end aimed at is the representation not of qualities of character but of some action" (1450a). As Jones makes clear: "Mutability is Aristotle's tragic focus, not misfortune" (47). Aristotle explicitly calls into question the focus on the hero: "A plot does not have unity, as some people think, simply because it deals with a single man *(hena)*" (1451a). He praises Sophocles' *Oedipus,* beginning a long tradition of focus on this play, and argues that the best sort of tragedy concerns the mean between worthy and wicked persons who through some *hamartia,* "missing the mark," fall into misfortune. He also says that character *(ethos)* must be good, relative to the class of person concerned: "Even a woman is 'good,' and so is a slave, although it may be said that a woman is an inferior thing *(kheiron)* and a slave beneath consideration *(holos phaulon)*" (1454a).

Aristotle's comparative evaluations of epic and tragedy confirm his views on the superiority of aristocracy to democracy. He considers the argument that tragedy is *phortike,* "vulgar," compared to epic: "The whole tragic art, then, is to epic poetry what . . . later actors were compared to their predecessors, since according to this view epic appeals to a cultivated audience which had no need of an actor's poses, while tragedy appeals to a lower class *(phaulous).* If then it is vulgar, it must obviously be inferior" (1462a). Although Aristotle says this is a criticism of actors, not poetry, the vulgar democratic audience of tragedy is a part of the spectacle; Aristotle recommends *reading* tragedies, instead of watching actors, obviating the ritual and political circumstances of its fifth-century performance. He concludes by calling tragedy the superior form, using instrumental criteria, because of its vividness and economy of length, unity, and effectiveness in producing pleasure *(hedonen)* (1462b).[20] In line with his advice concerning the reading of tragedy is his neglect of the collective nature, for example, of the tragic chorus: "The chorus must be regarded as one of the actors" (1456a). Such a comment reflects the ahistorical nature of Aristotle's experience of tragedy and leads to the history of misrecognition outlined here. Jones argues that readers project a modern self onto Aristotle's treatise: "Probably not much of the ancient tragic experience is recoverable by us, but we can avoid forcing upon Aristotle the local and no doubt transient self of the modern West" (36).

Later readers do force upon Aristotle, and tragedy, the "tragic hero" with his "fatal flaw." Influential readings focus not on *praxis*, on action, or mutability of fortune, but on *characters*, transferring to the ancient form what soon becomes a modern, individual, internal, and psychological self. Hegel's reading of the *Antigone* locates its meaning in its two central characters. As Michelle Gellrich points out, while restoring the notion of conflict to tragedy, absent from Aristotle's view, "Hegel understands the conflict in pervasively binary terms: Antigone versus Creon, family versus state, female versus male, unwritten divine law versus written civic edicts."[21] In Hegel's description of the drama, what matters is the collision between two characters, one identified with the ethical world of the family, the other with the city; Hegel contrasts male and female with a view to their individuation, albeit in the context of their ultimate unity in spirit: "These two universal beings of the ethical world have, therefore, their specific individuality in naturally distinct self-consciousness, because the ethical Spirit is the immediate unity of the substance with self-consciousness."[22] In the *Aesthetics* he goes further in attributing a romantic self to the characters of drama: "However far the individual and his inner life is the center of the drama, . . . a drama must display situations, and the mood they arouse, as determined by the character of an individual who resolves on particular ends and makes these what he wills in practice."[23]

For Freud, Sophocles' tragic hero Oedipus has the flaw of every man, the desire to kill his father and sleep with his mother; this is every human being's destiny. Freud looks only to the individual as he reads the Greeks. For him, Oedipus stands for each man, and for Greek tragedy itself, in a metonymy that ignores other characters, the chorus, the language, and other myths that serve as the matrix for the very many Athenian tragedies that fall out of the tradition.[24] As confirmation for the crucial role of the Oedipus complex in psychic life, Freud discusses not just the myth, but also the drama of Oedipus: "What I have in mind is the legend of King Oedipus and Sophocles' drama which bears his name."[25] Freud argues that Sophocles' tragedy is a tragedy of destiny, and that Oedipus' "destiny moves us only because it might have been ours—because the oracle laid the same curse upon us before our birth as upon him" (296).[26] Freud goes on to consider not another Greek tragedy, but *Hamlet*, citing it as proof of the gathering repression that characterizes the psychic life of mankind.[27]

Jacques Lacan, following Hegel, sees only Antigone, fatally beautiful; she is the death drive, living between two deaths. As a reader of Sophocles, he is blinded to all but Antigone: "*Antigone* reveals to us the line of sight that defines desire. This line of sight focuses on an image that possesses a mystery which up till now has never been articulated, since it forces you to close your eyes at the moment you look at it. Yet that image is at the center of tragedy, since it is the fascinating image of Antigone herself."[28] He rewrites Hegel's version of the tragedy to locate conflict not in the antagonism between the two characters Antigone and Creon, but rather as internal to a tragically split and insatiable self. Antigone becomes the sign of death, of the unreachable, the limit of the human, the incest taboo: "Her life is not worth living" (263). For Lacan, "Antigone goes beyond the limits of the human . . . Her desire aims at the following, the beyond of *Ate*" (263). So he too reads the tragedy, brilliantly, but within a modernity that focuses on the individual and the split, suffering self.

Judith Butler, in *Antigone's Claim,* discussed more fully in chapter 10, offers not a reading of Greek tragedy, but a utopian meditation on the place of the character Antigone in the invention of a possible new psychoanalysis, in which the focus would be not on Oedipus, as the father who slept with his mother and killed his father, but rather on Antigone, who reveals a culturally unacceptable, even incestuous, desire for her brother.[29] Butler uses Antigone's deviant desire to stand for all culturally new desires, forms of family and intimacy and community, forms of loss and lamentation that cannot be assumed into the conventional heterosexual nuclear family. She follows Hegel's reading closely, and Lacan's, and like them, even as her argument seeks a revolutionary recognition of new families, new forms of affiliation, she concentrates her analysis on the characters in the family, reading the tradition of philosophical and psychoanalytic readings of tragedy rather than the unruly and disturbing thing that is Greek tragedy itself. If I want to restore some of the unmanageability of Greek tragedy, it is in part in light of such work as Butler's, in which the historicity, permeability, constructedness, and groundlessness of personality and selfhood are theorized. Those modern or postmodern readers, not classicists, who still read *Antigone* as well as *Oedipus Rex* when they consider Greek tragedy, even allegorically, are the exceptions; the other tragedies fall from modern and postmodern view.

In his critique of conservative theorists of the death of tragedy, and of Butler and other postmodern theorists, Terry Eagleton, writing about tragedy in *Sweet Violence: The Idea of the Tragic,* seems ultimately to want to return to a model of sacrifice: "Christ is one of many tragic scapegoats thrust beyond the city and sacrificially dismembered, reduced to a piece of butcher's meat in a savage parody of kingship" (283).[30] In his formulation, Eagleton follows the influential characterization of Jean-Pierre Vernant concerning "tragic man" and Oedipus. Vernant argues that Sophocles' Oedipus can be illuminated by a consideration of two institutions of the Greek city, the *pharmakos,* or scapegoat ritual, and the procedure called ostracism. In the scapegoat ritual, the city selected the most abject of inhabitants—ugly, wretched, imprisoned victims—and beat them and drove them from the city's limits, so ritually expelling baseness from the body politic. Eagleton, like many readers, follows Vernant on the scapegoat ritual but neglects his formulations concerning ostracism, which cast light on the relationship between Oedipus and the tyrant, the most high, the almost godlike ruler of the city. Athens conducted an ostracism, a sort of anti-election, in which the citizens voted every year to expel, in a ten-year exile, anyone they chose from the democratic city; ostracism has been understood as a mechanism for ridding the city of those who have become too powerful, in order perhaps to deflect the envy of the gods, but also to maintain the putative equality of the citizens and to discourage demagogues or those with tyrannical ambitions. Vernant writes:

> In the person of the ostracized one, the city expels whatever it is in it that is too high and that embodies the evil that can fall on it from above. In that of the *pharmakos,* it expels whatever is most vile and threatens it from below. Through this double and complementary rejection it sets its own limits in relation to what is above and what is below. It takes the true measure of man as opposed on the one hand to the divine and the heroic and, on the other, to the bestial and the monstrous.[31]

If Eagleton does go beyond the tragic hero, the focus on the individual, and sees the possibilities of transformation in the multitude, he is nonetheless caught up in a model of sacrifice based on what seem to me anachronistic Christian notions, anachronistic, that is, in relation to ancient Greek polytheism, for example, and the worship of the god Dionysus, of which tragic performances were a ritualized feature: "There is a sense in which the *pharmakos* is the very paradigm of that nowadays much derided notion, objectivity. To strive for objectivity of judgment in fact demands a fair amount of courage, realism, openness, modesty, self-discipline and generosity of spirit; there is nothing in the least bloodless about it" (289). These are notions foreign to ancient Athenian conceptions of the wretched and persecuted *pharmakos.*

In a book much influenced by the work of Paul de Man, Michelle Gellrich argues that theory itself produces misreadings of tragedy: "While the sense-making, organizing operations of dramatic theory serve systematic interests, they also perform a definitive cultural function; they so digest tragedy into a form both intelligible and safe that its threatening, enigmatic aspects are transformed."[32] This is an illuminating critique, problematic only in that it anthropomorphizes "theory," making it an agent in centuries of reading tragedy. I would rather see the readings of various "theorists" of tragedy historically, from Aristotle to Eagleton, considering the ways in which theories work in their historical situations to turn audiences'—readers' and theorists'—gaze toward heroes, male or female, and instead insisting again on the "threatening, enigmatic aspects" of tragedy. If we return to Jones' insight concerning the *transference* of modern ideas of character onto ancient tragedy, to see what is happening in Greek tragedy besides the intractable character, the hero, the subject, we discover the threat, the enigma of works of dramatic art that challenge our ideas concerning life centered on the individual self.

I want to point to just three ways in which Greek tragedy exceeds the individual character, the tragic hero, the great man or woman dear to the tradition: in its haunting by the slaves, born as possessions in the homes and farms of Greeks or sold or captured and made part of the households of ancient Greek society; in its access to mourning, the lamentations over loss central to the genre; and in its presentation of choral song, necessarily collective and diverse and heterogeneous.[33] Readings of tragedy that focus on the individual, even the abject, sacrificial *pharmakos,* cannot take account of such moments as this in Euripides' *Hecuba:*

O Ilium! O my country,
whose name men speak no more
among unfallen cities!
So dense a cloud of Greeks
came, spear on spear, destroying!
Your crown of towers shorn away,
and everywhere the staining fire,
most pitiful, O Ilium,
whose ways I shall not walk again!

At midnight came my doom.
Midnight when the feast is done
and sleep falls sweetly on the eyes.
The songs and sacrifice,

the dances, all were done.
My husband lay asleep,
his spear upon the wall,
forgetting for a while
the ships drawn up on Ilium's shore.

I was setting my hair
in the soft folds of the net,
gazing at the endless light
deep in the golden mirror,
preparing myself for bed,
when tumult broke the air
and shouts and cries
shattered the empty streets—
Onward, onward you Greeks!
Sack the city of Troy
and see your homes once more!

Dressed only in a gown
like a girl of Sparta,
I left the bed of love
and prayed to Artemis.
But no answer came.
I saw my husband lying dead,
and they took me over sea.
Backward I looked at Troy,
but the ship sped on
and Ilium slipped away,
and I was dumb with grief.[34]

Anonymous and newly enslaved women, from the Asian community of Troy, sing this chorus, a group of men performing as women, recalling the fateful moment when their city fell, when these women, speaking as one, became slaves. This song from the chorus evokes the catastrophe of the fall of Troy, with its breached wall and devastation emblematic of the end of civilization for all of antiquity. It also speaks to the disaster suffered by this anonymous woman, with her husband killed, herself suffering the social death of enslavement, seeking in the worship of Artemis a return to virginity, to protection from sexual possession by new masters.

The choruses of tragedy offer an impressive array of difference, of a collective, always anonymous body, from another group of slave women in Aeschylus' *Libation Bearers* ("From our fathers' houses / they led us here to take the lot of slaves" [77–78])[35] to the votive slaves of Euripides'

Phoenician Women, who regret the delay in their arrival at the oracle of Apollo at Delphi: "I came, I left the wave of Tyre, / the island of Phoenicia, / a prize for Loxias, slave to Phoebus' house."[36] Not only are these women slaves, they are Phoenicians, not Greeks, and therefore an anonymous barbarian, ethnically distinct group, pledged to serve the Greek god Apollo, resident in Thebes because of the genealogical relation of the Thebans to Tyre. Their voices call up not only the presence of barbarians in tragedy, but also the thousands of slaves resident in Athens, in houses and on farms, working in factories and serving citizens.[37]

At many moments in Greek tragedy, the omnipresence of slaves and the horror of enslavement arise in the course of the drama, marking it with the specter of social death, anonymity, and ethnic difference. In Sophocles' *Trachiniae,* the wife of Heracles, Deianeira, about whom some debate has arisen concerning whether she is the "tragic hero," regrets the return of her husband from conquest with a new slave bride. She addresses the chorus, the anonymous women of the city of Trachis:

> Dear friends, while our visitor is in the house
> talking to the captured girls before he leaves,
> I have come out to you, unobserved. I want
> to tell you the work my hands have done, but also to have
> your sympathy as I cry out for all I suffer.
> For here I have taken on a girl—no,
> I can think that no longer—a married woman, as
> a ship's master takes on cargo, goods that outrage my heart.
> So now two of us lie under the same sheet
> waiting for his embrace. This is the gift my brave
> and faithful Heracles sends home to his dear wife
> to compensate for his long absence![38]

The situation of the new woman is ambiguous; is she a wife or a slave? Deianeira's address to the women of Trachis, the chorus, speaks to the omnipresence of slaves in the houses of the Athenian audience; their sexual availability to citizens; and their effects on relations of power, domesticity, kinship, inheritance, and difference in the city.

Even in the most canonical of Greek tragedies, *Antigone,* second only to *Oedipus Rex* in its overwhelming status for post-Aristotelian and post-Hegelian readers of tragedy, the issue of the ubiquity of slaves in the city emerges ineluctably. As Robert Goheen noted in 1951, the language of slavery in the play is linked to bestial imagery: "In his first speech when Creon describes Polyneices' crimes and concludes by branding him as one who has come 'to feed on kindred blood and lead the remnant into slavery' (202), the mention of enslavement is climactic and presumably is one of the strongest of his charges against Polyneices."[39] Creon uses the language of slavery with the image of a bridle to threaten Antigone; Antigone claims that Polyneices is entitled to burial precisely because he was not a slave; Creon calls his son Haimon a woman's *douleuma,* a "slave-thing" (756).

Rather than focusing solely on the characters' character, ethical position, and destiny, the plays engage in a complex and often contradictory debate concerning many issues, including slavery, slaves' disturbing presence in the city, the legitimacy of their enslavement, and the possibility of enslavement for free persons represented in the tragic performances and in their audiences. In fact, the inhabitants of cities defeated in war in the fifth century B.C.E. were subjected to death and enslavement, as the historian of the Peloponnesian war Thucydides reports: "Around the same time [421 B.C.E.] during this summer, the Athenians captured Skione by siege and killed the adult males, enslaving the children and women and giving the land to the Plataeans to occupy."[40] When the Athenians were at last forced to recognize defeat in the Peloponnesian War, according to the historian Xenophon, they feared retaliation for such brutality:

> As the news of the disaster was told, one man passed it on to another, and a sound of wailing arose and extended first from Piraeus, then along the Long Walls until it reached the city. That night no one slept. They mourned for the lost, but more still for their own fate. They thought that they themselves would now be dealt with as they had dealt with others—with the Melians, colonists of Sparta, after they had besieged and conquered Melos, with the people of Histiaea, of Scione, of Torone, of Aegina and many other states.[41]

Although ancient playwrights set their tragedies in a legendary past, situations like those represented in ancient Troy saturated contemporary experience. The ubiquity of slaves in the city, some captured in war, made them an inevitable and haunting presence and a reminder of the possibilities of disaster in the present.

Nicole Loraux has written about the aspect of ancient tragedy that resembles the oratorio, its moments of grief and mourning, its capacity to call forth sorrow in its spectators and to console, an aspect she sees as distinct from the political.[42] The theater of Dionysus is not the *agora,* the marketplace, one of the centers of civic activity in the *polis;* tragedy is not only political, it is even antipolitical in the sense that it goes beyond the city defined by a practice of consensus or even by conflict. The city seeks to limit lamentation; tragedy extends it to eternity. Tragedy embodies the oxymoron, the incompatible, playing on the prescriptions and oppositions of political discourse. Loraux argues that lamentation and lyric songs of mourning, the evocation of loss, go against the prescription of the city to forget and bring the spectator to a moment of recognition that exceeds the homogeneous civic community, to an acknowledgment of his or her place among humankind, as mortal (137). This aspect of tragedy is lost, too, with a focus on characters, character, and ethical choice alone.

Jean-Pierre Vernant argues that the form of tragedy itself produces a sort of centripetal force, in which the city produces itself for itself in the theater. In its engagement with a living past, tragedy expresses itself through a tension between the collective entity that is the chorus, and the characters, played by individual actors. While the characters, names from the legendary past, might be expected to speak in an archaic language, and the anonymous group of persons that resembles the collective of citizens should perhaps speak the language of their day, in fact the reverse occurs. In a chiasmic or centripetal form, the choruses sing in archaic lyric language associated with the past, with the aristocratic age, while the characters speak a prosaic language presumably closer to that of the audience.[43] As we accept Loraux' caveat that tragedy exceeds the political and the civic, this aspect of the form of tragedy especially resists assimilation to the familiar. The drama is not a treatise, not a philosophical dialogue, not purely an examination of character and ethical choice. Terrible events occur, characters and chorus are caught up in them, and the strangeness of tragic form is part of the experience of reading or viewing tragedy.

Tragedy probably developed from choral song; the standing out from the chorus of a single character appears retrospectively as the beginnings of drama. Such an occurrence may be said to mark the emergence of a Western sense of "character," the persona carved out in the separation of an individual from a collective. Charles Segal points to the connections linking writing, literacy, theatrical space, and the developing notion of an interior self in the fifth century B.C.E.:

> The hiddenness of the tragic poet's text in the performance is the negative sign of something always hidden from view, on the other side of the palace wall, which is also the side of the Other. As a poet/writer who manipulates

real bodies in real space on the stage, the dramatist becomes sensitized both to the invisible graphic space of his text and to the hidden, interior space of the self. What is concealed behind doors and gates—the gates of the palace, of the mouth, or of the body—becomes the problem of his writerly art . . . The inner life of the self . . . appears not on the stage but in the behind-the-stage implied by the invisible text . . . This interplay between interior and exterior space parallels the increasing awareness of the interior realm of the psyche, the individual personality.[44]

Rather than see this as an increasing "awareness" of something already existent, as Segal and Bruno Snell do, we might now argue that in tragedy we are witnessing the *construction* of that self, that interiority, that individualism, in a process concomitant with Athenian democratic ideology concerning equality and the interchangeability of citizens.[45]

The radically uneven surface of tragedy, moving as it does from song and dance to speech and back again, makes it different from epic, for example, with its continuous flow of the bard's song, or from lyric, the voice of chorus or singer alone. Choruses in tragedy sing not simply to experience the events for the audience—as Lacan puts it, "doing emotional commentary for you"—nor do they stand for the citizens themselves, since they often represent foreign, inassimilable persons, slaves, barbarians, or ecstatic maenads.[46] Readings that focus on character, destiny, and ethical choice tend simply to ignore such passages, rendering them invisible; they are vestigial remnants of archaic lyric that deprive the reader of the sense that he or she has mastered tragedy and insist on the radical strangeness and historical distance of tragedy. Attempts to contain such appearances within civic ideology or the history of absolute spirit must fail; they cannot come to terms with the lyrics' striking strangeness, inassimilability, and representations of difference.

In a recent essay on the "sociology" of tragedy, Edith Hall offers an important, though sanguine, interpretation of the diversity on display in tragedy. Hall observes: "Tragedy offers a range of characters of all statuses from gods and kings to citizens and to slaves, all ethnicities from Athenian, Theban, and Argive Greeks to 'barbarians' (the generic term for non-Greeks) such as Persians and Egyptians, all age groups from babies to the very old, and an overwhelming insistence on the troubled relationships between women and men."[47] She attributes a utopian quality to the presence of women, slaves, and barbarians in tragedy; while they were excluded from public debate in the city, an unexpected array of speakers is included in tragedy on the stage: "Tragedy postulates in imagination a world . . . which is 'democratic' in something akin to the modern Western sense; it is a world in which characters of diverse ethnicity, gender, and status all have the same right to express their opinions and the same verbal ability with which to exercise that right" (125). This formulation may exaggerate the degree to which slaves and barbarians, who usually speak with sorrow, deference, or fear on stage, have achieved a democratic parity with the kings and tyrants of the tragic stage, and return to a familiar model of celebration of the Greek miracle; yet it registers with great force the insistent presence of a multitude, a collective and inassimilable otherness on the Athenian tragic stage.

Mark Griffith uses a modified psychoanalytic model to account for tragedy's representation of monarchy, tyranny, and return to order, arguing that the space of tragedy allows for a play of desires, including an unconscious one on the democratic citizen's part for a childhood governed by a father and a polity governed by a monarchy or aristocracy. This is an exciting and provocative argument that relies for the most part on readings of Aeschylus and Sophocles, more amenable to such claims than Euripides, and is stimulating in its willingness to confront a programmatic conservatism in Greek tragedy, which sometimes is subject to a comforting idealization, couched in new terms. Tragedy is in fact a site of contradiction and struggle for the city, not perhaps as hegemonically concerning patriarchal sovereignty as Mark Griffith has argued, but nonetheless a more conflictual and troubled space than some describe.[48]

If tragedy has something to offer to readers and spectators in the present, it should be more than nostalgia for the private, individual subject of modernity, cherished or lamented by many readers precisely because it is receding in a world of postmodern globalization. Rather, a reading that sees all the *differences* in tragedy—its geographical extent; its slaves and free people; men and women; kings, queens, and citizens in action, conflicted, contradictory action—can speak to us now. The presence of a multiplicity; slaves, foreign and domestic; the attention to mourning; and the formal complexity of tragedy make it a richer, more contradictory, less familiar object than we are accustomed to find in the pages of Hegel. To read Greek tragedy, tragedy, the tragic, as a discourse on the individual, even one conceived within the narrative of absolute spirit, or split by incestuous desire, is to reveal perhaps a nostalgic desire for a sovereign, individual, heroic subject, one who can still make choices, even catastrophic ones, that determine his or her fate, that exhibit will and efficacy now eroded in the face of globalization and transnational corporate power. Even as the legacy of modern slavery in the Americas has produced a misrecognition of ancient societies, a failure to see all the slaves of the past, so the disintegrating modern self, the supposedly once sovereign, individual subject, reaches nostalgically for its past in ancient Greek tragedy, which in fact stages very different sorts of struggles and engagements and includes a multitude of characters, anonymous and named, from far distant domains of the global ancient world.

6

ALEXANDRIAS

The ancient city of Egyptian Alexandria, capital of the Hellenistic kingdom of the Ptolemies, was founded by Alexander himself in autumn of 332 B.C.E., in the course of his journey south and east from Macedon bent on exploration and conquest. Arrian describes the scene:

> On reaching Canobus he sailed around Lake Mareotis and disembarked at the site of present-day Alexandria, the city named after him. The site struck him as very beautiful for a new settlement, and he imagined that a city founded there would prosper. A sudden passion for the project seized him, and he himself marked out where the agora was to be built and decided how many temples were to be erected and to which gods they were to be dedicated—the Greek gods and Egyptian Isis—and where the wall was to be built around the city. With these plans in mind, he offered sacrifices, and the omens proved favorable.[1]

At its very beginnings, at its heart, Alexandria contained hybrid religious practices, worshipping the ancient Egyptian goddess Isis, sister and wife of Osiris, alongside the gods of the Greeks.

Alexander founded many Alexandrias, some of which survive, their names altered, reflecting fusion with indigenous languages and centuries of survival. In a capacious catalogue that includes several traditions, including the many cities listed by Plutarch, P. M. Fraser records fifty-seven cities founded by Alexander, not all named for him; they include forty-four Alexandrias, whose names have suffered many changes over time.[2] In the lands that once held the sages of the Mesopotamians, and the wise Rsis of the Vedas, people came to live in complex amalgams of indigenous traditions and layers of Hellenistic settlement and translation.

The Hellenistic world contained populations in unaccustomed proximity to one another, especially in Egyptian Alexandria, created and transformed through Macedonian conquest into a Hellenic, Hellenistic metropolis, one sheltering Nubians, Africans of other sorts, Greek African colonists from Cyrene, Jews from Palestine and the Persian Empire, and a vast variety of immigrants from such sites as Sicily—immigrants like the comic poet and writer of mimes, Herodas.[3] Richard Armstrong locates Freud's affinity for ancient Greece as against Rome, a stance shared by many Germans and Austrians, in Alexander's foundation of this great city:

> It was Alexander, after all, who created Alexandria, the city that saw the birth of a unique Hellenic-Jewish culture that led, among other things, to the Septuagint, a translation of the Hebrew scriptures into Greek, the universal intellectual language of the time. In sum, Alexander represented a figure of *inclusive* imperialist Hellenism . . . Alexander, as a son who had overcome his father and was yet fulfilling a paternal mission (the conquest of Persia), conforms to Freud's pattern of both the hero and the Great Man of History.[4]

Yet Alexandria was more than its foundation by a "great man." As Dan Selden points out in a fascinating article on Alexandria and one of its poets, Callimachus,

> The Lagid capital was a complex mosaic of peoples, tongues, religions, social and religious practices, drawn from every quarter of the Levantine world and never fully assimilated to one another . . . The Macedonian regime did not promote the effacement of ethnic difference or conceptualize Alexandria as a "melting pot," but, to the contrary, institutionalized heterogeneity at every level of the social order.[5]

There was a hierarchy dominated by newly arrived and slightly barbaric Macedonians, who had reverted to ancient monarchic and tyrannical ways. Discriminations were drawn among all the ethnic populations present in the new city; perhaps the distinction between slave and free stood as a displaced sign of all difference, one that included ethnic difference but also allowed for complex relations of domination, buttressed by threats, physical violence, and brutality, necessary in a new cosmopolitan, multiethnic Hellenistic civilization. Peter Parsons points to Hellenistic continuities with the classical period—that is, with high-classical fifth- and fourth-century B.C.E., mainland Greek, mostly Athenian, literary works—but adds that, while a practical view might be that more monarchs mean more money, "the psychologist's view might be different: the bibelot poetry and folkloristic antiquarianism, the combinatorial amiabilities of New Comedy, the rectilinear cities, universal histories, systematic philosophies, and encyclopedic textbooks show the Hellenistic Greeks variously denying or dominating the unease of widened horizons: the key to the age is cultural agoraphobia."[6] The vanguard thinkers of the third century confronted the heterogeneity of the new situation in Alexandria and made something new of all the cultural materials then at their disposal, from Nubian bodies to Jewish textual scrutiny and purification, to Egyptian traditions of chronicling.

In the later Hellenistic period, the circumstances of slaves may have deteriorated dramatically, as the Romans captured vast numbers of formerly free persons and set them to work. Mikhail Rostovtzeff declared that the "traffic in slaves was one of the most profitable branches in trade."[7] As the cities in the Hellenistic world became richer, there was a sharper conflict between what he, perhaps anachronistically from our point of view, called "the working classes and the government, which enjoyed in general the support of the *bourgeoisie*" (807). In the lands around the Mediterranean, the altered social, political, and intellectual situation of the Hellenistic kingdoms may have produced a new emphasis on distinction, on the difference between slave and free maintained through mockery, comic exaggeration, threats, and, if necessary, threats made real through torture and tattooing. In his more recent history, published in 1990, Peter Green also points to greater wealth inequities and the potential for slave rebellions that seems to have troubled rulers of the period: "Both Alexander's and Demetrius Poliorcetes' treaties with the cities that formed the League of Corinth contained a specific clause calling upon Macedonia and League members to suppress any movement involving abolition of debt, redistribution of land, confiscation of personal property, or the freeing of slaves to promote revolution."[8] Slave revolts were recorded not only in Southern Italy and Sicily, but also in Greece; two were attested in the Attic mines (Orosius 5.9.5).[9] Athenaeus recorded the resistance of Drimakos on Khios; slaves revolted on Delos, in what Green calls "desperate protests against intolerable conditions" (393). In this chapter I look at various moments in the rich history of the post-Alexandrian Hellenistic world. There are instances of cruelty, of Hellenic barbarity, of increased social differentiation, and also of contact and even fusion with remote peoples, stretching far into Africa and Asia.

Herodas

The Hellenistic writer Herodas presents some of the most brutal and disturbing images of slave ownership and management in all of ancient Greek writing. The violence and contempt and comic ridicule directed toward slaves were aimed principally at those who were not part of the dominant class of Hellenistic Greeks, from the old cities of the mainland, Macedonians, or islanders of traditionally Hellenic societies. The slaves came from elsewhere and received the brunt of literary and perhaps literal cruelty. Herodas, whose name may in fact be Herondas, probably wrote his *mimiamboi* during the third century B.C.E. His work carried on the traditions of Attic comedy and of the writer of mimes Sophron; some of the extant poems refer to Alexandria, others to the island of Kos. Herodas may have written for a reading audience, although some scholars argue that the scripts were performed by a single mime or by an acting troupe. In his representations of pimps, housewives, and cobblers, readers are given glimpses of what purports to be everyday life in this slave-owning culture. Although it is difficult to ascertain who is the audience for these mimes and whether they draw on popular culture or represent it for an élite audience, the mimes themselves display scenes of considerable cruelty. Mime 2, a monologue spoken by a brothel keeper, parodies a law-court speech and opens up strange possibilities of humor. The speaker, Battaros, complains about an opponent, Thales, once called Artimmes, that is, bearing a Phrygian name changed to suit his new circumstances. Headlam notes, "The Greeks had abundant opportunity of studying the Phrygian character, since their slaves were largely drawn from Phrygia; and the result was that the Phrygian became proverbial as a worthless and contemptible barbarian."[10] This antagonist, who does not speak in the mime, allegedly thrashed Battaros, came to his doors at night, set fire to his house, and took one of his *pornai,* his prostitutes, away by force (34–37). Battaros shows her off to the court, as silent evidence of his claims: "Come here, Myrtale—it's your turn. Show yourself to all; don't be ashamed. Consider that those whom you see trying the case are your fathers and brethren. Look, gentlemen, up and down, at her rents, how threadbare these were rent by this villain, when he mauled and tousled her" (65–71). Battaros does not object to his opponent's beating this woman; if the man were to buy her, he then would be free to beat her as much as he likes (83). As proof of his sincerity, Battaros offers himself up for torture: "If all he wishes is to damage the bodies of slaves, and challenges to the ordeal [*basanon*], I give myself freely; here, Thales, take me and torture [*streblou*] me" (87–89). The violence already committed against the slave girl Myrtale can be repeated here, in the law-court's torture, or *basanos;* violence and the violation of slaves' bodies, even or perhaps especially in this comic context, are taken for granted by the speaker, who mocks himself, his property, the *porne,* exposing his own vulnerability to torture, as a slave himself, or as a noncitizen, probably a eunuch, having undergone the violence of castration.[11]

In other mimes, these forms of violence recur, directed against schoolchildren and other victims, especially slaves, on the island of Kos and in Alexandria. The most brutal concerns the slave Gastron, named in Mime 5 by a jealous slave owner who believes her slave is pleasuring another woman: Gastron's mistress, Bitinna, threatens him repeatedly: "Bind this fellow . . . loose the rope of the bucket quickly and bind him" (10–11). "Strip him . . . Pinion his elbows behind him, and let the rope cut into his flesh" (20–25). The slave himself offers to be tattooed if ever he commits such crimes again: "*stixon*" (tattoo) (28). Bitinna commands: "Take him to the gaol to Hermon and bid him lay a thousand blows on his back, and a thousand on his belly" (32–34). "Kydilla, hit this villain on the beak, and . . . tell Hermon to give him a thousand here, and a thousand there" (41–49). The mistress's other slaves brutalize Gastron as well (58–62); and the girl Kydilla recalls the ankle shackles of the slave Pyrrhies. Then, although she finally relents, Bitinna calls for the tattooer herself, to tattoo her renegade slave on his forehead: *en to metopo to epigramm' ekhon touto* (79).

Interspersed throughout the mimes of Herodas are insulting and threatening remarks made to the slaves who surround the personae of the texts like furniture and are part of a constant social practice to establish the distinction between slave and free, to keep slaves in their place, to produce solidarity among the free. The insults serve to bind the free characters themselves, to establish them as belonging to a class apart, with rights and concerns that produce a social network.

The violence of the Gastron mime, with its threat of a forehead tattoo, is echoed in a fragment of another popular mime, edited by I. C. Cunningham in the Teubner edition of Herodas (1987) and summarized by the editor:

> The mistress has been rejected by Aesopus [a slave] in favour of Apollonia [also a slave]. In the first scene she rails against him, and orders the pair to

be taken away and killed. Next it seems that they have escaped, but the girl is recaptured; Aesopus is to be sought and killed. Then he is present, seemingly dead . . .

> [ ] that I may [ ],
> I now desire the boy.
> [ ] him to fuck me. [*binesei*]
> What then [ ] whips [*ma*]*stigas*] . . .

Aesop stands expecting to receive the slave

> Girl [ ] I'll hit his teeth and shake them out . . .
> Sirrah, if I ordered you to dig?
> And if to plough? [*arotrian*]
> And if to lift stones?

So compared with all the things that have to be done on the farm, my cunt has appeared harsher to you who were raised in a womanly fashion . . . I'm speaking to you, take them away and tie them by both extremities [to] the neighbouring trees, dragging one a long way apart from the other, and see that you don't show one to the other, in case being full of the sight of each other they should die happy. And when you have slaughtered them, meet me [inside].[12]

The mime fragments record sexual violence, whips, beating and the shaking out of teeth, tying by extremities to trees, and killing. This popular, undated, anonymous mime appears even more brutal than that of Herodas.

Milder moments of such comic relief abounded as well in fifth-century comedy, where abuse of slaves formed a crucial part of the representation of Athens to itself; here they call attention to the generic specificity of this mime, which is different from those Hellenistic poems featuring epic or bucolic subjects. Slavery, slaves, and abuse of slaves form part of the landscape. All these manifestations, these representations of violence and contempt, might be read as manifestations of *fear,* as expressions of the desire to manage, through the hegemony of coercion and consent, the desirable passivity of the slave class, often alien, potentially violent, and interspersed everywhere among the free.

We might conceive of several reasons for a more explicit degree of brutality and mockery, especially evident in the mimes of Herodas, where threats and humiliation abound. We could point to the lowness of the genre of mime, which may have its sources in popular entertainment and therefore exhibits more vulgar and explicit forms of domination than the elegant idylls of Theocritus, much as comedy differs from tragedy in the classical city. Yet it is not clear that Herodas is in fact producing low texts; his verse forms, diction, and allusions may in fact suggest that he is representing the low for the élite, that his audience enjoyed a representation of such characters as dildo makers, cobblers, pimps, and schoolteachers but were themselves of higher orders. It may be that the more sinister aspects of Herodas' mimes, the threat to beat and tattoo Gastron, for example, echo such scenes as that in Aristophanes' *Frogs,* in which the torture of Xanthias is comically evoked, and the innocence of the spectacle is misread by those in postmodernity appalled by the notion that torture on the rack, with whips and such, is the subject of laughter. But the possible acceleration of violence in representation may have to do with the changed circumstances of the Hellenistic era, mentioned above, in which the tiny classical *polis* was replaced first by the immensity of the incipient Alexandrian empire and then, when that huge provisional entity collapsed, was itself transformed into kingdoms dominated by Macedonian monarchs. This is a world in flux, in which Greek writers such as Theocritus, Callimachus, and Herodas, whose traditions responded to and were conceived within individual *poleis,* had to accommodate themselves to new forms of polity, the huge kingdoms of the Hellenistic heirs of Alexandria, whose empires eventually stretched far to the east of Alexandria itself, incorporating new aliens, new barbarians to be Hellenized, who ended by maintaining crucial differences within new hegemonies.

"Ekphrasis": Establishing Hegemony and Difference

Hellenistic *Ekphrasis*

In an essay on Hellenistic *ekphrasis,* a rhetorical form that often consists of the description of a work of art, Simon Goldhill has written of "the history of the formations of a viewing subject."[13] I want to use his formulation but to emphasize the history of the formation of viewing subjects, in the plural, the history of how the representation of the object viewed, along with its viewers, has its impact on questions of power and authority in the new world of the Hellenistic kingdoms left behind after the struggles among Alexander's heirs, an era of expansion and even vertigo for its writers. I will look at two ekphrases of the special sort, ekphrases of notional works of art, both written in the Hellenistic period, one by Theocritus and the other by Herodas. Goldhill discusses both Theocritus and Herodas, as I do, but considers Herodas' "a more restricted mime" and uses it simply as a foil to point to the complex ironies of the Theocritean ekphrasis (222). I argue for an elaboration of difference in these ekphrases, for the production of a set of responses, a variety of viewing subjects that takes in questions of historical knowledge, of ethnic difference, of gender and of class, as the narrators write, probably for élite audiences, and describe not just notional works of art, but also characters reading the writing on their walls. These ekphrases occur in the works of Greek authors from traditionally Greek regions, long colonized from the mainland cities, and reflect the necessity to respond to changed circumstances, a world in which not only the slaves are ethnic others, but also where the cultural élite mixes with new aliens, new barbarians.

In his fourth mime, thought to be set on the island of Kos, Herodas represents women looking at works of art in a religious setting. Because Herodas is closely linked to the comic tradition of Sophron, the fifth-century writer of mimes from Syracuse in Sicily, generic pressures push the scene low. Herodas' women are on Kos, probably, at the shrine to Asklepios there, and there are comic moments of jostling with slaves.[14] The text is uncertain at various points, so even the names of the characters cannot be ascertained with confidence. Yet Herodas concerns himself both with the description of works of art and with the mediation of the gaze upon them by silly women. The generic pressures of comedy and mime conspire to create these women, to paint them as ridiculous and ignorant. We have also blind or invisible slaves and women who do not speak, who are addressed in the standard comic tropes of insult and deprecation. A party goes to view the shrine and the works of art, but only some of those present are licensed to speak and to comment on what they see. Naive and gullible women provide a foil for the writer, and for a more sophisticated and learned listener or viewer, who learns how not to look at art.

The first women, Kynno, begins with praise of Apollo; she sacrifices a cock. She orders someone, perhaps named Kokkale, to set up a table for Hygieia. And Kokkale marvels at the statue, the *kalon agalmaton*. Sons of Praxiteles are said to have made them: "See dear, the girl yonder looking up at the apple; wouldn't you think she will swoon away suddenly, if she does not get it? . . . Why, one would say the sculpture would talk, that is if it were not stone when one gets close. La! In time men will be able even to put life into stones" (169). The woman's gushing amazement brings the listener back to another age, that of Daedalus and his marvelous statues that moved on their own and the golden automata of the god Hephaistos, whom he orders about to produce the shield of Achilles, the first verbal description of a work of visual art.[15]

The door is thrown open to the sacristy, and further marvels await within. Kokkale thinks the works might have been performed by Athena herself (as also Theocritus); the naked boy "will bleed . . . if I scratch him, Kynno, for the flesh seems to pulse warmly as it lies on him in the picture" (171). The only criterion accessible to these viewers is that of truth to nature, of naturalness: "Have they not all of them the look of light and life?" Kokkale fears that the ox might hurt her, as he gazes at her with one eye. Her companion informs her that these are works of the great Apelles of Ephesus. "If any gaze on him and his works save from a just point [*ek dikes*] of view, may he be hung up by the foot at the fuller's"—that is to say, he will be hung upside down and carded like a piece of dirty laundry (171). Violence and torture enter the scene, destined for the ignorant.

A bit of formulaic slave abuse reminds one that the slave, while present, cannot speak or express any reaction to the wonders. Kynno says, "La! Not an atom of notice does she take of what I am saying, but stands and stares at me for all the world like a crab" (169). For the slave, her mistress is the spectacle; she is not represented as capable of registering the presence of the objects seen in amazement by the two free women. I remark on this not as an incidental observation about slave societies in general, but to point out a feature constitutive of these discriminations; the connoisseur emerges in this period, by necessity in relation to the ignorant and the blind.

Theocritus' Idyll 15 also represents two female characters, Gorgo and Praxinoa. Praxinoa receives Gorgo in her house, and the two comment about husbands and children. They set out to see the Adonis at King Ptolemy's palace, a great spectacle that commoners were admitted to visit.[16] Unremarked by many commentators is the discourse about the slave girl at the beginning of the poem, which comically precedes the visit to Ptolemy's palace. Praxinoa brusquely orders her slave to set out a chair with a cushion for her guest, then after complaints about husbands, commands her slave girl Eunoa to take the spinning away: "Go on, move! Quick, bring some water. I need the water first, so she brings soap.

Give me it anyway. Not too much, you lazy slut. Now pour the water. You fool, you're soaking my blouse." Such moments of comic relief abound in Athenian comedy; here they call attention to the generic specificity of this idyll, different from other Theocritean poems featuring bucolic subjects in pastoral settings. As the two women leave the house, Praxinoa addresses another slave, her nurse, telling her to mind the baby, play with the baby, call in the dog, and lock the door.

Ethnicity as well as gender enters this poem; the two women are Syracusans from Sicily, resident in Alexandria in Egypt, and thus, like Theocritus, the poet himself, not Egyptian and not Macedonian like the ruling Ptolemies, part of a very different population used to life in a wealthy Corinthian colony long established in the west. These matters also frame the *ekphrasis*; the women talk, as they walk through the Alexandrian streets, about criminals who used to mug pedestrians "Egyptian fashion"; they call the Egyptians "ruffians to a man, born criminals. To hell with the lot of them." They are Greeks, reveling in their superiority, tentatively appreciative of the crack-down on crime they attribute to Ptolemy, the Macedonian king. They complain about the crush in the streets: "They are shoving each other like pigs" (72). Eunoa, the slave girl, is present but never speaks (76).

When the women arrive at the palace to gaze at the spectacle, the display, set up in honor of Adonis, they marvel at the tapestries in their naive and awestruck manner; the weaving is "so delicate and pretty," fit for the gods, in a phrase that recalls admiration of the weaving of Circe in the *Odyssey* (10. 222–223). They are struck most by the naturalness, the "truth," of the designs: "Such artists, to make their designs appear so true to life. How naturally, the figures stand, how naturally they move." They admire Adonis reclining on his silver couch, beautiful in his youth, "with the first downy growth spreading from his temples" (85). They listen to an Argive singer who praises Aphrodite and whose hymn is also an *ekphrasis,* in several senses, an epideictic tour de force and a description of the work of art all present are gazing at. One viewer points to features of the display: "See how after a year the soft-footed Hours have brought you back Adonis . . ." She includes praise of Berenice, mother of queen Arsinoë, who "pampers Adonis: Before him are laid in season the burden of fruit trees . . ." This *ekphrasis* draws in both praise of Ptolemy Philadelphus' queen and her ancestry and a careful description of the work of art: fruits, plants, perfume, jars of gold, cakes; creatures of the air and earth attend Adonis. "Boy loves" fly above, and there is an allusion to Ganymede, to gold, ebony, and eagles of white ivory that carry off the boy to perform as Zeus' cupbearer. Other elements of the shrine, or perhaps images on the tapestry, are coverlets of fine red wool, "softer than sleep." (This is a phrase that recalls a moment in Herodas' Mime 6, where dildos are described in similar terms.) The singer describes Aphrodite's embrace of Adonis: "His lip is covered with nothing but reddish down." The singer goes on to refer to the subsequent moments of the ritual, the women's carrying the image of Adonis to the shore, with lamentations, and she addresses the god directly, ending with a prayer for his return.

The Adonia, recalling the tragic death of Aphrodite's lover Adonis, brought from Syria and celebrated in Athens itself, was a ritual of lamentation and mourning profoundly contaminated with Asianism; the Lesbian Sappho mentions it in her Fragments 140 and 168: "Delicate Adonis is dying / Kythereia / what should we do? Strike yourselves, maidens, and tear your garments" (fr. 168). Marcel Detienne discussed it fully, in an argument that set the sedate ritual of the Thesmophoria, participated in by citizen-class women of the classical city, against the Adonia's urban worshippers, perhaps prostitutes or women who defined themselves in relation to Aphrodite and her young lover rather than Demeter and her daughter. The Orientalizing strategies of Theocritus, allied with the queen, assimilate worship of Aphrodite and Adonis to this new site, Alexandria, now a center of Greek culture set in Africa, a bridge between Asia and Africa that looks also to Macedonia, to European mainland Greece, and beyond to Sicily and the Greek colonies in Italy. If the observers are oblivious to these dimensions of the art they see, the poet communicates with other Greeks in a new Kosmopolis.

The *ekphrasis* is interwoven with byplay between the women and a stranger who calls attention to their accents. They are Syracusans, from Sicily, come to Alexandria, speaking with Doric accents ("twittering endlessly, cooing like doves. They'll exhaust me with their great broad vowels"). Richard Hunter allows for a differentiated response to the *language* here (122), but he doesn't connect it with issues of colonization, occupation, ethnic difference, gender, and slavery. Praxinoa defends herself, claiming a noble ancestry not just from Syracuse, but further back, from Corinth all the way to that city's hero Bellerophon: "So we speak Peloponnesian." Her snobbery calls up issues of ethnicity, Greek superiority to Egyptians, issues of dialectal and cultural difference among Greeks; in the hybrid, heterogeneous, ethnically mixed world of Alexander's foundation, negotiations about power and hegemony involve not just gender, but also questions of the old world, the new, and the newest, Alexandria herself.[17] If the Syracusan tyrants of Pindar's day were *nouveaux riches* and needed him to legitimize their sovereignty in relation to the old aristocratic families of mainland Greece, in this new center of culture in Africa, a comic pedigree that goes back to Bellerophon raises the stature of these women in their own eyes not only in relation to native Egyptians, but also in a hierarchy of newly arrived and slightly barbaric Macedonians who eschew the mainland Greeks' traditions of aristocracy, oligarchy, or democracy for a new Pharaonic kingdom.

In the Theocritean case, we falsify the ancient situation by considering it as a parallel to a modern setting in an art museum, with all the decorum and cultural discipline now associated with looking at art. In Theocritus' representation of the Syracusans gazing at the spectacle of the Adonia, however it may be visualized, with figures of divinities, then contained representations of other divinities such as Ganymede, enclosed within another medium, the coverlets, the appropriate reactions are not just aesthetic, but also have to do with reverence or irreverence, and with worship or cynicism about the importation of this Asian cult into the Greek pantheon and its adoption by these newly Egyptianized Macedonians.

The women also appear oblivious to the association between Adonis and Osiris, the dead god of Egyptian religion, the god of the River Nile who ruled over the underworld and, like Adonis, was cared for by an attentive goddess, in his case his sister and wife Isis. In the Theocritean scene and its evocation of Thetis' preservation of Patroclus' body in the *Iliad,* in a description of Aphrodite's deification of Berenice (106–108), there may also be reference to mummification, or at least to the synthetic practices of the ruling Ptolemies, descended from one of Alexander's generals, who skillfully deployed Egyptian ideology alongside Greek to authorize and legitimate their authority in the new capital of Alexandria. Like Adonis, Osiris died but was thought to be resurrected; his body was reconstituted by Isis, aided by Anubis, and so he is associated with mummification and also with recurrence, with the flooding and recession of the Nile. There may be an allusion in Theocritus' poem to this connection, in his reference to the lamentations of women worshipping Adonis at the shore. The Syrian Adonis, "lord," thus becomes a Greek version of the god Osiris, the god who absorbed each pharaoh after his death. Joan Burton points out that the relationship between Aphrodite and Adonis "shared traits with those of Phoenician Astarte and Tammuz, Phrygian Cybele and Attis, Sumerian Inanna and Dumuzi," as well as the Egyptian gods.[18] As mentioned earlier, Sappho herself spoke of Adonis, and the Adonia in her poetry, and her verses may mark the moment at which this Near Eastern consort of the goddess entered into Greek celebrations of the goddess Aphrodite.

Scholars have disagreed about the hymn contained within Theocritus' poem, unsure if it is merely bad or a parody. Burton reads it more charitably:

> A problem in composing a hymn for a public celebration of the Adonia is, how could it speak to the traditional audience members of the Adonia (mostly housewives and prostitutes) and make them feel welcome in a public festival enacted on the palace grounds? A description of how cakes are made and a mention of a shepherd's contribution to the making of coverlets might represent a suitable rhetorical strategy to draw in less elite audience members, those who normally feel excluded from the glittering palace society of Alexandria. (144)

I would argue rather that the connection of this *ekphrasis* with Sophron, and the ironic representation of these women, would lead to other conclusions, especially when the *ekphrasis* is compared, as it is by Burton, with Herodas' fourth mime.

In both of these texts a wedge is driven between the naivete of female onlookers, even though they are Greeks and have the genealogy of colonists from the mainland, and the gaze of a more sophisticated readership, with different criteria of judgment, which go beyond a purely Hellenic pedigree.[19] These poets are participating in new forms of culture, establishing new kinds of order and hierarchy, and allowing for the possibility that élites from populations once considered barbaric may have powers and capacities of synthesis and understanding unavailable to women, even women who are part of the dominant Greek population, now overshadowed by the ambitious and hybridizing Macedonian Ptolemies. Richard Hunter observes, "It does not require a long survey of history of discussions of 'mimetic realism' to realise how closely the reactions of the women foreshadow familiar modes of critical response. We might not naturally choose Gorgo and Praxinoa as models for ourselves, and their reactions might seem 'unsophisticated,' but the poem forces us to consider the basis and validity of our own critical judgments" (117). That difference, the distance, the irony established between these women's lack of sophistication and the listeners, and readers' response, is precisely the point. The situation calls up not just the comedy of a naive Theocritus coming to the Alexandrian court. Rather than valuing the truth to life, and naturalism, and the deceptive appearance of things, so lifelike as to invite touching and verification of their artificiality, the authors of these texts are moving toward other ways of seeing that may be glimpsed behind the screen of these unsophisticated lookers who appear ridiculous in their marveling at the works of art.[20] For the reader or for listeners seeing through or trapped behind the eyes of these characters, the ironic tension produces a desire for something else, for more, for an assessment of a tradition, an appreciation of the brilliant incorporation of indigenous Egyptian beliefs into a cult of Greek gods and Macedonian rulers, a judgment of the limitations of these viewers.

Consider the prescriptions of later Skepticism on judgment—for example, Sextus Empiricus (second century C.E.) on the earlier Carneades, who was Cyrenaic, that is, an African Greek (214/3–129/8 B.C.E.): "Just as at the place of judgment there are both the one who judges and that which is being judged, and the medium through which the judgment takes place and the spatial dimensions, place, time, . . . we judge the particular character of each of these things in turn: e.g. we examine whether that which is judging has sharp vision or not, whether that which is being judged is sufficiently large to be judged, whether the medium, for instance the atmosphere, is dark" (Sextus, *Adv. Math.* vii 183). If there are slaves who cannot be seen to see, and women who see naively, there is another, at the height of the hierarchy, who communicates with the reader over the heads of these viewers and stands perhaps for ekphrastic hope, as W. J. T. Mitchell puts it, for the dream of an adequate description, one that will *master* the work of art, or at least give it as a gift to the listener.[21]

The vanguard thinkers of the third century B.C.E. confronted the heterogeneity of the new situation in Alexandria and made something new of all the cultural materials then at their disposal, from Greek mythography to Jewish textual rigor and purification to Egyptian traditions of chronicling. The Hellenistic poets share with their hybrid fellow-Alexandrians a concern with forms of reading and interpretation, and such interests include ways of looking at and interpreting works of visual art. In their conscious or unconscious project of creating adequate readers, viewers of works of art, both writers use the naive and unsophisticated presence of babbling women to point to a hierarchy of viewers. Slaves are invisible, don't speak, can't be said to see anything at all. The women see but don't understand. The reader or listener, set in a position of ironic mastery over both slaves and mistresses, sees something new, over the heads, literally, of the characters of these poems. One does not come into the world knowing how to look at art. Coming to see *ek dikes,* "justly," is a long and complex cultural process. The Hellenistic age stands at a crucial intersection in the recognition that there must be experts, learned eyes, to guide the looker, and for us, that there are issues of power and hierarchy implicated in looking.

The Hellenistic age also saw utopianists, dreamers who argued for new cities without social classes, such thinkers as Iamboulos, who may have been "a Hellenized Nabataean Arab,"[22] contributing yet another ethnic element to the great heterogeneity of this period of an extended ancient "Greece." Even as the poets establish hierarchies of seeing, Iamboulos describes people "who have women in common, and love as equals the children that are born, bringing them up as the children of all" (Diodorus 2.57.1, 2.58.1). Perhaps the sites of Hellenistic capitals produce both the intense hierarchization, a new and formally sustained differentiation among kinds of seers—slave, female, and educated, eventually the "educated viewer," *pepaideumenos theates,* of the so-called second sophistic (60–320 C.E.), but also utopian fantasies of real equality, of which more in the next chapter.

Peter Weiss

In another description of a Hellenistic work of art, one that survives and persists and turns up, rhizomically, in twentieth-century Berlin, the narrator begins a novel:

> All around us the bodies rose out of the stone, crowded into groups, intertwined, or shattered into fragments, hinting at their shapes with a torso, a propped-up arm, a burst hip, a scabbed shard, always in warlike gestures, dodging, rebounding, attacking, shielding themselves . . . These only just created, already dying faces, these tremendous and dismembered hands, these wide-sweeping pinions drowning in the blunt rock, this stony gaze, these lips torn open for a shriek . . . thus they clashed with one another, acting at higher behest, dreaming, motionless in insane vehemence, mute in inaudible roaring, all of them woven into a metamorphosis of torture, shuddering, persisting, waiting for an awakening.[23]

The description comes at the beginning of Peter Weiss' monumental three-volume *Aesthetics of Resistance,* its first volume published in 1975. The *ekphrasis* is pronounced by the narrator, who stands before the Pergamum Altar in Berlin in 1937, ready to depart for the civil war in Spain. Eumenes II, the post-Alexandrian monarch of the kingdom of Pergamum in Asia Minor, built the altar to Zeus in the 170s B.C.E. to celebrate his victory over the Galatians, raiding and invading tribes originally from Europe. In Weiss' novel, the narrator's comrade Heilman interprets, explaining not only that the great frieze depicts a gigantomachy but also that the representation conveys other messages: The conquest of tribes who had invaded from the north became a victory of aristocratic purity over wild and barbaric forces. These museum-goers see in the battling figures not just giants and Olympians, but also an allegory of defeated Celtic Galatians and victorious Attalids. They see also the slaves captured by the victorious Hellenic forces, the workers who carried the blocks of stone to be carved, their very bodies represented in these stones. Weiss goes on, in other *ekphrases* in this brilliant, immense, and exhausting novel, to describe Gaudi's cathedral of la Sagrada Familia in Barcelona, Géricault's *Wreck of the Medusa,* and the temples of Angkor Wat, in an immense synthesis of political spaces and political education. Weiss writes: "Heilman says that works like those from Pergamum must be constantly reinterpreted until a reversal is achieved and the earth-born awake from darkness and slavery" (44). For the characters in the novel, the elaborate *ekphrasis* of the Pergamum Altar conveys the encrypted presence of slave bodies, the labor of the slaves effaced yet nonetheless registered in the work of art, and becomes a touchstone, a point of departure for reflections on art, on museums, on culture, on history, and on the hunger for culture felt by uneducated, self-educated proletarian laborers about to be caught up in the atrocious events of a new gigantomachy.

Reading the Hellenistic objects backwards, from the perspective of 1975, and from an incipient postmodernism, in an act of deliberate and self-conscious anachronism, recognizing the influence of such texts as Lessing's *Laocoön* on Weiss' *ekphrasis,* reveals other things besides the beauties and self-reflection of a poet's gaze, and marks a strong contrast with the ignorant women of the Hellenistic poems by Herodas and Theocritus. The narrator of Weiss' novel sees differently, reads not just the art historical object, the power and brilliance of its sculpture, but also what is not seen by others, what centuries of education have taught us not to see: the slaves, the workers, those who fashioned the stones and whose bodies served as models for the sculptors. And the utopian hopes embodied tentatively in the example of the revolution in the Soviet Union remind the narrator of the novel of all that can be hoped for: justice, peace, and an education in the history of human works of art, literary and visual, once inaccessible to the likes of such as he.

As another man who had undoubtedly stood before that same Hellenistic work, the great altar of Pergamum taken from the Turks by the Germans to Berlin, Walter Benjamin, wrote in 1940:

> Empathy with the victor invariably benefits the rulers... Whoever has emerged victorious participates to this day in the triumphal procession in which the present rulers step over those who are lying prostrate. According to traditional practice, the spoils are carried along in the procession. They are called cultural treasures, and a historical materialist views them with cautious detachment. For without exception the cultural treasures he surveys have an origin which he cannot contemplate without horror. They owe their existence not only to the efforts of the great minds and talents who have created them, but also to the anonymous toil of their contemporaries. There is no document of civilization which is not at the same time a document of barbarism. And just as such a document is not free of barbarism, barbarism taints also the manner in which it was transmitted from one owner to another.[24]

Benjamin's oft-cited, yet especially pertinent words bring up crucial methodological questions. As discussed in the introduction to this book, there are still those who want to quarantine antiquity, to set it off from contamination by the more recent past, or the present, to take a purely antiquarian approach to ancient culture. Yet it is impossible to look at these poems and these imaginary objects as if they were transparently accessible artifacts from the past. Interrogation of our own place in the history of their transmission seems part of the obligation to the past. If we identify with the élite viewers, the poets, philosophers, and ekphrasists of antiquity, we cannot see barbarians, slaves, for example, as presences, as artists' models, as workers, as silent bystanders in the process of making intellectuals and culturally sophisticated viewers for the present. Weiss acknowledges the death of one utopianism, the fantasy of a savior Lenin and a Stalin, who turn into historical monsters. But if we resign ourselves to the position of the élite viewers, cultivated and produced by all the efforts of the past to establish difference, we surrender to indifference, to exclusion, and participate in the shutting out of some from the utopian possibilities of history, and in a purely Athenocentric vision of the legacy of ancient Greece.

Other Alexandrias

The other Alexandrias that dot the map of Eurasia have their own practices of slave holding, art making, and fusing Hellenic and Hellenistic ways with their traditions. Ai Khanum on the Oxus River, the site of the discovery of the Seven Sages reference, in Bactria, discussed in Chapter 4, had a Greek *polis* plan, yet contained in its architecture elements both Greek and Persian: "It has Greek-style buildings such as a theatre, cult sanctuary, *gymnasion,* and long stoas . . . , though buildings and architectural elements reminiscent of Achaemenid architecture were also found"[25] Here I consider just two examples of the effects of the Greek diaspora eastward into the Middle East, and of the Indian, especially Buddhist, diaspora westward: one, the effects of Greek and Hellenistic art on Gandharan and Buddhist representational practices, and the other the literary-philosophical text "The Questions of King Milinda" *(Milindapanha).* The areas concerned are especially important in the history of Buddhism and its spread from northern India both westward and eastward.

Bactria had been a province of the Persian empire, where the Persians last resisted the conquest of Alexander, in 329 and 328. It occupied territory now claimed by Afghanistan, Uzbekistan, and Tajikistan, land contested furiously to this day. The ancient Bactrians fought first with the Persians against Alexander, joining Darius after the defeat at Gaugamela (Arrian 3.16). In the invasion of India, Bactrian troops fought with the Macedonians in the Punjab, at the battle of the Hydaspes River, against Porus (5.12). And on the terrible journey back toward Babylon, Alexander reminded his mutinous troops—who resented the fact that the Bactrian cavalrymen, among others conquered, had been distributed into his élite corps, the Companion Cavalry (7.6)—that he had given them Bactra, capital of Bactria, when they threatened him on the banks of the Tigris (Arrian 7.9).

Arrian, historian after the fact of Alexander's conquests, sums up his impression of the Indians, trying to sift out the true from the fabulous:

> I have not, in this history, recorded the Indians' customs, nor whether the country produces any extraordinary animals, nor the quantity or kind of fish or sea monsters to be found in the Indus, Hydaspes, Ganges, or other Indian rivers; nor have I mentioned the ants that mine their gold, nor the guardian dragons, nor all the other tales that have been written (more from pleasure

than for describing what actually exists), as I presume that all the bizarre tales invented about the Indians will not be verified or refuted by anyone. But Alexander and those who shared his campaigns tested most of them—as many, at any rate, as they did not themselves invent. They proved that none of the Indians had gold . . . that they had no taste for luxurious living; that they were physically tall, in fact the tallest men in Asia, most of them eight feet tall or nearly so; that they were blacker than all the other races except the Ethiopians; and that they were by far the noblest warriors among the inhabitants of Asia at that time. (Arrian 5.4)

The modern historian Graham Shipley records the connections of these regions with Alexander and his heirs:

Conquest of at least the north-western frontier of India was never achieved by the Seleukids, but had to wait for the expansion of the Graeco-Bactrian kingdom in the mid- and later second century, particularly under the so-called Indo-Greek (or Graeco-Indian) kings Demetrios II (c. 185–175?) and Menandros (Menander, r. c. 155–c. 130). Demetrios II was the first Graeco-Bactrian king whose title, "Aniketos" (Unconquered), was rendered into an Indian language on coins. (285)

The effects on Buddhist art of the Hellenistic works of art in Gandhara are well documented, although subject to critique from those who rightly argue that Western critics catalogue only the effects of Western civilization on the east, and never the reciprocity that must result from contact, hybridity, diaspora, and diffusion. Robert Fisher describes the differences from traditional Indian representations of the Buddha, "an essentially humble image" and those typical of Gandhara:[26]

By contrast, the Gandharan Buddha, despite having many of the same attributes—the lion throne, yogic posture and radiant nimbus—remained a mixture of Roman styles. Its most striking characteristics are the toga, an inappropriate garment for the climate of India, and the facial features, with a combination of realism about the mouth and cheeks but with deeply cut, stylized eyes. (46)

The hybrid Gandharan style persisted, in an almost ganglionic pattern, across vast stretches of Asia. Chinese Buddhists, who traveled to India, travelers who recorded their adventures, brought images as well as teachings back to China. Gandharan elements traveled into Central Asia and to

China itself during the high period of Buddhist belief. According to Fisher, "By the sixth century, the Wei empire of northern China had some thirty thousand monasteries, while Buddhist art had moved beyond the introductory phase and assumed a distinct Chinese character. The earliest images suggest Gandharan sources. A Buddha figure, with its moustache, topknot, toga, flaming shoulders and lion throne, could even have been made in Gandhara and carried to China" (91). In discussing the cave shrines of Yungang and Longmen, Fisher suggests that "the artists may have worked from drawings or sketches carried back by pilgrims from holy sites in India, especially in the north-western Gandharan regions" (93). As Fisher further notes, the iconography of Gandhara, especially in the representations of an emaciated Buddha, which he attributes to the "Roman love of portraiture and dramatic realism" (47), but which is rarely found in Indian depictions, finds its way to Japan, where it "belongs to a branch of Buddhist art devoted to acts of extreme asceticism," "of special appeal to Japanese artists" (147). Alexandria stretches from Egypt to Japan, and further, with the more recent diaspora of Buddhism, into the New World.[27]

The rock edicts of the Mauryan emperor Asoka, a Buddhist convert, claim that he sent missionaries westward to monarchs identified as Antiochus, Ptolemy, Antigone, and Alexander of Epirus.[28] Menander, king of the Graeco-Bactrian kingdom in the second century B.C.E.,[29] was said to have been converted from philosophy, the Greek practices of dialectic and inquiry, and then from Brahmanic worship to Buddhism by a missionary, Nagasena.[30] The Buddhist treatise that bears Menander-Milinda's name, preserved in Pali, describes his city: "In the land of the Bactrian Greeks there was a city called Sagala, a great centre of trade. Rivers and hills beautified it, delightful landscapes surrounded it, and it possessed many parks, gardens, woods, lakes and lotus ponds."[31] A company of enlightened Buddhists, arhats, sent for the Venerable Nagasena to come to the Greek king, Menander, called Milinda in this text, who was "bothering" local monks, presumably with metaphysical inquiries, and so "the Elders went to Sagala, lighting up the city with their yellow robes which shone like lamps, and bringing with them the fresh breeze of the holy mountains" (146–147). King Milinda went up to the Sankheyya hermitage, where Nagasena was staying with eighty thousand monks, Milinda arriving with a retinue of five hundred Greeks. In the text recording their conversation, the king engages with Nagasena on metaphysical questions, in a form of question and answer that has affinities not only with Platonic *elenchus,* or cross-examination, the dialogue or dialectic characteristic of Plato's texts, but also with the conversational and didactic forms of the Upanishads.

One of the "questions," for example, called the simile of the chariot, concerns the transitory nature of material reality. If, as he has declared, "there is no permanent individuality implied in his name," Nagasena asks, "What then is Nagasena?" Is it nails, teeth, skin, perception, consciousness? Nagasena illustrates his point that he is all these together by pointing to the king's chariot:

> "What is the chariot? Is the pole the chariot?"
> "No, your Reverence."
> "Or the axle, wheels, frame, reins, yoke, spokes, or goad?" . . .
> ". . . your Majesty, I can find no chariot . . ."
> When he had spoken the five hundred Greeks cried "Well done! . . . your Majesty, get out of that dilemma if you can!" (107)

In this public performance, this debate, the Greeks side with Nagasena against their ruler, and goad him on, as he concludes that the chariot is called a chariot "on account of all these various components," that "it is . . . a generally understood term, a practical designation" (107). And Nagasena agrees, concluding therefore that he himself, Nagasena, is the same, that it is "on account of the various components of my being that I'm known by the generally understood term, the practical designation Nagasena" (107).

Plutarch seems to have known of the Buddhist Greek king, and there is evidence of exchange westward of these "questions." The *Letter of Pseudo-Aristeas,* which refers to the Library of Alexandria, appears to be modeled on the *Questions of King Milinda,* according to W. W. Tarn.[32] And one of King Milinda's coins, according to the somewhat controversial Thomas McEvilley, has been found as far from Bactria as Wales (377).[33] Tarn suggested that the extant text, in Pali, may come from an original Greek text.[34] The form of the exchange resembles not only Upanishadic teaching techniques, but also the Platonic form of the dialogue, as noted, which itself has roots in the law-courts of the city of Athens, in mimes, and in Athenian drama.

McEvilley remarks:

> There is some reason to believe that Indian ascetics traveled this route [from Central Asia] and interacted at the northern end of it with Black Sea shamans, ultimately influencing Greek philosophy through Diogenes of Sinope, who seems to have brought Indian-derived ascetic practices into the Athenian philosophical milieu. It is perhaps through this route that an Indian yogi came to Athens to talk with Socrates, according to a story told by Aristoxenus and

thus extant at least as early as the fourth century B.C. (ap. Eusebius, *Prep. Ev.* XI.3.8). (10)

The Greek philosophers asked: Is the soul, for example, a thing, immortal, or an attunement, as the Pythagoreans taught? The Greeks considered the question of identity using the paradox of Theseus' ship, recorded in Plutarch's *Life of Theseus:*

> The ship wherein Theseus and the youth of Athens returned had thirty oars, and was preserved by the Athenians down even to the time of Demetrius Phalereus, for they took away the old planks as they decayed, putting in new and stronger timber in their place, insomuch that this ship became a standing example among the philosophers, for the logical question of things that grow; one side holding that the ship remained the same, and the other contending that it was not the same. (23)

A. S. Long and D. N. Sedley discuss this argument in their work on Stoic ontology:

> The Academics made great play of the Growing Argument . . . just as a number or measure when added to or subtracted from becomes a different number or measure, so too a person who grows or diminishes becomes a different person . . . The Growing Argument was invoked in connexion with the Ship of Theseus, which was said to have been preserved for centuries at Athens . . . Was it still the same ship?[35]

This debate, like Nagasena's simile of the chariot, draws on questions of the nature of being; of change in time; of naming, identity, and language: If every piece, every atom of Theseus' ship, which had sailed to Crete and brought him back from his conquest of the Minotaur, had been over the centuries replaced, did it maintain its singular being, its identity?[36] It is impossible to track precisely the flow between Greek and Indian civilizations at this period in history, just as the exchanges between thinkers in the earlier period of the pre-Socratics, elude specificity. Yet clearly information, philosophical speculation, material goods, persons, and iconography pass in both directions throughout antiquity.

The Alexandrias of the world survive into the recent past and present in many forms, including Peter Weiss' historical novel of the Nazi period.

The still-thriving Alexandria of Egypt, founded by the Macedonian conqueror Alexander himself, was in antiquity the site of a complex microcivilization, composed of a polyglot population from throughout the Mediterranean world. It implicates issues of diaspora, translation, xenophobia, and hierarchy, as in the works of the mime writer Herodas, who had an ambivalent and critical relationship to the traditions of the mainland Greek *poleis*. Although he participates in the class differentiations expressed and created by such literary forms as the *ekphrasis,* shared by Theocritus, his works express a new interest in domination. And the *ekphraseis* of Theocritus are even more intensely engaged in the projects of assimilation and cultural hegemony of the Ptolemies. In the farthest reaches of the land conquered by Alexander and his generals, we find the long-lasting impact of Hellenistic art forms on Asia, and the fruitful nexus of Buddhism and Platonism in the Graeco-Bactrian kingdom of Menander/Milinda, paradigmatic of the reticular cross-fertilization of ancient worlds.[37]

7

HISTORIES OF THE IMPOSSIBLE

In a gesture of what Michel-Rolph Trouillot, historian of the Haitian Revolution, might see as "erasure" or "trivialization," the great classicist Moses Finley excluded from his modern consideration of ancient utopianism the schemes of both Alexarchus of Ouranopolis, and Aristonicus of Heliopolis.[1] In an essay on Utopianism ancient and modern written in honor of Herbert Marcuse,[2] Finley argued that Alexarchus, who invented his own language for an Ouranopolis, a "heaven-city," "carries us all the way back to lunacy and its personal fantasies" (188). Apropos of Heliopolis, the sun city, Finley pointed to the "link in Near Eastern religion between divine sun and justice," noting that Near Eastern religions had devotees among slaves and the lower classes in the second century B.C.E. (184); he drew an analogy with millenarian Christianity in the modern period. Because of its "near-easternness," an exoticism, or orientalism, he declared the Aristonicus revolt "outside the Graeco-Roman orbit for all meaningful purposes" (184). Ancient utopias, he insisted, are always hierarchical (187).[3] This gesture of dismissal might extend to the alien presence of both ancient Judaism and ancient Christianity, both alien monotheisms within the hegemonic culture of the greater Mediterranean world, to be discussed in the next chapter. But of course, as the history of the Hellenistic period comes clearer, the line demarcating west and east becomes more and less distinct, and the effort to demarcate most productively what is purely "ancient," Western, or Greco-Roman becomes less and less possible.

In *Silencing the Past: Power and the Production of History,* Trouillot discusses the forgetting of the Haitian slave revolution led by Toussaint Louverture: "Silences enter the process of historical production at four crucial moments: the moment of fact creation (the making of *sources*);

the moment of fact assembly (the making of *archives*); the moment of fact retrieval (the making of *narratives*); and the moment of retrospective significance (the making of *history* in the final instance)."[4] Trouillot insists that, given the categories and mentality of the late eighteenth century, the slave revolution of Haiti was impossible, unthinkable. He sees two "families" of tropes that have governed this history and its loss: "The first kind of tropes is formulas that tend to erase directly the fact of a revolution . . . formulas of erasure. The second kind tends to empty a number of singular events of their revolutionary content so that the entire string of facts, gnawed from all sides, becomes trivialized . . . Both are formulas of silence" (96).[5] In this chapter I attend to whispers, almost vanished marks of resistance, the other utopias of Greek antiquity, broadly defined, that we barely glimpse, that never achieved the textual monumentality of Plato's *Republic*.

Walter Benjamin, cited earlier, who killed himself in flight from the Nazis, wrote: "The only historian capable of fanning the spark of hope in the past is the one who is firmly convinced that *even the dead* will not be safe from the enemy if he is victorious. And this enemy has never ceased to be victorious."[6] These words, repeated so often, are perhaps because of their frequent repetition, difficult to read anew, but are repeated here because they are so uncannily appropriate to my subject. An heir of Benjamin and other Frankfort School writers, Fredric Jameson, reads utopia as an unexpected symptom, a figurative practice in narrative, a textual figuring that emerges out of seamlessness. This emergence is almost like an unconscious letting itself speak in history, revealing impossible desires, in ruptures that persist and disrupt sameness.[7] Louis Marin, in a work on Thomas More and his *Utopia*, wrote: "The utopic discourse occupies the unoccupiable place (theoretically because blocked by ideology; historically empty because 'times had not yet come') of the historical and theoretical resolution of contradiction."[8] I want to identify the snags, the acts of resistance, barely visible in the historical record, and call them utopic, impossible practices.

As I wrote in the introduction, reading, a listening attuned to resistances and countertransferences seems to me a more productive deployment of psychoanalysis in the present, in relation to classical antiquity, than projecting a modern psyche anachronistically, backward, onto ancient persons, characters in texts, and institutions, in the form of historical allegories, in which we see a modern pathology governing an ancient society, as, for example, in Phillip Slater's *Glory of Hera,* in which the case of the pedophiliac Kenneth Elton, psychoanalyzed in the twentieth century, provides a paradigm for analysis of Greek mythology and the ancient Greek family, used to account for ancient Greek misogyny and male homosexuality.[9]

In this chapter, I will recall a crucified grammarian, the inventor of a new/old language, a tattooed runaway slave, and the bastard grandson of a harpist, not so much from the point of view of a historian, but as a student of culture and in the name of extending classical studies beyond Athens, to include erasures in the historical record and the presence of utopianism, of "near-easternness," and of slave revolts, in what can sometimes seem like a seamless narrative of Roman seizure of power in the Mediterranean.

In his geographical survey of Asia Minor, sometimes called the ancient "near east," the geographer Strabo, in the first century B.C.E. and first century C.E., recalls a poetic act of resistance by the grammatikos Daphitas, in defiance of the post-Alexandrian Attalids, rulers of Pergamon, makers of the altar to Zeus described in the first *ekphrasis* of Peter Weiss' *Aesthetics of Resistance*:

> The city [Magnesia on the Maeander] lies on the plain near the mountain called Thorax, on which Daphitas the grammarian is said to have been crucified, because he reviled the kings in a distich: "purpled with stripes, mere filings of the treasure of Lysimachus, you rule the Lydians and Phrygia [*porphureoi molopes, aporrinemata gadzes / Lusimakhou, Ludon arkhete kai Phrugies*]." It was said that an oracle was given out that Daphitas should be on his guard against Thorax.[10]

Joseph Fontenrose associated this incident with Attalus III, who eventually left Pergamon to the Roman people in his will; Fontenrose read the crucifixion on the mountain Thorax as a symbolic allusion to the victorious armies of the Romans and their allies.[11] Attalus III had killed Daphitas' father's friends, as well as various generals and governors, and in retaliation for Daphitas' epigram imposed crucifixion, a punishment usually reserved for the low; for example, an inscription from Amyzon commemorates the crucifixion of a slave for killing his master's son, during the later Aristonicus revolt.[12] The stripes of Daphitas' epigram and the contempt expressed by the grammarian for the kings, associate the kings with slaves, with those beaten who paradoxically wear the purple and rule; the image condenses degradation, humiliation, and violence, the purple marks of flogging, with the luxurious clothing of kings. Strabo, geographizing, even discusses the dyeing of garments with madder roots in this region: "The water at Hierapolis is remarkably adapted ... to the dyeing of wool, so that wool dyed with the roots rivals that dyed with the coccus or with the marine purple" (13.4.14). The very water of these sites encourages both a regal apparel and that apparel's metonymy of blood. These records, the poetic weals on the backs of the Attalid, and a ferocious suppression of the epigram as a form of resistance to power, stand for the phenomena I want to consider, other utopias, the barely visible islands in an archipelago overwhelmed by victors.

One of the daunting aspects of an effort to discover signs of defiance, revolt, and utopian practices in the late Hellenistic period is the paucity of information concerning such activities.[13] The silence is evident at the level of material culture, the remnants of the past, and in the work of the ancient historians who most immediately recorded the history to which they belong. Crucial to this history is the perception of the inevitability of the victory of the Romans over the Mediterranean world. The history of Polybius, for example, which is the most extensive remaining account of these processes and is considered in the final chapter of this book, presents the Roman conquest as necessary and right and a proper object of historical fascination: "There can surely be nobody so petty or so apathetic in his outlook that he has no desire to discover by what means and under what system of government the Romans succeeded in less than fifty-three years in bringing under their rule almost the whole of the inhabited world, an achievement which is without parallel in human history" (1.1).[14] Like modern historians who follow his lead, Polybius sees universal history, the inevitable domination of the Romans, as his theme, and his narrative leads him to subordinate utopianism and rebellion to the narrative of conquest, of the victors.

Yet even with this would-be seamless linguistic narration of Roman victory, there are many tantalizing references to acts of resistance and rebellion, failures to accept monarchy and the inevitability of absorption into what became a new world system in the West, which extended in fact far east, to the Parthians, under Roman hegemony. As an example of resistance to imperial hegemony, the issue of the homogeneity of language itself had once been addressed by Alexarchus, soon after the death of Alexander in the late fourth century B.C.E., language as a feature of social life that could be altered through utopianizing reform. Athenaeus described the invention of a new language as part of the reformer's plans for the foundation of a new city: "Alexarchus, founder of Uranopolis, introduced peculiar expressions, calling the cock 'dawn-crier,' the barber 'mortal-shaver,' the drachma 'a silver bit,' the quart-measure 'daily-feeder,' the herald 'loud bawler'" (3.98d–3.98f).[15] Athenaeus also records a strange message sent by Alexarchus to Cassandreia, the city named after his brother Cassander, using such convoluted, archaizing, and improbable diction. Alexarchus' foundation of Ouranopolis, "heaven-city," may have inspired the later foundation by fiat of Heliopolis, the city of the sun.

Alongside Daphitas' distich, and Alexarchus' idiosyncratic, poetic, imagistic language, which seems to have been meant to put a new ruler's stamp on everyday life, using archaism as a form of resistance to the ordinary, or to remind its speakers of the novelty of his foundation, stands a runaway slave, a devotee of the sun, another fragmentary symptom of dissonance, the body of this slave bearing resistance in material form. We have a papyrus, an early wanted poster concerning a slave belonging to a Carian ambassador to Alexandria, which presents to postmodern readers the detailed, vivid presence of a recalcitrant ancient body: "Hermon, alias Neilos, Syrian, from Bambyke (Hierapolis), 'about 18 years old, of medium stature, beardless, with good legs, a dimple on the chin, a mole by the left side of the nose, a scar above the left corner of the mouth, tattooed on the right wrist with two barbaric letters.'"[16] The papyrus may attest to the connection between a sun god and some slaves; the "barbaric letters" are seen by some scholars, including Bagnall and Derow, as symbols of consecration to the gods of Hierapolis, Hadad and Atargatis—the first letters of their names in Aramaic. Atargatis was the goddess, called by the Greeks "the Syrian goddess," worshipped at Hierapolis, as well as in Egypt and in Macedonia itself. She was eventually worshipped in Aetolia in mainland Greece, on Delos, and in Rome, from which Roman soldiers carried her worship all the way to Roman Britain.[17] It is not clear in this view that the fugitive slaves bore the gods' signs as tattoos or whether these slaves dedicated themselves or were dedicated to the god. Erica Reiner argued that these marks were not religious symbols but rather Aramaic letters applied after a previous escape to mark the fugitive slave.[18] On the papyrus, a "second hand"—that is, a subsequent writer—raises the reward for the slaves' capture, since the first offer did not do the trick, proving that this vividly portrayed slave did for a time at least successfully evade capture. Just as this marked body resists captivity, the kind of utopianism he may represent also has eluded recognition by Finley, historian of utopianism.

The revolt of Aristonicus of Pergamum catalyzes my interest in these forms of defiance—resistance to uniformity of language, to the Olympian gods, to imperial conquest. In contrast to the utopianism of Plato, who imagined an eternally Laconizing, Spartan oligarchic aristocratic system, the little we can discover about the plans of Aristonicus reveals another sort of ambition for a polity.[19] And Strabo's intermittent history of the Pergamenes presents several provocative elements that color the account and suggest connections to slaves and the violence enacted against them. In his discussion of the foundation of the Attalid dynasty, he mysteriously describes the emasculation of Philetaerus, "who was a eunuch from boyhood." Philetaerus was the son of Attalus, himself probably a Macedonian, and a Paphlagonian mother: "For it came to pass at a certain burial, when a spectacle was being given at which many people were present, that the nurse who was carrying Philetaerus, still an infant, was caught in the crowd and pressed so hard that the child was incapacitated [*perothenai*]" (13.4.1). This decorously described child, whose possible castration recedes behind a respectful veil, remained loyal to the Alexandrian generals Antigonus and his commander Lysimachus for a time but quarreled eventually with Lysimachus' wife, Arsinoë, who slandered him, and so he deserted first to Seleucus, another of the rival heirs of Alexander, "caused Pergamum to revolt," and then died, leaving his nephew Eumenes in power. The emasculation of Philetaerus might be read as a representation of a premonition of the imminent enslavement of all the Pergamenes to the Romans, and of the ultimately failed resistance by Aristonicus to that enslavement.

This intriguing episode sets in motion a whole series of questionable genealogical elements associated with the Attalids; beginning from an emasculating injury, which might allude in some way to the castration of slave eunuchs, it proceeds to the slander of the legitimate wife, and then to an almost papal succession of nephews, rulers of a kingdom to which Aristonicus, an illegitimate heir, eventually laid claim. Reciprocal violence and the mixing of kinds—Macedonians, Greeks, and indigenous peoples of Asia Minor—trouble this history throughout.

According to Justinus, "There was a son of Eumenes, named Aristonicus, not born in wedlock, but of an Ephesian mistress, the daughter of a harpist, and after the death of Attalus, this young man laid claim to the throne of Asia as having been his father's" (Justinus 36.4.6).[20] Strabo recalls the revolt of Aristonicus, which we know of from other sources, in his survey of the landscape of Asia Minor:

> After Smyrna one comes to Leucae, a small town, which after the death of Attalus Philometor was caused to revolt by Aristonicus, who was reputed to

belong to the royal family and intended to usurp the kingdom. Now he was banished from Smyrna, after being defeated in a naval battle near the Cymaean territory by the Ephesians, but he went up into the interior and quickly assembled a large number of resourceless people, and also of slaves, invited with a promise of freedom [*kai doulon ep'eleutheria katakeklemenon*], whom he called Heliopolitae.[21]

The association with the sun, Helios, led to speculation about "near eastern" cults of the sort rejected by Finley, such as those of Atargatis and Hadad, connected to the runaway slave Hermon/Neilos; about Stoicism and a link between the sun, which gives its light to all equally, and a utopian city of the sun described by Iambulus, mentioned earlier, who had a Scythian name but may have been an Arab from Nabataea, writing in the third century B.C.E. Various authors confirm other elements of the story; some say that the Roman Marcus Perpernas captured Aristonicus after the defeat of his forces, and that he died in Rome, in prison.[22] Yet one further intriguing aspect of this episode, besides the dangerous eruption of this rebellion, silenced by the paucity of material remains, by the accidents of extant histories, is the issue of the Roman Empire, its inevitability, and the attribution of the masterminding of the rebellion to the Stoic philosopher Blossius of Cumae. Blossius had been the advisor of the Roman populist Tiberius Gracchus (clubbed to death by irate senators), and after the defeat of the Gracchi came to join Aristonicus and died in Asia Minor.[23]

One of the most tantalizing and ambiguous pieces of evidence concerning Aristonicus' revolt is a provocative shred, a vestige, that appeared only when the archaeologists Louis and Jeanne Robert, in excavating the ancient oracle of Claros, near Colophon in Asia Minor, found an inscription recording a decree that honored Polemaios, a notable of Colophon. In the course of the decree, a fascinating biographical-autobiographical text in its own right, worthy of serious generic study, the text mentions a site otherwise unattested, a *Doulon Polis,* or "City of the Slaves": "looting and armed attacks taking place with damage at the city of the slaves" *(ginomenes harpages kai ephodou meth'oplon kai adikematon epi t[e]s huparkhous[e]s [he]mein khoras epi Doulon poleos)*.[24] This mysterious and tantalizing reference, set in a genitive absolute, that is, unmoored grammatically, and therefore without clear agency and tactfully, diplomatically vague, stands out in the context of praise for the man of good deeds, prominent benefactor of Colophon. Where is this city of slaves somewhere in the territory of Colophon? Who are the slaves? Are they still there? How can there be a city of slaves?

The Roberts connect the city of slaves tentatively with Aristonicus; they explain the inscription with reference to a decree of Pergamum, a threat against those who would leave the city and the territory of the city shortly after the death of Attalos III, that is, after the bequest of the city to the Romans.[25] They conjecture that some residents must have left and joined Aristonicus (38). In their view, the place retained, a little later, at the time of the Polemaios decree, the name City of the Slaves and was favorable for "social unrest, pillaging, and damage *(dégâts)*" (38). They argue that for the Roman senate to have intervened, as the decree states it did, the attacks must have been made by Roman soldiers. Again, very tentatively, they ask if it might be possible that these designations would serve simply to recall that place where Aristonicus' people had held sway before the defeat, and where Roman bands afterwards had imposed themselves (38)? All this, in the process of passing from occupation to normal order in the new Roman province of Asia.

Is it possible that the city of slaves remained the site of slave habitation, or that the supporters of Aristonicus were called as a group "slaves," a collective noun, by metonymy naming them all, in an effort perhaps to discredit them all by association? And that Romans were ordered by the senate to eradicate the problem but without damaging the *demos,* that is, the good people of Colophon who remained safely within the bonds of the *polis* and its ideology? The slightly nervous care with which the inscription cites this particular good deed of Polemaios, its genitive absolute, its unwillingness to name the actors and subjects of the pillaging and damage, could, of course, be attributed to the fact that the Romans were responsible, but there is clearly some felt danger, even years later, in this episode so deftly steered to the right end by Polemaios.

One question remains: What is a *doulon polis?* The degree to which the phrase is an oxymoron can only excite speculation.[26] A *polis* cannot be made up of slaves, except in some utopian world. In terms of Greek thinking, a *polis* has citizens, free persons, perhaps *metics*—that is, noncitizen but free persons from elsewhere—and slaves. A city consisting only of citizens existed only in the imaginary, the fictional realm, in the work of a writer, for example, like Iamboulus in his account of a remote island and city of the sun, detailed by Diodorus Siculus:

> The islanders do not marry but they have their women in common. They raise the children born of their unions in common and cherish them equally. When these children are still infants, the wet nurses will exchange the children they are nursing so that not even their actual mothers can recognize

their own children. Thanks to this institution no rivalry arises among them and they live their lives free of internal discord, setting the greatest value on social harmony.[27]

Although Finley believed all ancient utopias to be hierarchical, Iambulus' islanders exhibit a remarkable degree of equality and indifferentiation of status; the only ruler is the oldest man. Iambulus points out, too, that the islanders sing hymns to the gods, especially to Helios, "who has given his name to both the islands and their inhabitants" (58.7). There is no mention of slaves.

This, then, is a thought experiment that has been entertained: the city of the free. But a *doulon polis,* a city made up of slaves? Is it possible to think such a thing? Who would own the slaves, and if no one owned them, would they be slaves? What model of identity is being assumed here? Are these former slaves, now free, runaways, or the mass of resisters once led by Aristonicus, who take their name from the least among them?

Aristotle in the *Politics* says, "Every state [*polin*] is as we see a sort of partnership [*epeide pasan polin horomen koinonian tina ousan*]."[28] For him, the partnerships are male-female, ruler-ruled, and in the latter he includes master and slave: "For one that foresees with his mind is naturally ruler and naturally master, and one that can do these things with his body is subject and naturally a slave." Can there be a master without a slave, a slave without a master, a *doulon polis,* a city of slaves, in such a world?

Aristotle describes the necessity of relation, of reciprocity, in the *Categories:* "All relatives are referred to their correlates, provided they are rightly defined." Perhaps because the master-slave relation is fragile, or arbitrary, impossible to naturalize exhaustively, Aristotle returns to it repeatedly in his discussion of correlation. The master-slave correlation is not immediately legible, perhaps, or even presumptively legible, as is a kinship relationship, for example, and therefore must rather be compulsively insisted on: "Let 'slave' be defined in relation to 'man' or to 'biped' or what not, instead of its being defined (as it should be) by reference to 'master,' then no correlation appears, for the reference is really inaccurate [*ou gar oikeia he apodosis estin*]." And again:

> The correlative of "slave" [*doulos*], for example, is properly said to be "master" [*despotes*]. Suppose we remove all his other—I mean, his irrelevant—attributes, such as his being "two-footed," "receptive of knowledge," or "human," and leave but his being "a master," then "slave" will be still the

correlative, "slave" *meaning* slave of a *master* [*ho gar doulos despotou doulos legetai*].

And again:

On the other hand, let us suppose one correlative named incorrectly. Then, if we strip off its attributes, saving that only in virtue of which it was called a correlative, all correlation will vanish. Let "a slave" be defined as [of a man] "a man's" [*anthropou*] . . . Take the attribute "master" from "man": then indeed, the correlation subsisting between "man" and "slave" will have vanished. No master, in short, then no slave.[29]

And again:

Correlatives are commonly held to come into existence together, and this for this most part is true, as, for instance, of double and half. That a half exists means that the double of which it is half must exist. The existence of a master involves the existence also of a slave. If a slave exists, then must a master . . . Moreover, this holds of them also: to cancel one cancels [*sunanairei*] the other. (7b15–20)

Actually, the word Aristotle uses here, *sunanairei,* translated by Cooke as "cancels," can be taken as "destroy," "destroy together with," "destroy altogether," or "utterly," suggesting a more violent end to both master and slave; if one is destroyed, so is the other.

The logic here attempts to master difficulties that may have become even more unmanageable in the fluidity of the new social circumstances of the Hellenistic world, in the time after the conquests and death of Alexander the Great, the period of the monarchies of his heirs, on the threshold of the conquest of Greece and Asia Minor by the Romans. Aristotle may already be looking beyond the *polis,* already figuring in his text new instabilities, working on the problematic of the master-slave relationship in light of new imperial possibilities.

New ideas about universalism in works of the philosophers of the day emerge in the utopianism that so indistinctly surfaces in these late Hellenistic conditions, subject to the erasure and trivialization cited by Trouillot. Doyne Dawson has discussed in great detail the utopian thinking of the ancient Greek world,[30] arguing that the utopian tradition that has survived intact is for the most part Spartanizing and conservative, looking to an aristocratic oligarchic model for ideas of perfect societies, ones that serve as a thought problem for the élite, or for guiding reforms for less sophisticated, less philosophically inclined residents in ancient cities. He points to the supposed utopian thinking of the Cynics and the Stoics as offering alternatives to these more conservative models, showing that even when Plato imagines a communist utopia, that is, a situation in which there is a community of shared property, and of shared women, this is in the interest of aristocratic rule: "The utopian writings of Plato and Aristotle were meant to reassure [the propertied]. They provided a new ideology to reform and revitalize traditional aristocratic values; their practical goal was the creation of a unified and disciplined upper class, generous with patronage and immune to the temptations of faction" (102). Although one might find fault with this characterization of the Platonic project as a whole, setting aside its commitment to *paideia*, critical thinking, and the invention of philosophy as a way of life, this account does point to a crucial element of Platonic thinking on social structure: the necessity for specialization and hierarchy among men.

The Cynics and Stoics had, at least in the beginning, different ideas about ideal societies, and in the turmoil of the fourth and third centuries B.C.E., when the form of the *polis* was being called into question by the conquests and legacy of Alexander, these new forms of thinking about community had their effects. The fictional utopias of Euhemerus and Iamboulus may owe a debt to philosophical discussions of polity. The sources concerning Cynic utopian thinking, however, are for the most part lost to us, themselves erased or trivialized.

Stoicism, following Cynicism, written "on the tail of the dog," has its own history, one that by the time of the Roman Stoics had lost the critical power of the earlier Cynic influence. Yet Stoic universalism went beyond the city, to the cosmos, "a whole world of ideal cities."[31] Plutarch makes this clear:

> The amazing Republic of Zeno, founder of the Stoic school, is directed by one principle: that we should not live in cities and demes separated by different laws, but should regard all men as our demesmen and fellow citizens, and there should be one way of life and one world order, like a herd feeding together under the care of a common law. Zeno wrote this to create a model based on a dream or vision of an orderly philosopher's constitution. But out of these words Alexander produced deeds.[32]

"Zeno, and . . . Chrysippus after him, were assuming a world in which all people would be completely rational followers of nature in the Stoic sense.

All existing cities, by contrast, they described as based on slavery of some kind; and Plato's attempt to reform such a slave system by education of the rulers they dismissed as useless."[33] The Stoic utopia would contain only the wise, and therefore no one would be a slave. All subordination is unwise, is slavery; in the best of all worlds, there would be no subordination, and therefore no slavery. The impact of these ideas on political life is difficult to assess, but it does seem that speculation and critique flourished among these philosophical tendencies, in the context of a mutable political situation. Dawson points out that "Zeno [founder of Stoicism] lived at Athens as a metic or resident alien for about fifty years (ca. 312–ca. 261). During that time there were seven constitutional changes, several of them brought about by the intervention of kings, three unsuccessful revolts, and four sieges, in two of which the city was taken" (197).

The philosophers' utopian imaginings, now mostly lost, erased, or trivialized in Trouillot's sense, mark a transition. The change from focus on the ancient *polis* to focus on kingdom and empire must be considered as a radical break, a shift from one world to another, even if ruptures in history are now unfashionable, the "event" discredited, and many historians arguing for the preservation and persistence of the city and its institutions as they caution against seeing radical transformation and abrupt difference. Yet a profound change marked the difference between identity defined in terms, say, of Athenian citizenship of the democratic *polis,* based on autochthony and *oikos,* and identity as a Roman citizen, one who may never have seen Rome herself. Emile Benveniste pointed to this radical difference in his essay on *polis/polites* and *civis/civitas,* where the Greek name for "city," *polis,* logically precedes the derivative word for "citizen," *polites,* while the Latin *civis,* "citizen," produces *civitas,* "city, empire, civilization," as an extension of its primary meaning.[34] The citizen is the atom, the unbreakable unit of the Roman Empire, and the *civitas* is the huge and extended body of all its citizens.

If as students of ancient culture, we cannot appreciate this difference and are fixed at the level of minute studies of particular details, then we lose the analytic power of the difference in the inertia of the *longue durée,* which has its own analytical power but risks missing significant forms of resistance and change. The Roman Empire was not the same political entity as the Greek *polis,* and Greek cities within it took and take their meaning very differently than they did in a period of relative autonomy. The break between these two great systems, although impossible to locate punctually, afforded, briefly, the opportunity for new kinds of ideological imaginings.

Our own utopianism, desire, presentism, and anachronism inevitably contaminate our scholarly practices. In light of the collapse of the Soviet Union, there emerges a certain embarrassment in relation to scholarship of the recent past that celebrated revolutionary impulses and such seemingly suspect categories as universal humankind, smacking of dreams of world government, as in W. W. Tarn's view of Alexander:

> Before Alexander, men's dreams of the ideal state had still been based on class-rule and slavery; but after him comes Iambulus' great Sun-State, founded on brother hood and the dignity of free labour. Above all, Alexander inspired Zeno's vision of a world in which all men should be members one of another, citizens of one State without distinction of race or institutions, subject only to and in harmony with the Common Law immanent in the Universe, and united in one social life not by compulsion but only by their own willing consent, or (as he put it), by Love. The splendour of this hopeless dream . . . etc.[35]

These sentiments, subject to thorough demolition by such scholars as Ernst Badian, were coeval with economic analyses of ancient society that projected modern categories into the ancient past.[36] Mikhail Rostovtzeff, for example, in his account of the Hellenistic economic situation, used what many would see as the anachronistic language of capitalism; in the Hellenistic period, in his view, there was a sharper conflict "between the working classes and the government, which enjoyed in general the support of the bourgeoisie."[37] He identified the transformation of Aristonicus' war of independence, which turned "into a war of the 'oppressed' against the oppressors" (808). All this may now seem ill fated, sentimental, and utopian, tainted by association with twentieth-century fantasies of revolution and progress. Some scholars argue that the offer of freedom to slaves, as made by Aristonicus, was simply a customary tactic in war, for example. The hard-nosed contemporary historian must eschew fantasies of liberation.

But while we need to be wary of anachronism and a perspective confined by our present, we might also be suspicious of the notion that knowledge of the past can exist in a form unmediated by our context, and by our desire. Questions of globalization, empire, and resistance have come to the fore in the present, even as Trouillot points to the investment that academics have in their assessments of the past and the difficulty they have in relating the stories they tell to the present:

The traditions of the guild, reinforced by a positivist philosophy of history, forbid academic historians to position themselves regarding the present. A fetishism of the facts, premised on an antiquated model of the natural sciences, still dominates history and the other social sciences. It reinforces the view that any conscious positioning should be rejected as ideological. Thus the historian's position is officially unmarked: it is that of the nonhistorical observer.[38]

Yet we are all implicated in politics of the present; an historian such as Niall Ferguson cannot help but urge assumption of a new empire on the United States as he celebrates the history of the British Empire.[39]

Political programs that ultimately prove unrealizable, such as the Spartan reforms, or even Aristonicus' plans, such as we can discern them, emerge at moments when there is a sense of change without perceptible direction. One would not want to impose a teleological rhythm on these changes, see them as subject to a Hegelian inevitability, and especially not as irresistible progress from the individual *polis* to the empire. Yet change occurs, and it is in the break that a thousand flowers bloom; before the stabilization of Roman forms of Stoicism and acceptance of things as they are, new and radical and impossible events occurred: the revolt of the Maccabees, private languages, the defiant epigram, the refusal of Romanization, the fantasy of Heliopolis, and the *doulon polis*. These are instances of some "suspension of the political in the utopian moment," as Fredric Jameson calls it, a denial of the material limits of things as they are.[40]

In the unsettled conditions of the late Hellenistic period, oscillating between democracy, oligarchy, and monarchy, a new organization of the *oikoumene* was imminent, and it is in the border zone of a new arrangement of social and political relations that all can be put in question, critiqued, and rethought. New political, economic, and social conditions in contemporary globalization illuminate what is at stake in Hellenistic utopian thinking. We might draw an analogy between the circumstances of the present, and the opening up of boundaries and definitions of identity after the conquests of Alexander of Macedonia in the fourth century B.C.E.

Jameson considers the possibility of the utopian demand, of the demand that can "not be satisfied without transforming the system beyond recognition, and which would at once usher in a society structurally distinct from this one in every conceivable way." In the present, he contends, the demand would be for "universal full employment around the globe." Capitalism cannot in fact accommodate such a demand, and he argues that imagining a future of this sort serves a diagnostic and critical role. It seems to me that in the case of Hellenistic antiquity, Aristonicus' call to free Pergamum's slaves may serve a similar diagnostic and critical role, in that ancient society could not function, could not remain itself, if slavery were abolished; and therefore even the representations of such a scheme became impossible, trivialized, or erased, almost invisible in the historical record, even as a few historical traces of an experiment to bring it about are ineradicable.

In Jameson's view, utopianism, and the specificity of its modeling, come to the fore when

> the system really seems in danger of losing its legitimacy, when the ruling elite is palpably uncertain of itself and full of divisions and self-doubts, when popular demands grow louder and more confident, then what also happens is that those grievances and demands grow more precise in their insistence and urgency. We focus more sharply on very specific wrongs, the dysfunctioning of the system becomes far more tangibly visible at crucial points. (44)

This was the situation not only in Sparta, where revolutionary proposals concerning land redistribution took place in the third century B.C.E., but throughout the Greek world, where the model of Sparta and reform attempts by the Spartans rulers Agis and Cleomenes seemed to have had an effect on many cities and their projects for increasing freedom for those previously landless or disenfranchised, as in Sicily, but where these efforts at reform, resistance, and revolt were ultimately successfully repelled.

It is easy for us to disregard such moments, since nothing came of them, and remembering them, retrieving them, is nearly impossible; utopia's function is perhaps not in imagining a better future, "but rather in demonstrating our utter incapacity to imagine such a future . . . so as to reveal the ideological closure of the system in which we are somehow trapped and confined" (46). It is that entrapment and confinement within the system of slavery that the utopian proposals of Aristonicus reveal. It is indeed the very question of self and identity that a slave utopia calls into question, in a world in which social relations and identity require both the free and the unfree for its very existence.

Jameson, following Althusser, assumes that each of us is "shackled to an ideological subject-position" (46); just as postmodern persons establish pairs of opposites that define their existence, identity, and choices, such as oppositions between full employment and no employment (laziness), or between ecological planning and a naturalization of the market, so the moment of truth of each is realized through its negation, each offering an ideological critique of its opposite, in a double negation without cancellation of that opposite. Such a model is fruitful in relation to Aristotle's writings in logic, on correlation and on the necessary and enabling opposition between master and slave. A city of slaves as a real, material city is inconceivable, unrealizable, impossible. How can there be a city of free men, the universal freedom imagined in an early stoic utopia, all masters and no slaves, no slaves to allow for the possibility of freedom?[41] How can there be a city of slaves, a city of the unfree, where there are no masters? The slave in the real city becomes the citizen in the slaves' city, in an impossible rip, or ripple, in historical continuity, ephemeral as an invented language, a caustic epigram, a slave in perpetual flight. Yet in the present state of the world, with its troubled *oikoumene* threatened by new imperial initiatives, we should not forget, not abandon, trivialize, or erase, our fragmentary memories, the vestiges of hope, impossible demands, and struggles for a better world that can be discerned in the crevices of the great narratives of conquest, even if these liberatory experiments, like all those whom the gods love, died young.[42]

8

JESUS AND OTHER JEWS

One of the intriguing issues in the expanding of classics, in a new broader orientation of classical studies, is the baffling division of labor between classics and religious studies. The ancient Jews and Jesus are often ignored by classicists, shunted off to early Judaism and Christianity studies but not seen as inhabiting the world of the Romanizing Eastern Mediterranean. The barrier between classics and religious studies, between classics and Judaic studies and early Christian studies, or studies of the followers of Jesus, seems to me an artificial division, going back to a hermeneutic moment and to the investment of religious communities in their sacred texts. One could say also that the division owes something to language training, to the preparation of some scholars in ancient Hebrew, some in Greek and Latin, with a privileging of classical texts for classicists, texts written during the so-called golden ages of fifth-century Athens and first-century Rome. Yet especially in relation to the Hellenistic period, the early Roman empire, and the imperial period after Augustus, the social contexts and written texts of Judaism and Christianity, those produced around the ancient Mediterranean, should be part of our understanding of the ancient world as a whole, of a new ancient world that extends beyond the classical ages of Athens and Rome, that extends beyond the classical cities of Athens and Rome. In this chapter I want to consider various contexts in which the peoples of ancient Judaea lived within Alexandrian, Hellenistic, and Roman imperial contexts. The brilliant Daniel Boyarin, who has contributed a great deal to the analysis of the cohabitation and reciprocity of Jews and Christians in late antiquity, uses the work of Homi Bhabha to understand their relations: "In accord with much current cultural theory, with its focus on hybridity, and in accord with models of identity construction that are favored today, I will be offering here a revised model for understanding the historical relationship of the two 'new' religions of late antiquity," referring not just to Christianity, but to the new Judaism that arises dialectically with it.[1] Important as this project is, it seems necessary also not to lose sight of the fact that these monotheisms evolved in "not so late" antiquity and besides being hybrid forms of each other also drew from a "pagan," polytheistic, syncretic Hellenistic culture.

In this chapter, I extend my reflections on slavery, torture, and the marking of ancient bodies to some texts written in Greek, to the later books of the Hebrew Bible, and to the New Testament. Scholars of these textual traditions have often been more responsible in their openness to so-called classical—that is to say, perhaps "pagan"—culture than classicists have been to the religious studies scholarship.[2] Even though hampered by a limited or even nonexistent grasp of some of the languages here, classicists can nonetheless find much to learn, perhaps even something to contribute to the study of these subcultures within a widely defined Greek and Roman antiquity. The bibliographies of these fields, however, can be overwhelming, and I can here only refer the reader to other texts with huge bibliographies of their own and cite those studies that most helped me to begin to understand these vexed relations.

Slavery, Torture, and the Marking of Ancient Bodies

> When the guards had placed before them wheels and joint-dislocators, rack and hooks and catapults and caldrons, braziers and thumbscrews and iron claws and wedges and bellows, the tyrant resumed speaking: "Be afraid . . ."[3]

In New World slavery, the bodies of those enslaved were often different from their masters' bodies in that their skin color made them visible among the community of white owners. Although there were black slave owners and free black persons throughout the new world, the difference in skin color between so-called white and black persons was a significant marker that ideologically maintained a distinction of power between slave and free persons. In addition to the innate difference of skin color in Africans and those of African descent, there were the marks of punishment, torture, and branding imposed on African American bodies; slaves' bodies were scarred by beatings and torture, in scenes like those recalled by Frederick Douglass as he described his days as a slave seen to be in need of correction and taming by his master's overseer.[4]

In Greek and Roman antiquity, there were no dramatic differences in skin color between slaves and free persons. We recall the famous anecdote where two members of the senatorial class remark on the uppity behavior of slaves in Rome. One expressed a desire that the slaves be marked off from the free population with a special costume, and the other replied that this would be a terrible mistake, since it would only convey to the slaves how many they were and, he implied, encourage resistance and rebellion.[5]

We know that some ancient slaves had accents, that some did wear distinctive clothing, and that slave bodies were marked in various ways. Some wore slave collars, which have been recovered—collars in metal, with names or admonitions inscribed on them. Slave clothing often differed from that of free persons, especially in Greece, where few slaves achieved the levels of wealth and power that some Roman slaves acquired. In addition, slaves who misbehaved or ran away were sometimes tattooed. In one of Herodas' *Mimes,* discussed earlier, in Chapter 6, the mistress of Gastron, a slave used for sexual pleasure, threatens him with tattooing. Slaves sometimes were marked with the names or signs of the divinities into whose service they had willingly or unwillingly fallen; sometimes, as in the case of the Thracians, tattoos were part of the indigenous culture from which the slave came; sometimes they were tattooed as a sign of their belonging to a master, as in the case of prisoners of war; sometimes, especially in the case of unruly and rebellious slaves, prone to flight, slaves were tattooed with such signs as that recorded by the commentator on Aeschines, who tells us that runaway slaves were tattooed on the brow, inscribed with the message "*Katekhe me, pheugo*—Stop me, I am running away"—a motto that takes on particular significance when we recognize that most reading in antiquity was done aloud and that the reader looking at such a tattoo pronounced these words in the first person singular (4–5).

Many slaves, of course, were marked by scars from beatings. In Aristophanes' *Wasps,* a slave character comments ironically on the appearance of his back: "Ah, tortoises, I envy you your shells" (1292). One institution of the ancient city that might have produced the scars that marked ancient slave bodies, the *basanos,* as the Greeks called it, torture named for the touchstone, used the instruments I listed as I began: wheels and joint dislocators, racks and hooks and catapults and caldrons, braziers and thumbscrews and iron claws and wedges and bellows. In the ancient Athenian legal system, only slaves and noncitizens could be tortured; slave testimony was admitted in court only when it was obtained by torture.

Torture persists in a text of the Hellenistic period, an especially fascinating book of the end of the Hebrew Bible, 4 Maccabees, which reveals the ways questions of slavery, torture, and the marking of the body persist in the context of Hellenistic Judaism. 4 Maccabees was not written or preserved in Hebrew and thus never became part of the Jewish and Protestant canons, but the Roman Catholic and Orthodox churches print it in their Bibles. And it offers a fascinating narrative and philosophical argument, incorporating classical, so-called pagan thinking (the vocabulary on this difference is loaded, prejudicial, and inevitable) about rhetoric and reason and introducing scenes of Jewish martyrdom and redemption that swerve away from theological ideas of ancient Judaism.[6] 4 Maccabees has been dated between the publication of 2 Maccabees and 70 C.E., the date of the fall of Jerusalem, which is not referred to in the text. It may have been composed between 18 and 33 C.E., based on the date of an administrative change in the governance of Cilicia. Thus the text was composed around the time of Jesus, whose life also involved torture, martyrdom, and redemption. In fact, the Christian convert Augustine commemorated Eleazar, the seven brothers, and their mother, the martyrs of the Maccabees, with a Christian festival held on the first of August. Dayna Kalleres writes:

> The Jewish cult of the Maccabeean martyrs had long been established in the cave of the Matrona in Daphne and stood as vibrant testimony of the strong Jewish presence in both Antioch and Daphne. At some point, possibly in the early years of the reign of Theodosius I, these martyrs were posthumously converted to Christianity. In the Kerateion, the Jewish quarter of the city, a church of the Maccabees was erected, drawing crowds for the two-day festival that celebrated the bravery of seven sons and their mother who only after encouraging her sons' endurance could "travel to her beloved Jesus."[7]

Christianity absorbs or appropriates these Jewish martyrs.

One can discern a strong influence of Stoicism in 4 Maccabees, as the author stresses the importance of governance of the passions by reason, an idea that can be traced to Plato, with his concern that human beings not be enslaved to their passions, but that the passions be dominated themselves by reason.[8] The martyrs of 4 Maccabees dominate their passions with reason, enslaving their bodies to their masterly will, and in fact demonstrate their commitment, their subjection, their enslavement to their one god, who demands obedience on questions of diet and purity.

They are tortured, but they do not surrender to the will of the tyrant. The question of torture is central to this set of philosophical tropes, as it is in other philosophical reflections on *ataraxia* and the mastery of the emotions. And one intriguing issue here, which leads further to the question of the eventual conquest by Christianity of much of the ancient Mediterranean world, is how slaves, the tortured, and the marked, become the subjects of the new religion so foreign in spirit to "pagan," non-Christian, polytheistic, classical ideas, except perhaps in the worship of Dionysus.[9]

The issue of the slaves of the god of the Hebrew Bible is the subject of much important scholarship; the marking of the male body that is circumcision comes very early in the Hebrew Bible, in Genesis:

> God said to Abraham ... Every male among you shall be circumcised. You shall circumcise the flesh of your foreskins, and it shall be a sign of the covenant between me and you. Throughout your generations every male among you shall be circumcised when he is eight days old, including the slave born in your house and the one bought with your money from any foreigner who is not of your offspring. Both the slave born in your house and the one bought with your money must be circumcised. So shall my covenant be in your flesh an everlasting covenant. (Genesis 17:9–14)

Abraham obeys and is circumcised at the age of ninety-nine, along with his thirteen-year-old son, Ishmael, and all the slaves of his house (Genesis 17:23–27). And Isaac, when he is born later in the narrative, is circumcised on his eighth day (21:4). The worshippers of this god, Yahweh-Elohim-Adon, called themselves his slaves, and thus the mark of circumcision was in some sense a mark of slavery, of the economic relation signified by the cut, the covenant, the contract. The slaves of the Egyptians, who mythically became the Israelites, exchanged enslavement to the Pharaoh for enslavement to their god. As David Brion Davis points out in his classic text, *The Problem of Slavery in Western Culture:*

> Slavery was ... the clearest example of the total subordination of one individual to another, of the negation of personal choice and desire. It was associated in the Old Testament with religious humility and self-surrender, as when Abraham, Lot, Moses, Job, and David were referred to as slaves of the Lord. The Hebrews were perhaps the first people to think of God as a noble master, who might be persuaded to give aid and guidance to His lowliest slave. Moses used the same word to refer both to Israel's slavery in Egypt and, after deliverance, to their bondage to Yahweh.[10]

Although circumcision is sometimes understood as a symbolic sacrifice, the letting of blood that replaces human sacrifice, especially the killing of the eldest or favorite son, it can also be read as a mark of willed enslavement to the divinity. And this feature of Judaic culture takes on new and fascinating aspects in the works of the first followers of Jesus.

Related issues in the New Testament include the way Paul at the beginning of his letter to the Romans called himself *Paulos doulos Khristou Iesou*, "little slave of the anointed Jesus," or "Paul, slave of the Messiah Jesus" (Romans 1:1).[11] Giorgio Agamben points out in commentary on the use of the word *doulos*, in relation to "the markedly religious connotation that the corresponding Hebrew word *'ebed* (like the Arabic *'abd*) acquires in the Semitic world, that "in Paul, doulos refers to a profane juridical condition and at the same time refers to the transformation that this condition undergoes in its relation to the messianic event."[12] Not only is there slavery here, but there is also the marking of the ancient body, the crucial message of Paul concerning the question of circumcision, in which he says, "Circumcision indeed is of value if you obey the law; but if you break the law, your circumcision has become uncircumcision" (Romans 2:25). This is an intriguing translation: The word for "circumcision" in Greek, *peritome*, means "cutting around." The word Paul uses, which is translated as "uncircumcision," *akrobustia* (in classical Greek, *akroposthia*, and the singular form *to akroposthion*), literally means "the foreskin."

In this brief account concerning slavery, torture, and the marking of the ancient body as figured in Judaic and Christian texts of the Hellenistic and Roman age, the inscription or tattooing of Jesus in the last book of the New Testament, the Apocalypse, or Revelation, takes on special significance. Revelation teems with marked bodies, the 144,000 slaves *(doulous)* marked with a seal on their foreheads (Revelation 7:3), which resembles the mark on the doors of the Israelites in Egypt and recalls Ezekiel (9:4), where the Lord says, "Go through the city, through Jerusalem, and put a mark on the foreheads of those who sigh and groan over all the abominations that are committed in it." In Revelation, the others are killed; in Ezekiel: "touch no one who has the mark" (9:6). A beast, in contrast, "causes all, both small and great, both rich and poor, both free and slave, to be marked [*kharagma*] on the right hand or the forehead, so that no one can buy or sell who does not have the mark, that is, the name of the beast or the number of its name" (Revelation 13:16–17). "Those who worship the beast and its image, and receive a mark on their foreheads or on their hands, they will also drink the wine of God's wrath" (16:2); those who have the mark of the beast get "a foul and painful sore" (16:2). In 17 appears the great whore, on whose forehead was written "a name, a mystery: 'Babylon the great, mother of whores and of earth's abominations'" (17:5). The rider on the white horse, called the word of god, "on his robe and on his thigh . . . has a name inscribed [*gegrammenon*], 'King of kings and Lord of lords'" (19:16). These characters of the dramatic last book of the Christian Bible bear marks, the very sorts of marks worn by the slaves of the pagan culture in which they were imbedded. How can we map out the ways in which those bearing these marks of slavery and torture participated in, resisted, overturned the hegemonic ideas of the already heterogeneous culture of the ancient Mediterranean? What do such figurations, tropes of paradox, inversion, and repetition have to do with forms of identity and truth and a more cosmopolitan, diasporic, hybrid understanding of antiquity, one not so hermetically restricted to consideration of "pagan" culture, literary criticism of antiquity, for example, that focuses almost exclusively on the classical capitals or on questions of influence and intertextuality in Athens and Rome?[13]

Jesus as Magician

Jesus has affinities with other shamanistic, wise, magical figures, including Epimenides and Apollonius of Tyana, and should perhaps be listed among the sages of the ancient world.[14] In his controversial *Jesus the Magician: Charlatan or Son of God?* Morton Smith assembled the evidence that sets Jesus in the context of ancient magic.[15] One of the most fascinating features of this evidence concerns Jesus' tattoos. According to Smith, one of the early rabbinic stories about Jesus, from Eliezer, "of the generation that flourished from about A.D. 70–100," considers the question of whether "one who cuts (tattoos?) letters on his flesh during the Sabbath is guilty of violating the law prohibiting labor on that day" (46, 47). Eliezer uses the example of "Ben Stada," according to Smith a nickname for Jesus: "'But is it not (the case that) Ben Stada brought magic spells from Egypt in the scratches on his flesh?'" (47). Smith argues:

> The dispute about the tattooing almost certainly refers to Jesus because the same charges are specified by second-century pagan and Christian writers as elements in the Jewish account of him. (Magicians did write spells and the like on their flesh; directions for doing so are given in the magical papyri . . .)

Moreover, Paul claimed to be tattooed or branded with "the marks of Jesus," Gal.6.17—most likely the same marks that Jesus had carried [*ego gar ta stigmata tou Iesou en to somati mou bastadzo*]. (47–48)

Such evidence recalls also Revelation 19:16, mentioned earlier, where the rider on the white horse has written [*gegrammenon*] on his thigh: "King of kings and lord of lords."

Although some readers have seen the stigmata referred to by Paul as the marks of crucifixion, Smith takes them to be rather the tattoos borne by the magician who learned his craft in Egypt and brought back the corporeal marks of his special knowledge:

The rabbinic report that in Egypt Jesus was tattooed with magic spells does not appear in polemic material, but is cited as a known fact in discussion of a legal question by a rabbi who was probably born about the time of the crucifixion. The antiquity of the source, type of citation, connection with the report that he was in Egypt, and agreement with Egyptian magical practices are considered arguments in its favor. (150–151)

Smith assembles a great deal of contemporary evidence that Jesus was seen as a magician and his name used in "pagan" magic spells. Smith summarizes the evidence from the gospels and other sources:

The son of a soldier named Panthera and a peasant woman married to a carpenter, Jesus was brought up in Nazareth as a carpenter, but left his home town and, after unknown adventures, arrived in Egypt where he became expert in magic and was tattooed with magical symbols or spells. Returning to Galilee he made himself famous by his magical feats, miracles he did by his control of demons. (67)

Jesus shared freakish magical powers with the likes of Epimenides.

The life of Apollonius of Tyana is recounted by Flavius Philostratus, who recalls his birth in Anatolia. He studied in Tarsus, the city of Paul, and followed the Pythagoreans, members of the mystical, vegetarian, mathematical sect whose members believed in reincarnation. He was said to have traveled to Babylon and to have studied there with the magi, the *magoi*. Walter Burkert discusses the term:

An Iranian word that was to gain much prominence in Greek and European tradition is *magos,* which survives in the name and concept of magic. A special interest of Greeks in *magoi* in the fields of religion is marked already in Herodotus ... The word *magos (magush)* is incontrovertible evidence for Iranian influence in Greece ... The word is preserved in Old Persian, it is transcribed into Akkadian *(magasu)* and into Elamite *(makuis)*; evidently it was an Iranian term not at home in the current bureaucratic languages.[16]

The word survives, traveling through archaic and classical Greek into the life of Apollonius of Tyana, as well as into the New Testament with Simon Magus and the "three kings" of the Gospel according to Saint Matthew, and beyond, to J. K. Rowling's Hogwarts. Apollonius of Tyana left Babylon and visited the Brahmans of India, where he learned new techniques of transcendence, and returned to Greece performing magic tricks, or miracles, depending on the point of view of the spectator, ending, for example, a plague in the city of Ephesus. He also visited Rome, Spain, and Sicily, returning to Greece and then to Alexandria in Egypt. He was accused of killing a Greek boy, sacrificing him and using his entrails to predict the outcome of a plot to kill Domitian, the first-century emperor, and was forced to return to Rome, like Paul, to be put on trial. But he disappeared mysteriously, magically, from the Roman court and was said to have ascended to the heavens from Asia, and also to have manifested himself after death to an unbeliever. The emperor Caracalla engaged in worship of Apollonius as a hero, and others worshipped him as a god, and it may be purely accidental that there are not at present Apollonians among the religious of the world. His career in general has many resemblances, therefore, with the careers of other magicians of the day—with that of Epimenides and, indeed, with that of Jesus the magician who lived in the historical, geographical, textual context of such shamans and magicians as Apollonius, the sages, and even the Vedic Rsis.

Dionysus, Socrates, and Jesus

One experience of teaching the figure of Jesus in classical studies has been that many students in courses on classical mythology and ancient religion see him as the *telos* of the beliefs and practices encountered in their study of the ancient world. They interpret the "pagan" period of classical antiquity as an unenlightened prelude to the Revelation of the New Testament, a view sustained to some degree by philological studies. My understanding of these issues was profoundly influenced in earlier years by Erich Auerbach's *Mimesis: The Representation of Reality in*

Western Literature, as Auerbach says, was "written in Istanbul between May 1942 and April 1945," published in Switzerland in 1946, first translated and published in English in 1953.[17] As a student of comparative literature, I was assigned this text as a founding classic of the field. And I realize now that its narrative of Western civilization contained much more than a dazzling display of erudition, linguistic competence, and historical sense. Auerbach was exemplary of a generation whose members moved freely among European languages, read the classics they helped to define as such, and were committed to shoring up what they saw as the legacy of Western civilization in the face of Nazi and Fascist barbarism. In his account of the history of the representation of reality in the West, Auerbach defined a definitive break between the pre-Christian and the Christian worlds. The details of his history matter to me less here than the radical nature of the rupture he located between antiquity and the Christian era, a break recognized, from a different perspective, by contemporary students. He argued that there is a dramatic separation, an antagonism between sensory appearance and meaning, which "permeates" "the whole Christian view of reality," and that such an antagonism was absent from the Greco-Roman representations of reality, "perfectly integrated in their sensory substance" (49). His is, of course, a problematic move for us as contemporary readers. We are now led to believe that history does not change with such abruptness; and we recognize that in the Europe that provides the landscape for Auerbach's narrative were other important traditions: Jewish and Islamic textual traditions, for example, that must qualify our sense of Europe and the West as homogeneous and contained.

I disagree, also, with some of Auerbach's claims about antiquity; see, for example, that in such scenes of revelry as the Dionysiac symposium, there is indeed a separation, if not an antagonism, between sensory appearance and meaning. But this is incidental to my purpose, which is to return to some old issues, the relationships between Jesus and Dionysus and between Jesus and Socrates. These relationships have been much studied, and there is much scholarship that I cannot command concerning them. Nonetheless, there are new developments in the understanding of the ancient god Dionysus and the founder of philosophy, Socrates, and these affect their relationship to the figure of Jesus, especially as concerns the matter of gender. My claim will be not so much that the worship of Jesus was influenced by the widespread devotion to Bacchic worship and/or philosophy in the Roman Empire in the period of Jesus' life, but rather that the worship of Dionysus and the cultivation of philosophy may have made possible the transition to Christianity of the religious life of many inhabitants of this polytheistic empire over time, and indeed the synthesis of a more complex sense of *gender* in the identity of divinity than was possible in the inheritance from the patriarchal monotheism of ancient Israel. The polymorphous body of Jesus was made eventually to incorporate the complex, ambivalent gender of the ancient god and the philosopher, of Dionysus and of Socrates.

Dionysus

I want to focus on three different aspects of the worship of Dionysus here: his connection with the vine; the sacrifice and consumption of raw flesh, called the *sparagmos;* and his ambiguous gender. All of these seem to me to cast light on the figure of Jesus, even though we cannot locate them specifically in the practices and discourses of the life of Jesus himself.

First of all, of course, Dionysus figures in a complex polytheism, one in which there is a rich set of strata, of historical developments and local sympathies. Dionysus is but one of many. As such, he is often associated with the phallus, the detached and erect male genital, which was carried in phallic processions in his honor. He is also identified with the "wet," with the liquid domain of the cosmos, with semen, milk, honey, and, of course, wine, that food that supplements the "dry," grains and such, under the sign of Demeter. As Dirk Obbink makes clear, "The drinker of wine would be drinking the god himself. This was clearly not just a metaphor, but a way in which Dionysus was experienced, playfully theomorphized into the substance he invented and the sacrifice most often offered to him, in a form literally internalized and thus in turn *im*personated."[18]

Some episodes of the narrative of the myths of Dionysus concern the frequent and violent resistance to him, when he brings the new substance wine into various communities. Such initial rejection of his gift is interesting when considered in light of the recalcitrance of various communities toward the message of the apostles recorded in Acts of the New Testament. Dionysus, when he encounters resistance in these mythic narratives, exacts a heavy price. For example, in the story of Ikarios, this peasant of Attica is given the first vine shoot and shares the new drink with his neighbors. After consuming it, they fall into so deep a slumber that others who arrive at a banquet think them dead. They accuse and kill Ikarios for having poisoned them with this new substance. Dionysus is enraged, and he appears in person among them, in the guise of a seductive young man. The peasants fall in love with the young man and want to make love with him, and he incites them to seduce him, to violate him. Then he disappears, leaving them with an insatiable desire that can be eradicated only after consultation with the oracle at Delphi and the manufacture of terra cotta figurines offered there in place of their stubborn erections, which recede. What interests me most here is the association between the gift of wine—the new substance that transforms its drinkers and gives them peace, as Dionysus is known as the benefactor of the poor, the one who lessens and loosens the pains of everyday life for the poor—and the violent punishment he inflicts on those who resist this gift.

Dionysus' mother, Semele, was a mortal woman impregnated by a god, like Mary, mother of Jesus. The Greek tradition associated Dionysus with Asia Minor, with Phrygia and Lydia, especially. Walter Burkert points out that Dionysus' other name, Bacchus, might be "a Semitic loan word meaning wailing; the Greek women who search for Dionysos would then correspond to the women of Israel who bewail Tammuz."[19] Burkert believes there may have been early Cilician-Syrian connections with Dionysus and some influence of the Egyptian worship of the dismembered god Osiris. Other thought-provoking features of the Dionysus cult include the Agrionia festival, which had cannibalistic aspects. And the association of wine and blood, wine as the blood of the vine, is, according to Burkert, "ancient and widespread" (164).

In addition to the public festivals and dramatic presentations in honor of Dionysus, there were mysteries associated with his worship. Some of the rites of initiation involved homophagy, the eating of raw flesh, described by the messenger in Euripides' *Bacchae* who draws a picture of the maenads in their ecstasy on the mountain of Parnassus, tearing apart and consuming animals, children, and even perhaps Pentheus, the king himself, parodied in the scene of Crassus' head among the Parthians. The violence in the worship of Dionysus was not confined to those mortals who resisted his cult. Dionysus himself, in the form of Zagreus, suffered dismemberment and rebirth. The god was killed by the Titans as he played with toys as a child, according to this episode in the myth, recounted in a sacred tale attributed to Orpheus, and was dismembered. The Titans then consumed his flesh, and Dionysus was finally restored to new life.

There is some limited evidence that the Dionysiac mysteries also involved a hope of an afterlife, in the form of such texts as the gold leaf from Hipponion. Discovered in a tomb, and dating from about 400 B.C.E., the text ends, "You are going a long, sacred way which also other mystai and bacchoi gloriously walk" (293). Burkert interprets this and other inscriptions and literary material to suggest that "there are Bacchic mysteries which promise blessedness in the afterlife" (294). He also cites a gilt bronze krater decorated with Dionysiac scenes, which contained the ashes of a dead Macedonian and was buried in Derveni. Other representations on funerary objects show the dead in Dionysiac settings.[20]

Another aspect of the link between Jesus and Dionysus involves the *symposion,* the characteristic banquet of Greek men at which conversation, drink, and entertainment were graced by the presence of Dionysus, god of wine, and at which offerings, libations were made to him. And the cult of Dionysus, as stressed by Albert Henrichs, entails his "apparent humanity," which makes him exceptional among the Greek gods; his epiphanies have a "deceptive human quality, which exceeds the normal expectations of Greek anthropomorphism."[21] Henrichs also insists on the difficulty of modern thinkers, since Nietzsche, in coming to terms with the divinity of Dionysus, especially the "striking conceptual correlation of murder victim and immortal god that defines Dionysus as an immortal mortal, a god who has experienced human mortality but whose ultimate immortality confirms his divine status" (27).

In the myth of Pentheus of Thebes, mentioned above, Dionysus convinces the city's young king to dress as a woman to spy on the maenads and the women of Thebes, who have been drawn into the mountains by the god. Pentheus insists on the effeminate appearance of the stranger god:

> I am . . . told a foreigner has come to Thebes
> From Lydia, one of those charlatan magicians [*goes*],
> With long yellow curls smelling of perfumes,
> With flushed cheeks and the spells of Aphrodite
> In his eyes. (*Bacchae,* 233–237)[22]

It is remarkable that Pentheus refers to the god as a *goes,* a word used of Socrates in the *Meno* and explored in detail by Morton Smith in his book *Jesus the Magician:* "The common Greek word for 'magician' in Jesus' time was *goes* (plural *goetes*). It was usually, but not necessarily, abusive."[23] When confronted with Dionysus in the flesh, Pentheus comments on his curls and his fair skin: "It comes from the night when you hunt Aphrodite with your beauty" (457–458). Dionysus is here a magician but also exceptionally feminine in the moment of epiphany.

The implicit homoeroticism of the Dionysiac scene recurs in the story of Ikarios, where the peasants, men, fall in love with the young man who appears among them and cannot resist him erotically, a punishment they received for their unwillingness to accept the gift of wine. Michael Jameson, in an essay entitled "The Asexuality of Dionysus," discusses both the prominence of the phallus in Dionysus cult practices and the mountain dancing of the maenads, Dionysus' female worshippers. Jameson argues that "the communal Dionysia on the one hand and the mountain pilgrimage of the women on the other each emphasizes an aspect of human sexuality, the phallic and the female . . . The enigma is the central figure of such scenes, the god who is both male and female but isolated from the sexuality that flourishes all around him."[24]

Many of the features of Dionysiac cults have their analogues in the Gospels, in Christian belief and ritual, and in the representations of Jesus in graphic art. For example, the Last Supper of the Gospels depicts men, companions, dining and drinking together in an atmosphere of shared devotion. As a prelude to the Last Supper, with its symposiac aspects, we might consider the wedding at Cana: "When the wine gave out, the mother of Jesus said to him, 'They have no wine.' And Jesus said to her, 'Woman, what concern is that to you and to me? My hour has not yet come' " (John 2:2–4). This passage underlines the symbolism between wine and blood; if Jesus' time to act publicly or to die has not yet come, then it is time neither for the wine nor the blood. Yet he nonetheless orders that the stone water jars, used for rites of purification, be filled with water, and then orders that water be drawn out, which the chief steward at the wedding confirms has become wine, wine of the first quality. Morton Smith skeptically claims, as if all texts are not some form of "fiction," or shaped narrative, that "the Cana story is probably a . . . fiction; it has been shown to have been modeled on a Dionysiac myth."[25]

Although Smith says that scholars have read it as "an abusive deformation of *parthenos* ("maiden"), there is a persistent Jewish tradition that has given Pantera as the name of Jesus' father. "It was not a very common name, but we do know of a Sidonian archer, Tiberius Julius Abdes Pantera, who was serving in Palestine about the time of Jesus' birth and later saw duty on the Rhine. It is possible, though not likely, that his tombstone from Bingerbruck is our only genuine relic of the Holy Family" (61). Dionysus is often depicted in art riding on a panther.

In many passages in the New Testament, Jesus is associated with wine, vines, and vineyards. Such a connection may seem "natural" in the context of eastern Mediterranean culture, but, of course, nothing is "natural." Why should the vine figure so prominently in the discourses of the Gospels? One reason is the presence of wine and vineyards and vines in everyday life; as Auerbach points out, such a concern for the everyday marks the representation of reality in these Christian texts. Another reason for the prominence of vineyards and vines is their occurrence in the Hebrew Bible; see, for example, Psalm 80, in which Israel itself is represented metaphorically as a vine that Yahweh brought out of Egypt and is now threatened by its enemies; and Jeremiah 2, in which God pleads with Israel, "Yet I planted you as a choice vine, from the purest stock. How then did you turn degenerate and become a wild vine?" (Jeremiah 2:21).

It is in the context of these passages from the Hebrew Bible that John portrays Jesus speaking in an extended metaphor, with commentary:

> I am the true vine, and my Father is the vinegrower. He removes every branch in me that gives no fruit. Every branch that bears fruit he prunes to make it bear more fruit . . . Just as the branch cannot bear fruit by itself unless it abides in the vine, neither can you unless you abide in me. I am the vine, you are the branches. Those who abide in me and I in them bear much fruit, because apart from me you can do nothing. Whoever does not abide in me is thrown away like a branch and withers; such branches are gathered, thrown into the fire, and burned. (John 15:1–6)
>
> I appointed you to go and bear fruit, fruit that will last, so that the Father will give you whatever you ask him in my name. (John 15:16)

This is an exceptionally rich and extended metaphor, an analogy of the sort that Aristotle praises in his *Rhetoric,* as words "that make us learn something." It is metaphor, above all, he says, that produces this effect (1410b). "Men feel toward language as they feel toward strangers and fellow citizens, and we must introduce an element of strangeness into our diction because people marvel at what is far away, and to marvel is pleasant" (1404b).

The vine, once understood as the people and state of Israel, is here strangely and marvelously transformed into the body and person of Jesus. He embodies what was once an entire people and place, in the guise of the vine. The commentary in the *New Oxford Bible* points out that Jesus is the true vine, replacing the old Israel, which had failed in its vocation. The fruit of the vine, of Jesus as the new Israel, is the church, which "springs from union (actual incorporation) with him" (John 15:5). But surely there is much more to say here. This is a striking example of the rhetorical figure personification, in the first person, the speaker locating his own voice in the body of an animate but inarticulate entity. Jesus is the vine, and the metaphor looks back to the vine that is the old Israel, forward to the Christian church, and sideways to the cult of Dionysus.

First, let me note some compelling features of this analogy, personification, or extended metaphor. It contains connotations of mutilation, of the cutting off of members that do not flourish, a threat to those branches that do not bear fruit, interesting in light of the violence compressed in this image, in the stories of Jesus and of Dionysus. Even those branches that do bear fruit are cut, pruned, in imagery that suggests circumcision or castration. Yet earlier, or later in the evolution of Christianity, depending on where one locates such accounts of Jesus' teaching, of course, Paul argues that circumcision is not essential for the Christian: "Real circumcision is a matter of the heart—it is spiritual and not literal" (Romans 2:29; cf. Galatians 5:6).

This imagery does suggest castration, perhaps the state of the eunuch, and even a certain femininity. And such a female presence may also be inherent in the image of the vine that bears fruit, since similar language may be used of women, as in Deuteronomy 28:4: "Blessed shall be the fruit of your womb, the fruit of your ground, and the fruit of your livestock." This is a feminine image of fruitfulness, even as there is also a sense of masculine fertility in the notion that the followers of Jesus are the branches of the vine, the minor offshoots of its central trunk. Those who are incorporated, subordinated, accepting of this attachment, this embodiment, as branches will bear fruit, and those who do not will wither and be burnt. And even if we acknowledge that in this case there is a vine grower, the "father," this passage has compelling affinities with Dionysiac imagery. There is the famous image, for example, of the classical Greek vase painter Exekias, who represents the kidnapping of the "disguised" Dionysus by pirates. When they refuse to acknowledge his divinity, his shackles disappear, ivy curls around the masts of their ship, and vines sprout and entwine the mast and sail, vines represented as bearing fruit on Exekias' cup.

In Revelation, John connects the vine and violence, summoning imagery with affinities to Dionysiac worship. The author wrote:

> Another angel . . . called with a loud voice to him who had the sharp sickle: "Use your sharp sickle and gather the clusters of the vine of the earth, for its

grapes are ripe." So the angel swung his sickle over the earth and gathered the vintage of the earth, and he threw it into the great wine press of the wrath of God. And the wine press was trodden outside the city, and blood flowed from the wine press, as high as a horse's bridle, for a distance of about two hundred miles. (14:18–20)

The commentators in the *New Oxford Bible* connect this scene with the harvest of Matthew 13, but in that case the workers harvest wheat, the dry product of seeds. We must remark the violence in the pressing out of the blood, which is like wine, in the scene from Revelation, but also remark the analogy between wine and blood, wine that has the distinctive character of producing drunkenness and relieving the cares of the poor in the classical—that is, pagan—polytheistic understanding.

The *Secret Gospel of Mark,* edited by Morton Smith, about which some suspicion persists, suggests that there may have been aspects of the cult of Jesus that more fully resembled initiation rites, mysteries, and homoerotic bonding than have been registered in the canonical gospels.[26] Certainly, the symposium of antiquity was a site of homoerotic desire and even fulfillment of desire; Dionysiac symposia were participated in by men, often lovers, as we see in a scene such as that portrayed on the *Tomb of the Diver* in Paestum. The depiction of the symposiac scene, with two male lovers kissing, on a tomb, may also hint further at the associations between Dionysus, death, and the underworld. *The Secret Gospel of Mark* is accessible only through a letter of Clement of Alexandria, who is apparently denouncing the unspeakable teachings of the Carpocratians, who in their libertine understanding of Jesus' message may have advocated homoerotic love. The term *arrhetous* ("unspeakable") is used in reference to the sexual symbolism of the Eleusinian mysteries; the passage of the secret gospel of Mark cited by Clement, to clarify something he sees as exaggerated and illegitimate in the practice of the Carpocratians, does allow for the possibility of some kind of initiation rite, and for homoeroticism, although such an interpretation has been strenuously objected to by a homophobic tradition.

To a classicist, studies of Christianity can often seem "contaminated" by belief and by traditions of cult. Many scholars of early Christianity come from backgrounds of belief and piety, and these circumstances affect their relationship to the ancient objects. I say this not to find fault. Classicists, having the convenience of studying gods in whom (almost) no one still believes, are drawn to their objects for various reasons, sometimes having to do with a sense of élite privilege, the mysteries of languages unknown to the masses, or to what are imagined to be the joys of paganism, perhaps as a reaction against a hegemonic monotheism in Western societies, until recently dominated by Christianity and Judaism. In the case of masculinity, sexuality, and the social context of the earlier followers of Jesus, scholarship about these texts can approach the status of political interventions marked by desires and investments, in debates about gender; about religion, belief, and practices; and about the conduct of politics in the present.

Jesus is said to have raised a young man from the dead:

> Straightway, going in where the youth was, he stretched forth his hand and raised him, seized his hand. But the youth, looking upon him, loved [*egapesen*] him and began to beseech him that he might be with him. And going out of the tomb they came into the house of the youth, for he was rich. And after six days Jesus told him what to do and in the evening the youth comes to him, wearing a linen cloth over his naked body [*peribeblemenos sindona epi gumnou*]. And he remained with him that night [*nukta* (accusative of duration of time)], for Jesus taught him the mystery of the kingdom of God.[27]

Concerning this passage Smith argues the following:

> Since the Carpocratians had a reputation for sexual license, . . . it is easy to suppose that the Carpocratians took the opportunity to insert in the text some material which would authorize the homosexual relationship Clement suggested by picking out *gumnos gymno*. Similar developments might be thought to lie behind the celebration of baptism in *Acta Thomae* 27 as *he koinonia tou arrenos* . . . and sayings like Gospel of Thomas (Leipoldt) 108, "Jesus said: 'He who will drink of my mouth will become like me, and I shall be he, and the hidden things shall be revealed to him.' " (185)

Smith further points out that the word *neaniskos,* used of the resurrected youth, connects him with others (e.g., Mark 14:51, a youth wearing a sheet over his naked body was almost caught with Jesus late at night) (109). In any case, Clement cites the secret gospel of Mark, going on to deny that the words "naked man with naked man" *(to de gumnos gumno)* and, addressing his adversaries, "the other things about which you wrote," are found in the text. Later in Clement's letter, the youth is referred to as "the youth whom Jesus loved [*egapa*]" (109).

Certainly, in the context of early Roman imperial civilization, sexual acts between men were commonplace and unremarkable.[28] Paul refers to such homosexuality, condemning it, in his letter to the Romans, who like the male élite of the Greco-Roman world, especially in Athens, had long been practicing pederasty and homosexual acts: "God gave them [those who by their wickedness suppress the truth (Romans 1:18)] up to degrading passions. Their women exchanged natural intercourse for unnatural, and in the same way also the men, giving up natural intercourse with women, were consumed with passion for one another. Men committed shameless acts with men and received in their own persons the due penalty for their error" (Romans 1:26).

Jesus has not only been seen as inhabiting a homoerotic culture; recent scholarship has discerned feminine aspects in his representation. As the male god Zeus gives birth to Dionysus from his thigh, in a striking image of double birth, or masculine birth, so Jesus gives birth to the church from a wound produced in his side by a soldier's spear. Late medieval images depict a Jesus who feeds believers from the wound in his side.[29] Can we take the sexual ambiguity of Dionysus, as in his appearance in Euripides' *Bacchae*, and project it onto Jesus, simply because the two have so much else in common?[30]

The connection made by the early Christians between Dionysus and Jesus is produced and reflected in such works of art as the early-fourth-century mosaics of the ambulatory vaulting of the church of Santa Costanza in Rome, once a baptistery and the tomb of Constantia and her sister Helena, the wife of Julian the Apostate. The decoration includes vine tendrils and scenes from a grape harvest, where cupids take the grapes from their harvest baskets to fill wagons for the wine press. In *The Clash of Gods: A Reinterpretation of Early Christian Art,* Thomas Mathews argues against a reading of early Christian art based on the transformation of the iconography of the Roman emperor, claiming that this interpretation of Christian art derives from German scholars influenced by the "expectation that Germany ought to produce a modern emperor-savior."[31] Mathews cites the "entry way to a Bacchic cult hall in Spain," where "cup-bearing servants were represented in well-paced procession," as an example of the way in which "figures in procession were instantly identified by the spectator as making a religious statement" and incorporated into Christian art (152). Other Dionysiac elements in early Christian art include Jesus riding on an ass, a creature that appears as a commonplace of Dionysiac processions. Mathews points out, "Early Christian art is rich with Dionysiac associations whether in boisterous representations of *agape* feasting, in the miracle of water-into-wine at Cana, in vine and wine motifs alluding to the Eucharist, and most markedly, as we will see, in the use of Dionysiac facial traits for representations of Christ" (45). The relevance for Jesus and the question of gender comes with this last point. Mathews observes that Dionysus "was distinguished by unshaven cheeks and loose, untied hair," and he offers examples of such representations of the god. He cites the same scene of Euripides' *Bacchae* alluded to above, in which Dionysus is called a magician, more baroquely translated as " 'with essenced hair in golden tresses tossed' " (127). Mathews links Dionysus with Apollo, as well, arguing that "both of these youthful, long-haired gods had important androgyne aspects" (127). He cites Seneca, who called Dionysus "a pretended maiden with golden ringlets" in his tragedy *Oedipus* (420). Mathews claims that when Jesus let his hair down, "insofar as he copied the look of Apollo or Dionysos, he assumed something of their feminine aspect as well" (127–128).

Mathews argues powerfully for the feminine aspects of the early representations of Jesus, citing examples of his breasts, beardlessness (shared with some images of Dionysus), slender torso, and wide hips. He attributes the ancient femininity of the male gods to a celebration of their "life-giving fecundity" (135) and suggests, citing Gnostic sources, that this same motive may similarly inform fertility symbolism in the Christian representations.

Socrates

In *The Clash of Gods,* Mathews also devotes considerable attention to those representations in early Christianity that draw on the idea of Jesus as philosopher; there are numerous works of art in which the iconography identifies him as such. Mathews discusses a fourth-century Roman sarcophagus: "Like his colleagues, Jesus dresses in tunic and pallium, his right arm enclosed in the sling of the pallium the way a philosopher traditionally wore the garment" (28). The wise man, indifferent to worldly wealth, figures in the discourses of the Roman imperial period as a counter to the ambition and self-indulgence of imperial court circles; the emperor Marcus Aurelius, a student of Stoicism and of the works of Epictetus, exemplifies the synthesis of the philosopher and the emperor. And all the iconography of the philosophers, Cynic and Stoic and Epicurean, as well as Platonic, can be traced back eventually to the first philosopher, Socrates, founding martyr.

Although I can't discuss the links between Socrates and Jesus in great detail here, I want to draw on earlier work to suggest why the figure of the first philosopher, like that of Dionysus, allows for a richer, more ambiguously gendered body and person for Jesus than the anti-iconic and monist Yahweh of the Hebrew Bible. Socrates wrote nothing, like Jesus. He was executed by the state for his beliefs, and his death was the founding act of sacrifice that produced texts, and followers, for millennia afterwards. The philosopher asked difficult questions, spoke in parables, and encouraged a critical relationship to received ideas and petrified forms of worship. He was seen by others as a teacher, yet strangely took no pay for his conversations with his fellow men. He participated in a famous drinking party with his followers, one with distinctly homoerotic aspects. Most interesting to me, however, is the gender ambiguity of Socrates.[32] Plato, the writer who follows, says that Socrates called himself a midwife, like a woman, but one who helps others give birth to knowledge rather than to material bodies: "My art of midwifery is in general like theirs; the only difference is that my patients are men, not women, and my concern is not with the body but with the soul that is in travail of birth" (*Theaetetus* 150b). Veiled like a woman, he calls himself a "bacchante," a female worshipper of Dionysus (*Phaedrus* 234d–237). Plato alludes to Socrates' "pregnancy" (*Symposium* 206c). Socrates ventriloquizes the erotic wisdom of the Mantinean priestess Diotima. He appropriates the imagery of female reproduction to describe the birth into philosophy and erotico-philosophical transmission, down through generations of male lovers, of insight. In the *Symposium*, Plato transforms the imagery associated with women's bodies and their reproductive powers and reinscribes them for philosophy; Diotima says, "Those whose procreancy is of the body turn to woman as the object of their love, and raise a family . . . But those whose procreancy is of the spirit rather than of the flesh—and they are not unknown, Socrates—conceive and bear the things of the spirit" (208e–209a).

Dionysus/Socrates

Dionysus and Socrates present two different paradigms of gender complexity in antiquity. Dionysus stands between the genders, participating in both, sexually ambiguous in his own corporeal manifestations, encouraging worship in women, perhaps initiating young men in homoerotic symposiac settings. Socrates, in some ways sexually ambiguous as well, similarly leads a group of young men, encouraging the philosophical appropriation of female, material, corporeal reproduction and its transmutation into a life of spiritual knowledge.

In making these connections, I distance myself from the picture of Western civilization offered by Erich Auerbach, in which there is a radical rupture between the world of pagan antiquity and its forms of representation of reality, and the forms of representation in the New Testament, as I would argue against a progressive notion of history, against a master narrative that privileges the emergence of absolute spirit, even as Auerbach insists on taking the lives and truth-claims of ordinary people seriously.[33] And I point toward heterogeneity, hybridity, movement, and traveling, an opening in both directions, from antiquity into the Christian era, and backwards from the Christian period into antiquity, making a claim for the pagan location of the early followers of Jesus, rather than for a teleological direction for ancient religion. That is, I would identify a Dionysus who embodies asexuality, bisexuality, a doubleness of gender, and a putative origin in the "East"; an ambiguously gendered Socrates; and a Jesus who resembles both Dionysus and Socrates in ways that have only recently become more apparent through a scholarly focus, in feminist work and in studies of the history of sexuality, on gender in the study of ancient religion and philosophy, work that calls into question a Christian reinscription of the Hebrew Bible's God the father.[34]

John vs. the Whore of Babylon

I recall reading the book of Revelation, when I was first learning Greek as an undergraduate in a very small reading group, and recall the experience of translating very, very slowly, laboriously looking up each word in the dictionary, fearing as one does at this stage of learning Greek that one's life will be filled with such agonizingly slow progress, dictionary in hand, through every reading.[35] I have an especially vivid recollection of painstakingly looking up words for gems, and having each one land brilliantly in my translation—the experience of translation itself like a revelation because of the slowness of my understanding. This is the passage I remember most particularly, translating slowly, painfully, and exquisitely, the description of the holy city Jerusalem coming down out of heaven from God:

> The wall is built of jasper, while the city is pure gold, clear as glass. The foundations of the wall of the city are adorned with every jewel; the first was *iaspis,* jasper, the second *sapfiros,* sapphire, the third *kalkhedon,* agate, the fourth *smaragdos,* emerald, the fifth onyx, the sixth carnelian, the seventh chrysolite, the eighth beryl, the ninth topaz, the tenth chrysoprase, the eleventh jacinth, the twelfth amethyst. And the twelve gates are twelve pearls, each of the gates is a single pearl, and the street of the city is pure gold, transparent as glass. (21:19–21)

The *ekphrasis* of the imaginary city recalls the collection of poems by the Hellenistic poet Posidippus, who wrote a series on gems, including #14: "Pegasus etched upon misty jasper . . ." and also this:

> There's no feeling for women in my heart, but men
> Have set it ablaze, buried in coals unquenchable!
> This is the hotter fire: as the male is stronger than the female,
> So is desire for him sharper than desire for her.[36]

As a classicist, I have not mastered the vast, rich array of readings and interpretations of the book of Revelation, the Apocalypse, "the unhiding." As an example of interpretation of this difficult text, I take up Lynn Huber's *Like a Bride Adorned,* a recent rhetorical reading, which carefully analyzes the sometimes baffling imagery concerning marriage in the Apocalypse.[37] Huber uses conceptual metaphor theory to reveal how the author of the Apocalypse moves between what she calls the metaphor of the city as bride to the metaphor of bride as city. A less rigorous, more impressionistic reading of the nuptial imagery of the book would have obscured this crucial shift, which leads me to some points about the sexual politics of rhetoric and the imbeddedness of the text's author in the world of Hellenistic Greece and the Roman Empire.

Violence and bloodiness are threatened, against all that John excluded from the new Jerusalem, in the context of the nuptial imagery analyzed by Huber. Violence suppresses, and casts out, establishing a practice radically different from by which ancient polytheistic, "pagan" culture might have presented these same metaphors. I am concerned with the conceptual metaphor *The city is a human being is a bride,* and look at the sexual politics of such a metaphor as an ancient polytheist might have used it, rather than at its reinscription in the book of Revelation. Pagan homoeros and other practices of ancient classical societies provide some background to the violence and refusal of fornication and the ways of the whore of Babylon here.

The classicist Victoria Wohl, in *Love among the Ruins,* explores the legendary homoerotic founding of the classical capital Athens. She recalls how in the sixth century B.C.E., at the time when Athens was ruled by the sons of Peisistratos, one of the tyrants sexually approached the male beloved of the aristocratic Harmodios and was rebuffed. The tyrant then insulted the man's sister, and in revenge the two lovers killed Hipparchus, the tyrant, set free the city from tyranny, and mythically founded Athenian democracy. In memory of their great deed, a statue of the two lovers was erected in the *agora* of the city. In his funeral oration, reported in Thucydides' history, the great statesman Pericles alludes to the homoerotic beginnings of the city, calling on the assembled citizens in mourning for their warriors killed on the field of battle to become lovers of the city and of its fallen soldiers. The love of Harmodios and Aristogeiton, the model of aristocratic love, of pederasty, governs this exhortation. The *polis,* the *demos,* the body of citizens, are men in love with the city, which, as another great statesman says, is not its great buildings or its wall, but rather its citizens, its free men. Such homoeros lies at the heart of political culture in ancient Greece.

Huber's seems to me to be a dramatically censored version of antiquity in this regard; she mentions lesbians in Juvenal but sees their presence in his satire to be part of standard invective: "In both Juvenal and Horace unrestrained feminine sexuality or lack of sexual self-control serves as a metonym for the overall decline of the empire. It is important to remember, however, that this topic functions within moral argumentation and is not likely an accurate description of ancient reality" (122). In fact, in Juvenal, as in Horace and Martial, sexual love between males is a much more prominent topic, one that is treated frequently, and that evokes both pleasure and censure. See for example, Horace's ode *Persicos odi . . .* (*Odes* 1.38), a hymn to the simple life of the farm, without luxury, with a slave boy as companion.

The world of soldiers and war, as well as the worlds of rural leisure and eroticized politics, comprised an intensely homoerotic element of ancient social existence. Soldiers were thought to fight better if they were in love with fellow soldiers, if they fought alongside their lovers. In an excursus, Huber alludes to the war imagery of Revelation, recalling that "Stephen Moore suggests a metaphorical connection . . . between military imagery and masculine sexuality. Moore notes the double entendre implicit in Revelation's claim that Christ will rule the nations with a 'rod of iron,' which uses a phallic image to describe Christ's coming reign" (158). (In a footnote Huber reminds us that "masculine sexuality was understood as an active role. The masculine role in sexual intercourse was to penetrate and never to be penetrated; thus, males who were penetrated in homosexual intercourse would be described as 'having a woman's experience' [*muliebria pati*]" [158n68]). Of course, when considering the rod of iron, we are talking not just about heterosexual masculinity and military imagery, but about a world of homoerotic activity among Roman citizens, emperors, soldiers, Greek-speaking inhabitants of the empire, and many others who seem to have had much homoerotic experience, perhaps not always limiting their passive experiences to boyhood. It is crucial to understand that ancient Greeks and Romans, perhaps apart from Jews and Christians, did not disapprove of homoerotic activity per se. A normal, natural reaction to corporeal beauty was to be drawn to it erotically, and beauty occurred in every sort of body—a woman's, man's, boy's, slave's, and free person's.[38]

Intensely homoerotic episodes are reported of the emperors and begin to take the shape of the new discourses Michel Foucault described in *The Care of the Self,* the third volume of *The History of Sexuality,* which argues against the view that the Christians reformed pagan morals, claiming rather that there was a philosophical turn during the Roman Empire toward Stoicism and other philosophical disciplines, and a transmuted attitude toward pleasure, sexual practices, and desire. Foucault describes a new art of the self, which

> emphasizes the importance of developing all the practices and all the exercises by which one can maintain self-control and eventually arrive at a pure enjoyment of oneself. It is not the accentuation of the forms of prohibition that is behind these modifications in sexual ethics. It is the development of an art of existence that revolves around the question of the self, of its dependence and independence, of its universal form and of the connection it can and should establish with others, of the procedures by which it exerts its control over itself, and of the way in which it can establish a complete supremacy over itself.[39]

Restraint and decorum were part of an intensified philosophical *askesis*.

Yet in this same period love between men extended not only to erotic unions, but also to nuptial occasions, as reported by various ancient historians. Nero, the emperor who may be referred to as the apocalyptic beast whose number is 666, himself engaged in homoerotic weddings, according to Suetonius:

> He castrated the boy Sporus and actually tried to make a woman of him; and he married him with all the usual ceremonies, including a dowry and a bridal veil, took him to his house attended by a great throng, and treated him as his wife. And the witty jest that someone made is still current, that it

would have been well for the world if Nero's father Domitius had had that kind of wife. This Sporus, decked out with the finery of the empresses and riding in a litter, he took with him to the assizes and marts of Greece . . . fondly kissing him from time to time.[40]

And further: "He [Nero] was even married to this man [Doryphorus] in the same way that he himself had married Sporus, going so far as to imitate the cries and lamentations of a maiden being deflowered" (29). Emperor as bridegroom; emperor as bride.

Suetonius also reports that a letter was preserved in Domitian's hand by a man who was promised an assignation, and Domitian himself may have been the lover of the succeeding emperor Nerva (Suetonius, *Domitian* 1). Dio Cassius reports similar stories about the later emperor Elagabalus (218–222 C.E.), who "was given away in marriage as a woman; he was called 'wife,' 'mistress,' and 'queen,' and he spun wool, he bound his hair in a net, and he wore makeup on his eyes" (80.14). Strangely, Domitian himself, fearing assassination, "lined the walls of the colonnades in which he used to walk with moonstone, to be able to see in its brilliant surface the reflection of all that went on behind his back" (*Domitian*, 14). Walls of precious stone signify not just glory, but also paranoia.

My point is that we cannot, as Huber acknowledges, separate politics and cultural assumptions from conceptual metaphors; in fact, in some ways they provide an invisible paradigm through which people and their texts construct reality. The John of the Apocalypse is playing with a crucial cultural paradigm of antiquity by portraying the city as a bride. If we include the pagan metaphors *The city is a community of male lovers, and the bride is a man,* the nuptial imagery of the text takes on a further dimension. As he follows through the metaphor of marriage between a god and a city, John is both feminizing and homoeroticizing the citizens of the New Jerusalem, perhaps the 144,000, the Redeemed, "these who have not defiled themselves with women, for they are virgins" (14:4). There is violence, horror, bloodshed, and revulsion directed at the fornication of Babylon, yet the citizens of the New Jerusalem are the objects of desire of the bridegroom, in a shift that contradictorily perpetuates metaphorically the practices of homoeros that saturated ancient polytheistic, pagan culture even as it condemns them. And the followers of Jesus eventually emerge as radically opposed to assimilation and acceptance of what come to be condemned as the contaminated ideas of a polytheistic, pederastic, and disavowed tradition.

The disciplinary divides between classical and religious studies have produced a confusing and sometimes limited representation that separates "pagan" Greece and the Hellenistic world from the domain of Judaea and the followers of Jesus. Part of the extension of the idea of the classical, of a rethinking, an opening up of the definition of the classics, would of necessity include some coming to terms with the ways these heterogeneous multitudes inseparably constitute the ancient world, are saturated with its ethics and values, engaged together in its social practices. Their heirs continue to struggle over who owns the ancient holy lands and ancient sacred texts.

9

THE PERSISTENCE OF OEDIPUS

The ancient Greeks reach into the twentieth century, not only in the form of the enduring monotheisms of the Hellenistic kingdoms and the Roman Empire. Apollo, ancient patron god of Delphi, slew the Python, a monstrous dragon protecting an oracle possessed by an earth goddess; in a compelling transposition of ancient myth into modernity, following Sigmund Freud's resuscitation, rehabilitation, and reinscription of the Oedipus myth, Alain Robbe-Grillet used the garbled, distorted sound of a public address system in a railway station to echo the enigmatic utterances of the Delphic oracle:

> A tremendous voice fills the hall. Projected by invisible loudspeakers, it bounces back and forth against the walls covered with signs and advertisements, which amplify it still more, multiply it, reflect it, baffle it with a whole series of more or less conflicting echoes and resonances, in which the original message is lost—transformed into a gigantic oracle, magnificent, indecipherable, and terrifying.[1]

The oracle of Delphi, which uttered the truth yet led many astray with its riddling prophecies, found its analogue in the baffling crackle familiar to travelers. Robbe-Grillet's *Les Gommes,* published in 1953, alluded to, mimicked, intertwined itself about, and played endlessly with Sophocles' classical tragedy *Oedipus Rex*. Robbe-Grillet allowed the tragedy to appear in his novel through a palimpsestic scrim. His transmutation of the ancient plot perverts and reinscribes the narrative sequence of the myth.

The Oedipus plot, according to some psychoanalytic critics, may underlie all detective fiction, a genre only possible perhaps with the explorations of sexuality, human development, and a certain model of the psyche emerging in the work of such modern writers as Edgar Allan Poe and Sigmund Freud.[2] Richard Armstrong, in his exhaustive examination of Freud's relationship to the Greeks and Romans, *A Compulsion for Antiquity: Freud and the Ancient World,* sees Freud's resort to Oedipus as fitting into a pattern in his reasoning:

> Whatever his reasons were for aligning psychoanalysis so closely with Empedocles, [Freud's] recourse to this figure fits a pattern we have seen: a disturbance in his theorization leads him to adopt a figure of antiquity as he works toward his solutions. When his seduction theory of the neuroses collapses, he adopts Sophocles (or at least his Oedipus) . . . the recourse to figures of antiquity often hides a more troubling and proximate relation. Sophocles' Oedipus, as some suggest, came along in time to save Freud from troubling doubts concerning Wilhelm Fliess, his own father Jakob, or even his mother Amalie.[3]

For whatever reasons, if indeed as a technique of avoidance, Freud selected the figure of Oedipus out of a vast array of ancient mythological characters, and Oedipus came to haunt the twentieth century.[4]

Miriam Leonard, in her study of the twentieth-century French intellectual reception of the Greeks, discusses extensively the place of Oedipus in the story.[5] She argues that "post-war France's encounter with the Greeks gave rise to a new interrogation of the political" (3); Oedipus plays a central role in her account. For example: "For Foucault, Oedipus will represent the oppressive allegiance between knowledge and power which underwrites the dominance of modern liberal democracy" (5). In Leonard's view, "the fates of Oedipus, Antigone, and Socrates became the focal point of a questioning of the nature of ethical choice and political action in so-called structuralist and poststructuralist thought" (5). Although each of her chapters comes to grips with intense debates among major theorists, I draw attention here to Oedipus, the figure central to her first chapter, which explores "the question of the political subject" (20) as these theorists wrestle with the Theban tyrant so crucial to Freud's understanding of the history of the psyche.[6] Even though much of the writing concerning the figure of Oedipus was done after the events of May 1968, the debates she describes also form the context for Robbe-Grillet and even Simenon in their novelistic practice. She analyzes Sartre's choice to reinscribe the *Oresteia* in *Les Mouches,* written in 1943 during the German occupation of France, and argues that "the legacy of Sartre's Orestes haunts the post-war investment in antiquity."⁷ Orestes, whom Sartre represents as assuming responsibility, acts, in freedom, and finds that freedom that is not liberatory but burdensome.

Leonard goes back to show how the particular problem of Oedipus preceded Freud's investment in the ancient Theban tyrant, since it concerned both Schelling and Hegel, and how "Oedipus is in many ways the symbol of nineteenth-century philosophy and, in particular, German Idealism's appropriation of the Greek past for the projects of modernity" (31). In the French postwar intellectuals' "rediscovery of the tragic, and the figures of Oedipus and Antigone, in particular," we find "a different kind of political investment in the ancient world" (31). Leonard traces the differing attachments of Claude Lévi-Strauss, Louis Gernet, Jean-Pierre Vernant, and Michel Foucault to the tragedy of Oedipus, and the ways in which matters of structure and human agency are worked out, to some degree in response to, and also often as a rejection of, Sartrean existentialism. Always in the background is the Freudian, psychoanalytic investment in the figure of Oedipus, the object of explicit and implicit critique by Lévi-Strauss, Vernant, Deleuze and Guattari, and Foucault:

> For Vernant, although Oedipus' subjectivity is circumscribed by structures beyond his control, these structures are explicitly politicized, and through his emphasis on the *pharmakos* Vernant shows how democratic structures and democratic actions are not mutually exclusive. Foucault, on the other hand, will show how it is the structures of Oedipal power which have been responsible for the disempowering of certain sectors of our society from the madhouse to the prison. While rejecting the Orestean symbiosis of the individual and his actions, both Vernant and Foucault succeed in recuperating a political role for Oedipus—and for themselves. (221)

Leonard observes that postwar thinkers efface the role of Sartre in his wartime resuscitation of Greek myth, in an act of "parricide," preferring to return to the Germans, or to the Greeks themselves in their political appropriations of the ancient tragedies of Oedipus and Antigone, and to the Platonic character Socrates, the martyr of philosophy (223). Their political interpretations of the ancient myth restore agency to Oedipus, who strangely, for both Vernant and Foucault, escapes his position in a historicizing narrative that fixes him in the ancient *polis,* to become a sort of Everyman. In both their accounts, the Freudian appropriation of the Theban tyrant is rejected. Yet in the works of Robbe-Grillet to be discussed here, the fatedness of the Oedipus myth persists, even as the novelist overtly rejects psychoanalysis. Georges Simenon, the other detective novelist discussed in this chapter, a contemporary of Robbe-Grillet, makes a refusal of another sort, one that occludes his own history as a political agent.

The American tradition of psychoanalytically influenced literary criticism has often taken the Freudian paradigm more literally than do Jacques Lacan and his descendants, even in the interpretation of detective fiction. Lacan interpreted Edgar Allan Poe's story "The Purloined Letter" and set off a new train of commentary and responses.[8] In a chapter entitled "Two Ways to Avoid the Real of Desire," in his book *Looking Awry: An Introduction to Jacques Lacan through Popular Culture,* Slavoj Žižek discussed the Sherlock Holmes variety of detective story, in which guilt is located in a scapegoat, as opposed to the "hard-boiled" version, in which a femme fatale enters the narrative and brings with her "the real."[9] Earlier, Geraldine Pederson-Krag notoriously read in detective stories the "primal scene": "The reader addicted to mystery stories tries actively to relive and master traumatic infantile experiences he once had to endure passively. Becoming the detective, he gratifies his infantile curiosity with impunity, redressing completely the helpless inadequacy and anxious guilt unconsciously remembered from childhood."[10] Geoffrey Hartman pointed to the "fear that the murderer will prove to be not an outsider but someone there all the time, someone we know only too well—perhaps a blood relation."[11] Glenn W. Most notes that "the detective is, in fact, the figure for the reader in the text, the one character whose activities most closely parallel the reader's own."[12]

In Robbe-Grillet's *Les Gommes,* the reader is detective and murderer, a new Oedipus. Yet the darkest secret of the modernist-postmodernist plot of authors of the postwar generation in France, high and low, serious and popular, may after all be not desire for the mother, nor murderous impulses toward the father, but rather a bracketing of the most recent wars, international and colonial, and forms of postwar or postcolonial guilt. Especially in the case of the French novels to be discussed here, for the reader who is detective, Oedipus, or analysand, the authors show Paris before, Berlin after, never the thing itself, a hollow at these novels' center, unspeakable, the real secret that has come to replace for these authors—or perhaps rather to refigure—the murder of the father. Claude Lévi-Strauss himself, many years after an influential reading of the Oedipus myth that denies a sexual, Freudian interpretation in "The Structural Study of Myth,"[13] wrote in *The Jealous Potter,* "Take another look at

Oedipus-Rex: a point of constitutional law is at the crux of the whole matter (who can hold the power legitimately: the queen's brother or the husband?); it is a detective story whose puzzle is progressively solved in the course of a public trial."[14]

It may be that the trajectory of the average *policier* does have as its background an Oedipal scheme, but it is a scheme that diverts guilt and responsibility from the son onto an unknown and thus at least temporarily masters and suppresses Oedipal guilt. The obsessive character of some modern readers' consumption of these texts may be a symptom of the need constantly to manage an anxiety through a familiar narrative that consistently names another as the criminal, that occupies the imagination with a search, a relentless inquiry into the identity of a murderer, or that discovers that murderer at the end, the murderer who is not oneself, but that of course is oneself, someone who has expressed one's murderous impulses.

Analysis of Robbe-Grillet's telling of the Oedipus myth will here be juxtaposed with that of a contemporary 1953 novel of Georges Simenon, *Maigret et l'homme du banc.* How are murder, parricide, other violence, war, secrets, the unspeakable, and the drive toward the truth represented differently in high and low fiction?[15] And how does Robbe-Grillet himself return to this plot in 2001, in *La Reprise?* In *Les Gommes,* the reader is detective and murderer, a new Oedipus. Bruce Morrissette pointed out long ago the allusions to the Oedipus myth, and to classical tragedy, both Greek and French, in *Les Gommes.* His account in *Les Romans de Robbe-Grillet* lists briefly the novelist's references to classical antiquity.[16] I would add to his catalogue the *ekphrasis,* the rhetorical description of a work of art, here Robbe-Grillet's representation of an artist drawing from nature, one of several *ekphrases* in *Les Gommes:*

> He is putting the finishing touches on a carefully drawn landscape—which must actually be a copy of some master. It is a hill with the ruins of a Greek temple among cypress trees; in the foreground, fragments of columns lie scattered here and there; in the distance, in the valley, appears a whole city with its triumphal arches and palaces . . . But in front of the man, instead of the Greek countryside, stands instead of the setting a huge photographic reproduction of a modern city intersection.[17]

The rhetorical topos calls attention to the framed, staged, and repetitive quality of description. The observer Wallas, looking into a shopfront window, suddenly recognizes the house where the failed murder of Daniel

Dupont occurred; the *mise en abîme* draws the site of the eventual murder into ancient Greece, which is alluded to elsewhere throughout the text. As well as the *Boulevard circulaire,* the city of *Les Gommes,* unnamed, contains a rue de Corinthe (70), where the Juard clinic, sheltering Dupont, is located, a road to "Delft" (60), and a monumental statue of a chariot, sculpted by V. Daulis, Daulis the name of an ancient Greek city figuring in the Theban myth (80).[18] The *ekphrasis* of the pastoral scene is repeated later in the novel:

> The ruins of Thebes.
> On a hill above the city, a Sunday painter has set up his easel in the shade of cypress trees, between the scattered shafts of columns. He paints carefully, his eyes shifting back to his subject every few seconds; with a fine brush he points up many details that are scarcely noticeable to the naked eye, but which assume a surprising intensity once they are reproduced in the picture. (168)

This time the painter records the modern house, and the description might almost be a manifesto, before the fact, of Robbe-Grillet's technique in *La Jalousie* and other new novels, texts that often speak to a new context of colonialism and its undoing, to the situation of colonialists in a postcolonial world, with techniques slowly coming into being even in this novel of 1953, and in the works of Marguerite Duras. But here it alludes back in time, to an enormous cultural burden, the weight of Greek antiquity, its myth and tragedy, and perhaps as well, implicated in the representation of Thebes, the Freudian interpretation of Sophocles' tragedy in his invention of the Oedipus "complex."

Another *ekphrasis,* repeated, concerns curtains seen as Wallas paces through the streets of this city: "The curtains are decorated with a mass-produced allegorical subject: shepherds finding an abandoned child, or something of the kind" (45–46). Later, "Again, open blinds and that cheap net curtain: under a tree two shepherds in classical costume give ewe's milk to a tiny naked baby" (46). And again, "that same net curtain . . . It probably is not very healthy to make a baby drink from the ewe's teats that way: certainly not very sanitary. Behind the wide mesh of the netting, Wallas glimpses a movement, discerns a figure . . . a few seconds later there is nothing left, in the window frame, but the two shepherds carefully bending over the body of the newborn baby" (102). The Oedipus myth, toyed with throughout the novel, is ultimately unhygienic. Kristin

Ross sees Robbe-Grillet as an advocate of what she calls "redemptive hygiene": "The novelist, for Robbe-Grillet, must be eternally vigilant, on the lookout for the tell-tale stains of an outmoded romanticism that lurk in the form of animistic descriptive adjectives and metaphors . . . All projections of depth—which is to say, of human significance—must be eliminated.[19]

Wallas, the detective of *Les Gommes,* continues to look for a certain sort of "eraser," *gomme,* as he wanders through the unnamed city of this novel: "a soft, crumbly gum eraser that friction does not twist but reduces to dust . . . The manufacturer's brand was printed on one side, but was too worn to be legible anymore: only two of the middle letters were still clear: 'di'; there must have been at least two letters before and perhaps two or three others after" (126). The letters spell the Latin word for "gods," but also form the middle of the word *Oedipe.* The soft eraser has its double in another thing, enigmatic and recurrent in the text, a cube of gray lava (210, 211), remnant of a volcanic explosion remote in time.

The scenes and localities of the Oedipus myth recur incessantly through the novel; the fatal crossroads, where Oedipus encountered and killed Laios, comes in the form of the narrator's careful delineation of the detective's itinerary: leaving the police station, he heads for the rue de Corinthe by way of the rue Bergere (that is, shepherdess); "he found himself at an intersection of three roads" (217–218). The author combines Corinth, city of Oedipus' upbringing, with the shepherd who saved him when he was exposed, delivering him from Mount Parnassus above Thebes to Corinth, and with the intersection the grown Oedipus reaches after having been warned by the oracle at Delphi that he will kill his father and marry his mother. At the triple crossroads leading from Delphi, Oedipus chose the route to Thebes, avoiding a return to what he believed to be his parents' home, Corinth.

Other fragments, dispersed vestiges of the ancient story recorded in Sophocles' *Oedipus Rex* and reinscribed in *Les Gommes:* the plague (218), sign to the Thebans in Sophocles' *Oedipus* that their city is polluted, and another reference to the abandoned child, Oedipus, who was exposed and then found on a hillside: "A word that sounds like foundling keeps recurring, without any apparent reason" (113). Dupont finds in Doctor Juard's clinic a figurine of an athlete with a lizard, that is, Apollo with the Python, "and a blind old man led by a child" suggesting both Teiresias, the seer of Thebes, and Oedipus himself after his blinding, led by his daughter Antigone (208). In a mirror, the images repeat themselves: the two hands, the two blind men, the two children, the two empty candlesticks, the two earthenware jars, the two ashtrays, the two Apollos, the two lizards (217). In a programmatic move, Dupont is made to allude to narrative sequence, the practices of the novelist himself, as he rearranges the objects, arbitrarily reversing the last two: "the earthenware pot and its reflection, the blind man and his reflection, the candlestick, the athlete with the lizard, the ashtray" (209). Robbe-Grillet himself manipulates and plays with the order of events in the Oedipus myth, scrambling and distorting their linear inevitability.

As an observer stares into the dark water of the canal, he sees first fragments that resemble a human face: "Or else it is some legendary animal: the head, the neck, the breast, the front paws, a lion's body with its long tail, and an eagle's wings" (33). This is the sphinx defeated by Oedipus, as he answers the famous riddle and wins the queen of Thebes; the riddle too has its banalized equivalent in the question of a passerby (114), and in the banter in the café: "What animal is parricide in the morning, incestuous at noon, and blind at night?" The answer is, of course, Wallas himself, who, we learn eventually, piecing the clues together, once visited this city as a child with his mother, and who ends by killing Daniel Dupont, his lost father, realizing the fate of the parricide as well as completing the destiny of Dupont himself, bound to be assassinated. In a seemingly random and aleatory dispersal of the elements of the Oedipus myth, Robbe-Grillet scatters the legacy of Western civilization and simultaneously retains it, allowing this story of fatality and destiny to come to its inevitable conclusion. Although he suggests that this paradigmatic story of the West, the abandoned child and his act of parricide, has decayed and fragmented, it nonetheless exerts a compelling and irresistible force over the central character of this novel, suggesting that the myth is broken and dead, and yet that it survives, and fate triumphs.

Although Robbe-Grillet claimed to despise the consolations of traditional psychology, the examination of the internal lives and private musings of his characters, refusing to consider the trivialities of the self, he here dismembers and remembers a foundational psychoanalytic myth that some have argued, as noted above, provides the foundation for detective fiction, as well. Freud, of course, chose this myth, and Sophocles' tragedy *Oedipus Rex*, as paradigmatic of the individual's fate:

> There must be something which makes a voice within us ready to recognize the compelling force of destiny in the Oedipus . . . His destiny moves us

only because it might have been ours—because the oracle laid the same curse upon us before our birth as upon him. It is the fate of all of us, perhaps, to direct our first sexual impulse towards our mother and our first hatred and our first murderous wish against our father.[20]

If Robbe-Grillet consistently refused both the tragic and psychoanalytic as elements of his thinking and writing, we may beg to refuse the intentional fallacy and detect other motives at work. Like Vladimir Nabokov, who mocked psychoanalysis in his writing, Robbe-Grillet often exhibits the most unabashed forms of psychoanalytic figures, untrammeled fetishism, for example. Although he may be ostentatiously mocking the psychoanalytic reader, he nonetheless, especially in his teasing use of the Oedipus myth, solicits psychoanalytic interpretation to accompany his *chosisme,* itself perhaps commodity fetishism. In "Une écriture freudienne?" Jean Bellemin-Noel points out, "Alain Robbe-Grillet detested psychoanalysis. It is difficult to ignore this, since he never missed an occasion to remind us of it."[21] Yet Bellemin-Noel locates in Robbe-Grillet's texts denegation, the fetish, the unconscious: "He writes in lines of light with the black ink of the drive" (629).

Robbe-Grillet's work long circled around the detective, murder, and discovery. His first novel, *Un Régicide,* written in 1949 but not published until 1978, concerned the failed assassination of a monarch. He read and absorbed the works of such masters of detective fiction and espionage thrillers as Graham Greene, James Cain, and Raymond Chandler and drew them into the legacy of Kafka, he too concerned with the institutions of the law and its inexorability, its helpless victims. Even *La Jalousie,* set in a colonial world, which does not figure a murder among its nonevents, nevertheless allows for the possibility of killing and vengeance to be read behind the minute descriptions of verandas and Venetian blinds. *La Maison de Rendezvous* contains a murder, and murder and crime haunt other texts such as *Le Voyeur,* with its absent center.

Les Gommes sends out feelers in many directions, toward Greek antiquity, myth, Sophocles, Freud, and also toward the recent past of France, the war fresh in memory in 1953. Kristin Ross sees Alain Robbe-Grillet as a participant and an agent in the general turn toward sanitization and cleansing of the postwar period, his prose an analogue to the clean kitchens of the French housewife and to torture in Algeria. But in *Les Gommes,* the more remote past tantalizingly contaminates the present of the text; just as his own past, of incestuous desire and father seeking, determines his final act of murder, so the Greek myth shadows and haunts Wallas' investigation.

One of the most compelling features of the novel is its lack of affect; although Robbe-Grillet receives and reinscribes the tragic myth of Oedipus from both Sophocles and Freud, the tragic quality of the narrative is erased, expunged, deleted from the novel. Aristotle discusses the effect of the tragedy in terms of catharsis, a purging of the emotions of pity and fear in the spectator, as discussed in Chapter 5.[22] Robbe-Grillet's novel admits neither pity nor fear. Freud ascribes feelings of desire and hatred to the child who masters his emotion in development, suppressing his inevitable reactions to the nuclear family for the sake of being someday a man, with the phallic power to possess a woman of his own. The narrative in Freud's account suggests a struggle to master intense feeling. In Robbe-Grillet's novel, all proceeds without turmoil; the gun fires, the bullet strikes and kills the father, all without characterizing epithets of emotion: "He walks around the body, keeping out of reach of a possible reaction. The man still does not move. His hat has remained pulled down over his forehead. The right eye is partly open, the other is turned down toward the ground; the nose is crushed against the carpet. What can be seen of the face looks quite gray. He is dead."[23] Robbe-Grillet's account has neither the hard-boiled quality of a police procedural novel, nor the suppressed sentimentality of Raymond Chandler. The corpse has become *une chose,* one thing among many.

Georges Simenon's *Maigret et l'homme du banc,* published in the same year as *Les Gommes,* offers an interesting parallel to Robbe-Grillet's text, and a similar willingness to treat murder rather than the great violence of recent war and genocide. Simenon's Maigret *policiers,* unlike his more ambitious literary novels, rely on comforting tropes: the startling capacity for alcohol consumption of Maigret himself; Maigret's dependence on his wife, the excellent cook known only as Madame Maigret; Maigret's trance-like meditations concerning those responsible for the murders he investigates; and, most of all, an atmosphere, an ambience, a setting, usually in Paris but sometimes in provincial localities, in which there is a rich descriptive texture, an exploration of neighborhoods, houses, apartments, with decors, class hierarchies, all set in an indeterminate past, sometime in the thirties, the forties, the fifties, but with no historical markers or indications of any larger political events.

Simenon was accused of collaboration after World War II; nine films of his fictions had been produced during the Nazi occupation. He defended himself, but, although he was not formally prosecuted, he left France and wrote his succeeding Maigret novels, nostalgic for a certain lost past, from a distance, from Connecticut.[24] *Maigret et l'homme du banc* shares the features mentioned above, especially the indeterminate setting in a Paris from which historical markers have been effaced. However, especially notable in this text is Simenon's projection onto Maigret of a certain xenophobia; Maigret's police force has to this point been resolutely French but has now itself been penetrated by darker forces. One of Maigret's colleagues on the crime squad is a certain Santoni, a Corsican, an internal immigrant: "Maigret had never before worked on a case with Santoni. In the confined space of the little black police car, he was uncomfortably conscious of the powerful smell emanating from the Inspector, a little man, who wore high-heeled shoes. He used hair oil, and on his fourth finger wore a big yellow diamond, probably paste."[25] Need one say more?

This *policier* has other interesting features—for example, the victim had lived in a new housing development in Juvisy, and much is made of the "hundreds, maybe thousands, of detached houses all exactly alike in size and shape" (9). Simenon refers to successive devaluations of the franc (48). Modernization has come to this postwar world, even though in other ways the city of the 1950s remains identical to that of earlier Maigret novels, as Maigret moves through the old quarters, mapping the boulevards.

The most interesting feature of this novel, however, is Simenon's treatment of the Jewish question. The victim, who had worked for many years in a factory making party items, "false beards, cardboard trumpets, Christmas tree decorations of every sort, paper streamers, carnival masks, and seaside resort souvenirs" (29), had lost his job and taken to theft, concealing his unemployment from his wife. He was someone who owned "cheap editions, popular novels, cloak-and-dagger romances, and one or two detective novels" (91). The factory, Kaplan and Zanin, had closed three years earlier, and the reader might expect some reference to the confiscation of Jewish property during the Occupation and the deportation of the Jews of France, native and immigrants, to the death camps. In this case, any expectation of an acknowledgment of these facts, like any historical specificity in these novels, is disappointed. Police inquiry results in the following information: "There were no longer any Zanins in the firm when I came to this place twenty-six years ago. At that time, old Monsieur Kaplan was running the business singlehanded. Children would stop in the street and stare at him, because he had the look of an Old Testament patriarch" (28). When the police try to track the owner's heir, they learn that he is staying at his villa at Antibes (46): He remains prosperous, even privileged, having profited from the closing of his factory. The novel perhaps represents a wish that the old man, M. Kaplan, the father, and all the Jews of Paris had survived and prospered, while at the same time ambivalently "denegating," denying and suppressing the historical facts of confiscation, deportation, and mass execution. In a telling reversal, the owner's closing of the factory and consequent dismissal of its workers are in fact the first cause of the unemployed victim's death.

The murderer, it turns out, was a Marseillais of the pimping class: "They couldn't be shadier. The woman runs a bawdy house, and the man is a thug from Marseilles" (181). Of course this semi-ethnic characterization has its interest. Marseilles was an ancient Greek foundation, a colony established in the sixth century B.C.E., and retains some of the allure and strangeness of its foundation. Just as the Maison Carrée of Nimes stands in the middle of a modern city, recalling the presence of Greeks and Romans in its remote past, so Marseilles as a city is in some ways an inassimilable other within the homogeneous body of France, founded as a Catholic nation, according to right-way discourses that look back to Clovis and Jeanne d'Arc for the nation's purely Gallic origins. Marseilles more and more, from the moment of its foundation by Greek traders, received Mediterraneans of various sorts, North African immigrants, as well as native Nizzese Italians and others drifting north, to represent a southern, eastern, contaminated edge, a porous border that represents only a dubious claim to the ethnic Gallic purity of the north, even or perhaps especially in the hands of the Belgian novelist.

Simenon's *policier* has no pretensions to mythic shape, no tragic periodicity. It has the inevitable shape, however, of the detective novel; someone is killed, and the murderer is revealed after the obstacles to discovery are cleared away. Death is managed, made comprehensible through the agency of the detective, who labors through a network of human connections to find the contaminated or polluted actor and to remove him from society. Maigret, then, can return to dine in peace with his wife, public safety maintained, collaboration and the Jewish question successfully sidestepped.

There is no allusion to Oedipal energies in Simenon's novel, no rage at the father, no desire for the mother. If there is an Oedipal subtext, it is radically displaced. The victim's daughter and her younger boyfriend, a naive student who works at a book shop, are suspected of killing the father in order to escape to South America to avoid parental disapproval of their liaison, but in fact the boy retreats from his courtship and is absolved of responsibility for the murder. Her mother, an unsympathetic, ambitious, shrewish wife to the victim, exhibits no tragic sentiments concerning her loss. If there is an Oedipal dimension to this plot, as with so many other *policiers,* it evokes the Greek Oedipus rather than the Freudian, the inevitable linearity of a plot in which murder will out and the murderer be revealed. Simenon's is a weak shadow of the Sophocles plot, the Oedipus as further amplified by Freud, in which the one investigating the crime, the analyst, or Oedipus himself, turns out to be the perpetrator, actually or in fantasy, the one who wishes to kill and who is revealed at the end. It is in this sense that every detective is an Oedipus, if he is, as Freud says, a would-be killer like every man; in the detective novel, the perpetrator is reassuringly revealed to be an other, not the detective himself, not the reader, but someone quite different. In the Simenon *policier,* the murderer is comfortably named as especially other, as often in these popular texts, not only a hardened and experienced criminal, but also a Marseillais, that is, having southern tendencies, therefore almost foreign, at the very least Italianate, and thus suspect to a xenophobe of the north.

Robbe-Grillet's *Les Gommes* is of course Oedipal in another sense; rather than writing "an ingenious puzzle novel," as some critics have suggested, he does make the investigator himself perform the murder itself, and in this case, the detective-murderer is also the victim's son. One of the most interesting aspects of Robbe-Grillet's engagement with the symbiosis between the detective story and the Oedipus myth concerns his return to it in a novel, *La Reprise,* published in 2001, almost fifty years after the publication of *Les Gommes.*

La Reprise is in some ways indeed a retake, a repetition, a remake, some would argue a mis-take, of the 1953 *Les Gommes,* returning to the earlier novel in countless ways, and to Sophocles' *Oedipus* behind that earlier novel.[26] Themes of incest, murder, and detection constitute the labyrinthine plot of the text. There are many allusions to scenes, events, and objects of *Les Gommes* in the later retelling. Within the convoluted plot, which exhibits various flourishes, implicitly citing Borges, Nabokov, and Calvino, Kafka and Kierkegaard, Robbe-Grillet also cites himself. For example, as in *Les Gommes,* the shifting narrators engage in the practice of *ekphrasis,* the verbal description of a work of art, a rhetorical topos inherited from antiquity. One of the characters, Mathieu, known also by other names in the text, gazes at an image, *mise en abîme,* reflected twice and inverted in two mirrors. The images not only mimic the picture, but also recall another vision, where another version of this character imagines a statue. The picture

> represents some episode (perhaps quite famous, but he always wondered which one) of ancient history or of mythology, in a hilly landscape in which can be made out in the distance, to the left, several columned buildings in Corinthian style forming the background of the setting. Coming from the right, in the foreground, a horseman riding his black stallion brandishes a warlike sword in the direction of the old man in a toga who is facing him.[27]

Archers follow; the lone horseman wears Roman clothing, the old "king" a "vaguely Hellenic toga" (79). Earlier, in the prologue, the pseudonymous Henri Robin, who turns out eventually, it appears, to be the murderer of his own father, sees a pedestal, now empty of its "allegorical bronze group" (16); to him appears, in a sort of hallucination, a similar scene, an ancient chariot containing an old man crowned with a diadem, followed by two archers. The scene, repeated, recalls not only moments from *Les Gommes,* but also the crucial scene at the triple crossroads in the myth of Oedipus, where Oedipus, choosing the road to Thebes over the road back to Corinth, murdered the Theban king, his father. The image in *La Reprise* goes further, gathering into the system of reference also Plato's myth of the charioteer in the *Phaedrus;* the chariot is called "the flamboyant chariot of the mythological Eros" (21). Robbe-Grillet adds to his Oedipal plot references to Sade, Pauline Réage, and the pornographic novel *L'image,* with several pedophilic, sadomasochistic, and incestuous moments between the erstwhile narrator and his half sister. She works in a brothel called the Sphinx, "(or rather La Sphinge, since the word is feminine in German)" (106). Other works of art depict the girl Gigi in bondage; one of them alludes directly to Réage's *L'Histoire d'O:* "In the first image, entitled Penitence, the young victim is shown from the front, kneeling on two little round prickly cushions" (130). The central character, Robin-Mathieu-von Brucke (Marco who becomes Walther), is frequently called Wall, Wallon, in an allusion to Wallas, the detective-parricide of *Les Gommes.* Another character bears the name Pierre Garin, like Garinati, the failed assassin of the earlier novel. The detective's watch stops, as does the watch of Wallas in *Les Gommes,* which starts again once Wallas has successfully assassinated Daniel Dupont. The murdered man in *La Reprise* is Dany von Brucke—that is, a German version of Daniel Dupont. In the later novel, the mother character, here a stepmother, called at times Jo Kast, wife of the murdered father, herself "ran a modest neighborhood stationery shop . . . where children came to buy pencils and erasers" (74). This woman echoes the saleswoman of the earlier novel from whom Wallas seeks his erasers and for whom he feels attraction, the ex-wife of Daniel Dupont. Incest and parricide—in *La Reprise* the frustrated son of the murdered man, who visited Berlin as a child with his mother seeking his lost father, accused of his murder yet innocent, perhaps, eventually assumes the identity of his twin brother, who did commit the parricide. Marcus von Brucke, who becomes Walther, claims that the man trying to pin the crime on him is called Walther von Brucke, and that he is the victim's son. The son is not dead, as a conspiracy of liars claims. "And this collective, premeditated lie discloses . . . the murderer's identity." His motives? "A fierce rivalry of an openly Oedipal character. This accursed family is the kingdom of Thebes!" (159).

The myth of Oedipus, retold by Sophocles, by Freud, by Robbe-Grillet himself in 1953, here is reworked again, in a new setting, with new lines of incestuous force. All the old characters recur: the blind man, Teiresias, his daughter, Oedipus with Antigone, Apollo the oracular presence. In this novel, the older man requires a child as the object of his incestuous desire, replacing the child who desires his mother. The remembrance of things past jostles with other high cultural memorabilia like the Grail legend; Proust is invoked and Marcel drawn into pedophilia with his "vampire" mother, as Robbe-Grillet calls her, as in this passage: "the evening kiss of the vampire mama required by the little boy as a viaticum in order to be able to fall asleep" (118). Yet the novel has none of the enigmatic compression and dread of *Les Gommes* and remains tedious in its sadomasochistic interludes, which appear like senile naughtiness to gratify the pedophile reader, and which overpower gratuitous allusions to the war and the Nazi regime in Berlin.

La Reprise uses Berlin and the Wehrmacht as decor for its sadomasochism, but the novel nonetheless calls up not only Oedipus, but also the historical repressed of 1953. Beyond all the convolutions of plot, allusions, and sadomasochistic eroticism, this novel, unlike *Les Gommes,* is situated in an actual site, an actual city, at an actual moment in time, divided Berlin four years after armistice was declared (although this dating, made by the narrator, is denied in a footnote by an unknown, other Nabokovian detective who shadows and corrects the text of the first). Yet somehow the attempt to anchor the events, to link them to the devastation of the postwar city, its division, the Nazi past, and the Holocaust, expose the triviality of this repetition. The mysterious locale of the earlier novel, which alluded to the Baltic, to northern cities intersected by canals and an unidentified grayness, proves much more ominous and disturbing than the mere location of this novel in the capital of the Third Reich.

If Simenon cannot allude to the war, or to the fate of deported and murdered Jews who lost their property under the Nazi occupation, Robbe-Grillet's attempt to recuperate history, in oblique allusion to his experience as a forced laborer in Nuremberg, rings false when it appears on the page in 2001. His bricolage, with his own work, the work of others, and the Oedipus myth, in the new millennium, has less force here than in the compulsory trajectory of *Les Gommes,* ponderous and pretentious as it may seem at moments. The earlier novel—sly, mocking, teasing as it is—still has the power of a real meditation on the question of Oedipus, and set alongside Simenon's popular *policier* of the same date, exposes what may be the seductive power of the detective story for readers, the discovery of a murderer who is never oneself.

Oedipus has persisted, in large part because of Freud's interested retrieval of this one myth, among many, from the religious and tragic world of ancient Athens and Thebes. Although the garbled oracle of *Les Gommes* recalls in retrospect not one lost child, but many, trains of deportation carrying passengers to labor camps and gas chambers, the survival of this figure from tragedy speaks to the rhizomatic strength of these elements of the past, recognized in their new context in the twentieth century as addressing a new kind of family, psyche, and social order. If we were all Oedipalized then, as Deleuze and Guattari argued with regret, in this important novel of the twentieth century the recognition of the detective's failure to name the reader as the murderer drives her on to read, avidly to consume, the next detective novel, looking both for herself, and for continued assurance that the murderer is other than herself, and that the great violences of war and extermination of peoples can be suppressed and contained microcosmically, synecdochally, within a narrative of a single death as murder, by the pleasure of that murder's solution. The reach back into Greek antiquity tries to efface the realities of a new kind of war by reinscribing the familiar mythic narrative, however jumbled and distorted. The persistence of Oedipus seems to allow for an oblique recognition of the horrors of the history of the twentieth century, while rendering them manageable through the paradigm of the ancient myth and the literary and psychoanalytic formulae that depend on it.

10

TWENTY-FIRST-CENTURY HIGH THEORY AND THE CLASSICS

The ancient political theory that descends to us, especially from Greek antiquity, comes from the theorists of order,[1] concerns the avoidance of conflict, of *stasis,* and expresses the point of view of aristocratic, conservative strains of thinking usually opposed to any revolutionary sorts of ideas, unless they are directed toward the establishment of an aristocracy, rule by the best; an oligarchy, rule by the few; or a plutocracy, rule by the rich.[2] As Josiah Ober puts it, "The answers to the problem of civic conflict offered by Greek philosophers centered on eliminating the very possibility of strife by carefully managing diversity within the community at large, and by eliminating diversity within the body of active, participatory citizens."[3] Plato's republic is modeled to a great degree on what he admired in the Peloponnesian community of Sparta, notorious among the Greeks for its conservatism—its refusal of the use of coined money, for example; its rigid and violent control of its enslaved Helot neighbors; its adherence to archaic modes of bride theft, communal dining, and homoerotic bonding among the band of warriors that kept the Helots enslaved and provided the great infantry that defeated the Athenians in the Peloponnesian War.

In antiquity there were theorists of radical democracy, of materialism, of equality among all human beings, of antislavery even, perhaps, but they are lost to us, their writings almost without exception destroyed by a conservative tradition. Thinkers like the sophists, the early Stoics, materialists like Democritus and Leucippus, do seem like antecedents, ancestors of the thinkers of critical tendencies of the present. But as Eric Havelock argued long ago, in *The Liberal Temper in Greek Politics,* "It could be claimed that hypocrisy, considered as a method of conserving the morale of civilization, has been one of the West's specific contributions to cultural development . . . [Aristotle, for example] tried to make this system elastic enough to accommodate the pieces of a materialist, historical, and egalitarian system which he has dismembered in order to make them innocuous."[4] Thomas Cole attempted patiently to recover some of the traces of these lost theorists in his *Democritus and the Sources of Greek Anthropology*. But like the poems of Sappho, the works of these thinkers survive only in fragments and have been almost entirely overwhelmed and overshadowed by an aristocratic, antidemocratic tradition exemplified by the works of Plato and Aristotle, which have been preserved in greatest detail and passed on to the Romans, the middle ages in the Christian, Jewish, and Islamic traditions, and into the Renaissance, to dominate inevitably our understanding of ancient societies.

Yet contemporary high theorists of a left-leaning sort—whether invested in queer resistance; anti-imperialism; class struggle in the traditional Marxist sense; universalism derived from the enlightenment and ideas of the rights of man; anti-totalitarian, anti–death camp culture—the theorists of the present most read and debated, continue to return to the Greek and Roman classics as they think about the problems of the present.[5] This chapter focuses on recent work of Antonio Negri and Michael Hardt, in *Empire;* on Giorgio Agamben, especially in his crucial text, *Homo Sacer;* on Judith Butler's book *Antigone's Claim;* on Jacques Rancière's work on ancient Greek democracy and the *demos,* the people; and on the work of Alain Badiou, especially in his book *Saint Paul*. This is not an arbitrary selection, but one that attempts to point to crucial, influential contemporary theory, to present a mapping of a certain landscape, focusing on the details of these texts rather than presenting a more remote categorization of trends, since the strategies of these authors differ radically from one another even as they all return to antiquity. Classicists might find fault with much that is argued by these theorists, with their inadequate grasp of ancient history and ancient languages, and of recent scholarship within the discipline. I am interested here not so much in locating inadequacies; in evaluating these theorists' bodies of work in relation to the criteria of classicists, listing inconsistencies or contradictions; or in reconciling one with another. I engage with these theorists not to offer critiques of misreadings of the ancient world, but to call attention to their engagement with the same unstable, shifting elements of an ancient world that classicists themselves find endlessly compelling, and to argue for their inclusion in a broader definition of classical studies.

* * *

I'll begin by considering the work of Judith Butler and, in particular, her reading of an ancient myth and an ancient text, Sophocles' tragedy of Antigone, in *Antigone's Claim*, first presented as the Wellek Lectures at the University of California at Irvine and mentioned earlier in relation to the persistence of Oedipus in the twentieth century.[6] I look at this volume in particular in relation to the question of classicists' interpretations, treating the other theorists in this chapter in less detail, while still drawing attention to their resort, like hers, to antiquity as a site, a source, a stimulus for contemporary theory, for contestation of our current inherited arrangements of power and hierarchy.

In the case of queer theory, there may be more of a justification in looking to ancient society than in theorizing about revolution and resistance of other sorts. The gender and sexual arrangements of ancient Greece and Rome, as is well known, exhibit not just a tolerance of homoeroticism, but a celebration of same-sex pleasure, intimacy, and bonding. Sappho, the greatest woman poet perhaps of all Western poetry, an aristocrat of ancient Lesbos, wrote poems of desire and longing directed toward female objects of *eros* and was praised and admired as almost equal to one of the Muses by male poets and literary theorists of antiquity like Longinus, who in his treatise on the sublime praised her excellence (10.1). Pederasty, man-boy love, and man-man love were crucial not only to the Spartan and Theban military, but also to archaic symposiastic culture, to aristocratic *hetairiai*, or clubs, of the classical period, and to Plato's understanding of *eros* and the progress toward philosophy. It is the love of a beautiful boy or man that arouses a man or a boy, student of philosophy, first to understand what beauty is and eventually to move toward a sight of the gods and the good from which all emanates, in Plato's view.

So Judith Butler's finding in antiquity a source for undermining an argument in favor of coercive, normative heterosexuality made in contemporary America makes sense. What is more intriguing is her turning toward Sophocles and the myth of Antigone. Sophocles was, of course, not just the most conservative of the Athenian tragedians, but also a lover of boys. Yet Butler emphasizes not the normal pederastic habits of the classical citizen of Athenian democracy, which in fact rarely penetrate the decorous world of what remains of Athenian tragedy, but rather the exemplary figure of Antigone herself, using her allegorically, catachrestically, metaphorically, chiasmically, and metonymically.

Butler's argument on Antigone relies on her reader's familiarity with various crucial moments of the Western tradition, such as Hegel's progressive, dialectical view of history; Hegel's argument concerns Antigone, in the *Aesthetics* and elsewhere, where both Antigone and Kreon are seen as correct in principle, but where each of their principles is of limited validity, as each stubbornly insists on his or her absolute right.[7] Antigone represents the individual, the woman, the underworld, the autochthonous; Kreon, the principle of community, order, male domination, the outward material world and its law. They collide to form the ethical moment or act in which mutual destruction results; these forces are entwined like strands in a double helix, and they cannot mesh but must mutually destroy one another. The conflict between these two principles results in the emergence of a higher, more inclusive level of consciousness. Butler relies also on Freud's account of Oedipus, mentioned early on in *The Interpretation of Dreams,* where Oedipus is revealed as Everyman, every male child who dreams of overcoming his rival his father by killing him and winning the hand of his mother. Butler assumes knowledge of the arguments of Claude Lévi-Strauss concerning the elementary structures of kinship, the taboo on incest, evident in the Oedipus myth and Freud's discussion of it, that separates nature from culture, and Juliet Mitchell's subsequent argument for the abolition of the incest taboo as a feminist imperative.[8] Butler touches on Luce Irigaray's arguments on the question of Antigone, and focuses on Jacques Lacan, who wrote about the whole tradition of exegesis on this myth and tragedy in his work on the ethics of psychoanalysis.[9]

Butler explicitly links her argument to the genealogy of readings derived from Hegel, which "appears to assume the separability of kinship and the state, even as it posits an essential relation between them." Yet: "Antigone . . . absorbs the very language of the state against which she rebels, and hers becomes a politics not of oppositional purity but of the scandalously impure."[10] Butler deconstructs Hegel's opposition between kinship and the state and asks, "Is there a social life left for kinship, one that might well accommodate change within kinship relations?" (18).

In a preliminary statement of her position, Butler is also critical of Lacan's arguments, suggesting that "the distinction between symbolic and social law cannot finally hold" and "that radical alterations in kinship demand a rearticulation of the structuralist presuppositions of psychoanalysis and, hence, of contemporary gender and sexual theory" (19). Butler finds in Antigone an example of another relationship to kinship: "Antigone represents not kinship in its ideal form but its deformation and displacement" (24). She works through Hegel's reading of the play and offers a critique based on the Greek text:

> Antigone cannot exemplify the ethical consciousness who suffers guilt; she is beyond guilt—she embraces her crime as she embraces her death, her tomb, her bridal chamber. At this point in his text, Hegel cites Antigone herself . . . Note the extraordinary suspension of the question of guilt and the implicit rebuke to Hegel that enters with the most reliable translation, that offered by Lloyd-Jones: "Well, if this is approved among the gods, I should forgive [syggignosko] them for what I have suffered, since I have done wrong; but if they are the wrongdoers, may they not suffer worse evils than those they are unjustly inflicting on me!" (34)

In Hegel, she goes on to say, "Womankind does not act politically but constitutes a perversion and privatization of the political sphere, a sphere governed by universality" (35).

Butler also analyzes in some detail Lacan's reading of the figure of Antigone: "Antigone will emerge, then, for Lacan as a problem of beauty, fascination, and death as precisely what intervenes between the desire for the good, the desire to conform to the ethical norm, and thereby derails it, enigmatically, from its path" (46). For Lacan, in Butler's view, "the unwritten and unfailing laws prior to all codification are those that mark the far side of a symbolic limit beyond which humans may not cross. Antigone appears at this limit or, indeed, as this limit" (47).

And this is a condition tragic in our contemporary sense, one that Butler wants to resist. In an argument saturated with "rhetorical" questions, Butler offers another perspective on kinship, the family, and psychoanalysis: "What would happen if psychoanalysis were to have taken Antigone rather than Oedipus as its point of departure?" (57). And she suggests a potentially damning criticism of those who repeat the truths of psychoanalysis: "The one who with the present recites the curse or finds oneself in the midst of the word's historical effectivity does not precisely ventriloquize words that are received from a prior source. The words are reiterated, and their force is reinforced. The agency that performs this reiteration knows the curse but misunderstands the moment in which she participates in its transmission" (65–66).

The tragic situation of the Antigonean subject receives, in Butler's examination, affective, compassionate, and revealing exegesis: "What is produced is a shadowy realm of love, a love that persists in spite of its foreclosure in an ontologically suspended mode. What emerges is a melancholia that attends living and loving outside the livable and outside the field of love, where the lack of institutional sanction forces language into perpetual catachresis" (7). Butler concludes, as the tragic character offers a purchase on critique of the norm: "[Antigone] functions as a chiasm within the vocabulary of political norms. If kinship is the precondition of the human, then Antigone is the occasion for a new field of the human, achieved through political catachresis, the one that happens when the less than human speaks as human, when gender is displaced, and kinship founders on its own founding laws" (82).

The argument of *Antigone's Claim* rests on Butler's claim that previous writers about Antigone have taken for granted the necessity of received kinship order. Hegel and Lacan, in different ways, assume that this represents a necessary aspect of human civilization. Hegel argues that an ethical life requires acceptance of the law, that Antigone is embedded in kinship, a woman, standing for maternity, and that she exists outside the law. Lacan idealizes Antigone, seeing her as beautiful, as beauty, as the enigma of the drive of desire that pushes one toward death, and that places her between two deaths, at the limit of life. Butler wants to imagine another possibility, one that would speculatively found psychoanalysis not on the figure of Oedipus but on that of Antigone, and that would therefore think beyond the repetition of the law of the father, toward another kind of kinship. Antigone is at the center of this allegory, the masculine woman, the incestuous lover of her brother, the daughter of her brother, standing for the ambiguity and impossibility that disrupts the law, embodying the melancholia of those who stand between two deaths, unable to grieve.

Butler, a postfeminist, poststructuralist, postmodern queer theorist influenced by deconstruction, is here interested in undermining the feminist resort to the state as the source of reforms. Other contemporary theorists use antiquity as a common ground, a lingua franca, a point of common reference for all readers. Sometimes ancient texts or history provide a source for allegory, for negative or positive example, as Spartacus and Saint Paul do for Badiou, as Thucydides' Pericles does for the neoconservative classicist Donald Kagan. The reference to antiquity can persuasively authorize contemporary writers. Some see ancient Greece and Rome as a point of origin that lends them an authority based on that origin, suggesting even, as in Heidegger's case, for example, that we must go back to the beginnings to right our ways, to retrieve what has been lost. Etymology often, for Heidegger and some of his followers, affords a privileged access to ancient truths, as in his idiosyncratic excavation of the Greek word *aletheia*, "unforgetting," "unconcealing," "truth." Heidegger's "claim" is that the polarity between Being and thinking sums up "the entire Western tradition and conception of Being, and accordingly the fundamental relation to Being that is still dominant today."[11] He argues that this is "the real target of our attack. It can be overcome only *originally,* that is, in such a way that its inceptive truth is shown its own limits and thereby founded anew" (89).

In Butler's case the author uses the classical text first of all because others have. The myth of the family of Oedipus is a palimpsest, common ground, an origin, displaying, perversely, the failures that ensue from incest, producing therefore a certain normative structure of kinship, for Hegel and Freud; Antigone is an exemplum for Butler, a resource for allegory because she is a discursive catachresis, the daughter of her brother Oedipus, speaking when commanded not to, assuming a masculine role, refusing reproduction, disobeying the law, grieving for her brother whom she desires. Butler doesn't rely on the text as an authority but rather conceives of the text of the play, or the myth, as a fruitful site of investigation and even of productive misreading precisely because there is a long genealogy of interpretations of the play, including Hegel's, Holderlin's, Freud's, Lacan's, Irigaray's, even George Steiner's. The traces of many generations of interpretants of the myth and tragedy of Antigone can be tracked, revealing a variety of cultural investments. And most especially an investment in kinship as it has always been, with a nuclear, heterosexual family, and a law of the father that produces the superego. Butler implicitly accuses those who hold to such a view of a failure of utopian imagination in their incapacity to conceive of other structures of common life, and of reinforcing compulsory normative heterosexuality by reiterating and reinforcing these forms.

Where does Butler's reading stand in relation to traditional, conventional, or accepted analyses of the Sophoclean text made by contemporary classicists? Many readings take the conflict in the play as a gendered matter, of male versus female, and they often conclude by celebrating Antigone, as does Irigaray, as a feminist heroine resistant to patriarchal power. Kreon is at fault, Antigone the heroine, sustaining the old ways, the old gods, the unwritten laws, the family, the private sphere, against the state. This can be recast as a struggle between *oikos* and *polis,* private versus public, as in Arendt's discussion of the classical city, or as the spectacle of the heroic individual against the state, in which gender is less significant; this is an interpretation resorted to often in the allegorical presentations of Antigone seen as an exemplary resister to totalitarian regimes, as in a segment of the film *Germany in Autumn.*[12] Other readings center on the question of burial, sacrilege, and the cultural contexts of mourning and lamentation, following from the horror expressed at the mutilation of the corpse in *The Iliad,* discussed in an early work of Charles Segal.[13] Mark Griffith, in an ongoing set of essays on the essential conservatism of Athenian tragedy, argues that the genre typically allows conflicts in the classical *polis* to surface briefly, but that then tragedies end by closing down alternatives and the possibility of social change; the corpus of tragedies finally seems to present a public and political spectacle affirming that the status quo is best. Griffith sees this structure as especially visible in the extant plays of Sophocles.[14]

I read Antigone the character as occupying a conservative, aristocratic class position within the politics of the democratic city, framed in the person of the female, against the tyrant Kreon, with his son Haimon representing the dialectically advanced position of democracy. In this diptych form, with two inflexible characters, tragedy represents a failed dialectic, the inability of both to yield to rhetoric, to persuasion, to hear proofs, to listen to one another, this tragedy then monitory in the sense that *Oedipus Rex* is, another warning by Socrates against abandoning older values for the hubris and exhilaration of life in the new democratic city. In Sophocles' *Antigone*, in a passage that Butler does not stress in her reading of the play, Haimon, the betrothed of Antigone and son of Kreon the tyrant, makes a plea to his inflexible father that alludes to the question of democratic persuasion, rhetoric, and *logos,* in the context of Athenian and Theban politics:[15]

> Do not bear this single habit of mind, to think
> that what you say and nothing else is true.
> A man who thinks that he alone is right,
> or what he says, or what he is, himself,
> unique, such men, when opened up, are seen
> to be quite empty. For a man, though he be wise,
> it is no shame to learn—learn many things,
> and not maintain his views too rigidly.
> You notice how by streams in wintertime
> The trees that yield preserve their branches safely,
> But those that fight the tempest perish utterly.
> The man who keeps the sheet of his sail tight
> And never slackens capsizes his boat
> And makes the rest of his trip keel uppermost.
> Yield something of your anger, give way a little.
> If a much younger man, like me, may have

a judgment, I would say it were far better
to be one altogether wise by nature, but,
as things incline not to be so, then it is good
also to learn from those who advise well.[16]

In language that harmonizes with strains of Taoist thinking, this hopeful, soon to be disobedient son advises his father to listen and yield, to be persuaded by argument, in lines that evoke the archaic metaphor of the ship of state and recall the earlier chorus: "Many are the wonders, none / is more wonderful than what is man. This it is that crosses the sea / with the south winds storming and the waves swelling, / breaking around him in roaring surf" (368–372).[17] Mark Griffith comments on the Sophoclean ode: "To the Athenians of the 440s, heavily dependent on imported grain, victors of Salamis, and rulers of the Aegean through the Delian League, triremes and trade were indispensable sources of power and prosperity" (185). Griffith, in his notes, further points out that "Greek moralists debate whether men should maintain a pure and consistent character (like gold, or a lion; so Achilleus), or should be adaptable and resourceful in self-presentation (like an octopus: Theognis 215–18; so Odysseus). The opposition, which is sometimes presented as one between aristocratic and democratic values, is esp. marked in S[ophocles]" (243–244). The deaths of both Antigone and Haimon reveal the terrible consequences of the tyrant's inability to yield to his son's arguments for persuasion. Sophocles' tragedy exemplifies drama's rhetorical function, both comedy's and tragedy's role as political education in Vernant's sense, the city making itself into a theater and participating in intense local Athenian debates concerning class conflict, guilt and responsibility, piety and reverence, family and allies, wisdom or sense.

Butler's analysis overrides the rhetoric of the fifth-century tragedy and extracts the single character Antigone from its discursive, poetic, narrative, and dramatic situation. Butler's polemic leaves out a great deal of historical context that situates the play for classicists: the struggle over democracy, Pericles, the Persian and Peloponnesian wars, Dionysus and Eros, and the religious context of the play. In transmuting the rhetorical address of Sophocles' tragedy, which I believe communicates an anxious, monitory, conservative politics to its first audience, she appropriates it, pessimistically and most tentatively, for a radical reinvention of family, kinship, and subjectivity in postmodernity. An elegiac tone, a melancholic and affectively powerful rhetoric echo the regret and pessimism of Sophocles in the context of this call for utopian reimagining of the relationship between kinship and the state.

Jacques Rancière's *Disagreement: Politics and Philosophy,* first published in French in 1995, like Butler's *Antigone's Claim,* works from a classical Athenian cultural site to formulate his arguments concerning politics in the present. His style in this text differs from that of Butler, who presents a densely philosophical reading of the problematic generated by the figure of Antigone. French scholarly style has always allowed for fewer footnotes, more lyricism, and a tolerance for a writerly style different from the American scholarly traditions. In this text, Rancière is engaging with various political theorists—Michel Foucault; Jurgen Habermas; Karl Marx and later Marxists, including the important French Marxist theorist Louis Althusser; Jean Baudrillard; and Emmanuel Levinas—who stand silently present, rarely named but nonetheless addressed, haunting the text in a complex, many-sided dialogue.[18]

Disagreement argues that political philosophy is an attempt to get rid of politics, which Rancière defines idiosyncratically: "Politics exists when the natural order of domination is interrupted by the institution of a part of those who have no part" (11). He goes through a refutation of various moments of political philosophy, from Plato and Aristotle to Hobbes and Marx, in order to show that politics is "local and occasional," a temporary interruption of domination. He is especially interested in ancient "democracy," and in contemporary globalizing culture, and offers a critique of all these moments, including what he calls archipolitics (Plato), parapolitics (Aristotle and beyond), and the Marxist states that exhibited what he calls "metapolitics," the state claiming to speak for the proletariat.

Disagreement's preface argues that in fact political philosophy is how philosophy tries to *rid* itself of, rather than engaging with, politics. And Rancière intends to go back to politics, to return politics to political philosophy. He begins with the beginning of politics, with Aristotle's formulations concerning the wealthy and the best, *oligoi* and *aristoi,* and with his own definition of the *demos,* the people. If some scholars have identified *demos* with the whole citizen body of the ancient democracy, Rancière sees them otherwise. For him, politics is the struggle between the rich and the poor: "Politics does not happen just because the poor oppose the rich. It is the other way around: politics (that is, the interruption of the simple effects of domination by the rich) causes the poor to exist as an entity" (11). The poor, those who "have no part," interrupt that natural order of domination. Rancière recounts the anecdote of the Scythian slaves in Herodotus, in which rebellious slaves are put back in their place by the mere display of the whip by their masters, returned after a generation away. The domination of the poor by the rich is the antipolitical, the imposition of a naturalized order. The equality of the arithmetical must be substituted for, as philosophy replaces it with "the divine order of geometric proportion that regulates the real good, the common good that is virtually each person's advantage without being to anyone's disadvantage" (15). Plato sees the arithmetical order of democracy as scandalous and seeks to restore proportionality.

Rancière argues that politics begins with a wrong, "harm," *blaberon*—that is, inequality—and he constructs an opposition between what he calls police and politics:

> The police is, essentially, the law, generally implicit, that defines a party's share or lack of it ... The police is ... first an order of bodies that defines the allocation of ways of doing, ways of being, and ways of saying, and sees that those bodies are assigned by name to a particular place and task; it is an order of the visible and the sayable that sees that a particular activity is visible and another is not, that this speech is understood as discourse and another as noise. (29)

Rancière contrasts policing, the rule governing the appearance of bodies, with politics, which he calls "antagonistic to policing" (29). Politics can be "actions that reconfigure" space, shifting bodies from their assigned places, making "understood as discourse what was once only heard as noise" (30). Politics happens when the police process collides with the process of equality; "Politics acts on the police" (33). And questions of aesthetics are for Rancière crucial to the eruption of politics: "The aesthetic configuration in which what the speaking being says leaves its mark has always been the very stakes of the dispute that politics enlists in the police order" (57). His arguments implicitly call for a return to politics, for the interruption of policing in the name of those who "have no part," like those ancient participants in the Athenian *polis*.

For Rancière the classics produce an origin, that is to say, the beginnings of politics and political philosophy, both for good and for bad. That is, he finds in the ancient world the beginnings of attempts to get rid of politics, but also the beginnings of politics—for example, in the claim of the Athenian *demos* to be the whole, in the plebeian secession to the Aventine Hill in Livy (in Shakespeare, as well)—where the plebeians "conduct themselves like beings with names" (24). Rancière identifies as well a conservative philosophical ambition in Plato and Aristotle, an attempt to manage, contain, and diffuse politics through philosophical reflection, as well as these traces, vestiges, of something else, the people claiming to have *logos,* "reason," "the word," (26) rather than simply an animal voice, *phone.*

If the entire field of political philosophy is based on beginnings in Plato and Aristotle—where Plato is seen variously as a great utopianist, for example, or as the first totalitarian and Aristotle as the first great empiricist or as the encyclopedist who fixed a stranglehold over Western science for millennia—then Rancière is identifying a crucial presence, that politics opposed to the police, to whom one must after all assume that Plato and Aristotle belong. So for Rancière the Athenian *polis* is the site of possibility but also of the beginnings of that which he means to contest, the complicity of so-called political philosophy in silencing the claim of the people, that local and occasional outburst at the site of contestation that is politics.

Rancière is interested in a critique of political philosophy, since he sees its aim as removing politics from philosophy. He uses the tradition of Plato, Aristotle-Hobbes, and Marx to show how their various theories seek to eradicate politics—Plato by naturalizing hierarchy, in archipolitics; Aristotle by accepting democracy but eliminating politics through a distribution of offices; Marx—or communist states, rather—by substituting the party for the people, for the poor. With a more oracular, lyrical, and aphoristic rhetorical style than we are accustomed to in the work of Anglo-Saxon classicists, continually redefining and elaborating what he means by politics, Rancière also somewhat obscures basic historical points, alluding to them but not spelling them out. As the meta-historian Hayden White notes,

> In Rancière's view, the modern study of history must be scientific in the sense of seeking to become a systematic search for the latent (what is hidden and indeed unseeable) in, below, or behind the phenomena that manifest the existence of "a past." So, farewell to the older *empiricist* ideal of historical investigation. History must construct its objects of study rather in the way that, in psychoanalysis, the unconscious has to be constructed as an object

of study on the basis of its symptomatic effects or, in physics, electrons must be posited on the basis of the trails they leave in a bubble chamber, rather than by direct observation.[19]

For example, history as the revolution of the sixth century B.C.E. in Athens, when the poor were being indebted, then enslaved and sold by the rich, which led to, we must assume, some "politics" in his sense, some upheaval that claimed citizenship and equality of the poor citizens with the rich, using the myth of autochthony, which Rancière alludes to very briefly, to justify their equality with the aristocrats and the rich.[20] This led to Solon's reforms—the abolition of claims on the land, the *horoi,* ownership markers on others' lands, citizen enslavement for debt, the recall of slaves from other cities, the distribution of offices into classes—these leading eventually to Cleisthenes' reforms and the establishment of what was called the radical democracy, which Plato despised and which led him to invent his *politeia,* his ideas about a republican hierarchy, to "cure."

Rancière seems focused on the free citizen of the *demos,* the citizen who has nothing but his freedom to distinguish himself from the slave—that freedom that renders him equal to the patricians, or the aristocrats, or the rich—yet does not consider slavery as a crucial feature of Athenian democracy. Could one imagine another kind of ancient history of "politics," according to Rancière? One would begin with the upstart Thersites, move on to sixth-century conflicts concerning land and politics, the shape of fifth-century Athenian democracy, and the claims of those with no part, as well as the evidence in historical, forensic, tragic, comic texts testifying to the role of Samos at the time of the Peloponnesian War, to the Hellenistic slave revolts, to further developments in Rome and in the rise of Christianity. Rancière's arguments are firmly grounded in the history of the West, in classical and democratic Athens, because he is concerned with the history of political philosophy and sees its origin as a discipline and a tradition there. But there is no reason his arguments cannot be extended to include other places, other times, as we see in his discussions of immigration and of globalization and ethnicity. His resort to the Greeks derives from the project's focus on the question of political philosophy as a discipline, its beginnings in ancient Athenian democracy and the philosophers who lived within it, and from his insights concerning their investment in stability and control. His readings of Plato and Aristotle in particular lead him to advocate, implicitly, a new politics that will, locally and occasionally, open a site for aesthetic engagement, contestation, a claim on the part of those who have no part, like the poor of ancient Athens, in the current complacent world of consensus or postdemocracy. An intriguing, although perhaps peripheral, question: How can one reconcile Butler's arguments with Rancière's? Is what Antigone does "politics" in his sense, as she claims *logos,* a right to speak, a space for the claim where there is none?

I turn now to another text by Alain Badiou, his *Saint Paul: The Foundation of Universalism,* first published in French in 1997. But first, it might be necessary to point again to the division of labor that too often separates the study of ancient Christianity from the classics, that allows for a disciplinary chasm to persist.[21] The study of the later Roman Empire, especially after the conversion of Constantine, must take account of Christianity, and such polemical work as Badiou's can enliven our understanding of ancient people even as it participates in contemporary debates concerning universalism and militancy. How does an argument such as his affect classicists' understanding of ancient religion, ancient cult, ancient ethnicity?

In *Saint Paul,* Badiou argues that Paul is exemplary of a subject produced by an event, that is, a militant for a truth. This is a case study that illuminates Badiou's work in other texts, his claim that the task of philosophy is not to produce truths, but to set out criteria for recognizing and evaluating claims for a truth. Here he considers Paul as an example of what we need in the present, implicitly, someone to replace the militant of communism, Paul as the Lenin to Jesus' Marx. The classical texts Badiou reads as a source for his arguments concerning universalism are Paul's letters. The Acts of the Apostles were composed later, and in Badiou's view were too much influenced by Greek romance and fictional forms to be reliable informants concerning the beliefs of Paul. The Gospels, too, touched by narrative forms and the odor of the miraculous, came later. The letters of Paul are a precious source, evidence of communication from an ancient person, and Badiou's book is a reading of the letters, written between 50 and 58 C.E., texts of the ancient world. Badiou uses Paul as a positive example of an antidialectical antiphilosopher, a militant for his truth. Badiou argues that Paul understands "the event"—a crucial element of Badiou's thinking, discussed earlier in relation to Spartacus—to be the resurrection, the killing of death, and that Christianity is a new discourse, distinct from Greek philosophy and Judaic law, and also different from a discourse of the supernatural or the miraculous.

Badiou's is a rich and complex interpretation of the innovation of Paul, which nonetheless conflicts with another, more traditional interpretation of Paul arguing that Jesus is the radical, the revolutionary, Paul the conservative who builds the church and sticks to the law. While his short book does not provide a great deal of ancient historical context, Badiou situates the life of Paul as an orthodox Jew in Tarsus but doesn't spend much time considering other religions of the period, including the cult of the emperor (Augustus declared a god in Palmyra, for example). He does discuss the Judaism of Jerusalem, especially those followers of Jesus who considered themselves still to be Jews and required followers of Jesus to be circumcised and to follow Jewish law. He doesn't focus on the Maccabees, rebels against Antiochus, the Hellenistic Seleucid king, or on the later rebellion of 66 C.E., which resulted in Titus' destruction of the third temple, reflected in a Roman triumphal arch.[22] Hellenists may rarely use this text as a source, or as evidence for belief or practice in antiquity. Acts, for example, provides a vivid scene at the temple of Artemis in Ephesus—the silversmiths are angry when Paul comes there and preaches to the Ephesians, some of whom make their living producing figurines of Artemis and who hoot at him, "Great is Artemis of the Ephesians!" (Acts 19:28).

Badiou is interested in the case study of the event (as in the example of Spartacus, analyzed earlier), the subject produced by the event, the truth advocated by the militant for that truth; and he is concerned with particularity, the specific situation that produces an innovative, universal truth that is open and objective. Truths are about equality for him as well as for Rancière, and he does elsewhere consider the problem of evil, the Nazis as a perversion, a distortion, an evil that is not a truth, using exclusion, naming, old ways of belief.

From the beginning, Badiou distances himself from those who examine Paul's career as Christian believers themselves: "Basically, I have never really connected Paul with religion."[23] "For me, Paul is a poet-thinker of the event, as well as one who practices and states the invariant traits of what can be called the militant figure" (2). And further, he sets his reading of Paul within the context of an attack on contemporary multiculturalism and what he sees as an epidemic of fragmented social movements claiming victimization. He wants to restore universalism to the political domain and sets it against "cultural and historical relativism," the "intersection between culturalist ideology and the 'victimist' [*victimaire*] conception of man" (6). He opposes monetary abstraction, which he considers a false universalism, as well as state communism and capitalist parliamentarianism, and finds a clarion call in Paul: "A genuinely stupefying statement when one knows the rules of the ancient world: 'There is neither Jew nor Greek, there is neither slave nor free, there is neither male nor female' (Gal. 3. 28)!" (9). Badiou sets himself against the "'culture-technology-management-sexuality' system," in the name of a "universal singularity" (13), advocating a mission that he sees also in Paul, who would not allow his call ever to "be determined by the available generalities, be they statist [*étatiques*] or ideological" (13).

Badiou discusses Paul's relationship to Greek philosophy, drawing on the account in Acts in which, "hearing Paul speak of the resurrection of the dead, the Greek philosophers burst out laughing and leave" (27). He sees Paul tackling "the Greek intellectual milieu, whose essential category is that of wisdom *(sophia)* and whose instrument is that of rhetorical superiority *(huperokhe logou)*" (27). "Paul opposes a show of spirit *(pneuma*, breath*)* and power *(dunamis)* to the armed wisdom of rhetoric" (28). And he points out the crucial status of the Roman Empire to Paul's mission: "For him, the structure of the Roman Empire, which means the world between the Orient and Spain, is more important than the preeminence of Jerusalem" (34). He recalls the script of a film, never made, written by Pasolini in which Rome is New York City, Paris is Jerusalem, and the anti-fascist Resistance is the tiny Christian community. "For Pasolini, Paul, in revolutionary fashion, wanted to destroy a model of society based on social inequality, imperialism, and slavery" (37).

Badiou identifies two discourses, Jewish and Greek, "subjective dispositions," as he calls them (41). "Greek and Jewish discourse are both *discourses of the Father*. That is why they bind communities in a form of obedience (to the Cosmos, the Empire, God, or the Law)" (42). Paul argues in contrast that "one must proceed from the event as such, which is a-cosmic and illegal, refusing integration into any totality and signaling nothing" (42). "Only that which will present itself *as a discourse of the Son* has the potential to be universal, detached from every particularism" (42).

I won't go in to the intricacies of Badiou's analysis of Paul's new subject, which goes beyond the opposition between Jewish and Greek discourses, "a paradigm of a major difference for thought" still for Levinas (57): "This is the driving force behind Paul's universalist conviction: that 'ethnic' or cultural difference, of which the opposition between Greek and Jew is in his time and in the empire as a whole, the prototype, is no longer significant with regard to the real, or to the new object that sets out a new discourse" (57). Badiou sets out what is at stake for him in a revealing statement, for him as a believer in universalism and truth: "There is no doubt that universalism, and hence the existence of any truth whatsoever, requires the destitution of established differences and the initiation of a subject divided in itself by the challenge of having nothing but the vanished event to face up to" (58). And here again one senses Badiou's admiration for Paul: Ventriloquizing the disciple, he writes, "It is incumbent upon us to found a materialism of grace through the strong, simple idea that every existence can one day be seized by what happens to it and subsequently devote itself to that which is valid for all, or as Paul magnificently puts it, 'become all things to all men [*tois pasi gegona ta panta*]' (Cor. I. 9. 22)" (66).

Badiou points out how revolutionary such a program is, in the context of ancient Greek and Roman society: "Resurrection . . . suspends differences for the benefit of a radical universality, and . . . the event is addressed to all without exception . . . This is precisely what, in terms of the Roman world, constitutes a staggering innovation" (74). And in a formulation that echoes some of the themes of Jacques Rancière's *Disagreement,* Badiou points out what he sees as the resistant force of the Pauline call, against the law: "The law is always predicative, particular, and partial. Paul is perfectly aware of the law's unfailingly 'statist' character. By 'statist' I mean that which enumerates, names, and controls the parts of a situation. If a truth is to surge forth eventually, it must be nondenumerable, impredicable, uncontrollable" (76).

In his conclusion, Badiou points out that "real universalism" was already present in statements of Archimedes, "certain political practices of the Greeks" (unnamed), in Sophocles, "in the amorous intensity to which the poems of Sappho bear witness" (107), and in the Psalms and Ecclesiastes. But he identifies a break, "still illegible in the teaching of Jesus" (107): "The Pauline break has a bearing upon the formal conditions and the inevitable consequences of a consciousness-of-truth rooted in a pure event, detached from every objectivist assignation to the particular laws of a world or society yet concretely destined to become inscribed within a world and within a society" (107–108). "A truth . . . is the correlate of a new type of subject . . . entirely defined as a militant of the truth in question" (109). For Badiou, as for Rancière, *equality (égalité),* legacy of the French Revolution, is the essential element here, the necessary structuring principle of any utopic imagining: "Paul demonstrates in detail how a universal thought, proceeding on the basis of the worldly proliferation of alterities (the Jew, the Greek, women, slaves, free men, and so on), produces a Sameness and an Equality . . . The production of equality and the casting off, in thought, of differences are the material signs of the universal" (109). And Badiou ends his text on Paul with the authorial voice: "Many events, even very distant ones, still require us to be faithful to them" (111).

Badiou stands here as a critic of parliamentary democracy, in this resembling Butler, a critic of state communism and of fascism, generating a new theory, based on truth, the event, the subject produced by the event. Badiou gives us an interested, polemical, almost allegorical close reading of his ancient text, yet as he does so, he offers an account of a new kind of subject for the Roman Empire, one that can explain the transition from paganism to Christianity through his analysis of Paul's militancy. How could this work as a mode of writing ancient history? Such a history would differ radically from a chronology, or a history recounting the deeds of great men or women, or even of the struggle of social classes, with an emphasis on the subaltern. This new form of history would focus on identifying moments of truth, sparks in the fabric of everyday life that have their effects on a future.

I'll more briefly look at two other texts of contemporary theory that rely on ancient texts, ancient societies, in these cases on works of Rome—the first Giorgio Agamben's *Homo Sacer: Sovereign Power and Bare Life*.[24] Agamben writes that Western politics begins within the ancient *polis* of the Athenians, with a distinction between "bare life" *(zoe)* and political life *(bios),* and that this is a fundamental fracture or division or insurmountable opposition that stands at the beginnings of the West. *Zoe* was life in the *oikos,* or animal life, existence as simple, natural life, reproductive life; *bios politikos* is something else, life in a community. All this is based on an interpretation of life in the Greek *polis,* and on Aristotle's "politics." In a further development based on ancient Roman law, Agamben sees sovereignty as based on the power to decide who will be reduced to bare life—the *homo sacer* is the man who can be killed but not sacrificed, who is not formally executed or ritually committed to the gods— and it is the founding act of sovereignty to decide who is a *homo sacer*. The sovereign declares the state of exception; he is the law, he makes the law that suspends the law, so he is both of the law and outside it. The *homo sacer* is subject to the "ban," abandoned, cast out, and vulnerable. Anyone can kill him with impunity. In modernity, we have all internalized that sovereignty, but we have also become bare life, *homines sacri,* and the model for this state is the concentration camp, the death camp, the refugee camp, inhabited by those who live always in the state of exception, subject to being killed but not sacrificed; in postmodern America, such spaces include immigrant detention centers, public hospital emergency rooms, and prisons. Modernity means that the sovereign state has taken over the biological life of its citizens.

Agamben treats ancient Greek and Roman societies as a point of origin, the site as a founding distinction that has not been overcome, as it must be for a new politics. In some sense, he seems to see the Greek city-state as a model, in its indifference to the *zoe* of its citizens; they are not disturbed in their bare life, though classicists might differ, arguing that the city did intervene, through laws of inheritance, for example, to insure the perpetuation of the *oikoi* of the city.

There are cross-references here, among those scholars who look toward antiquity to conceptualize their own work. Judith Butler uses Agamben's concepts in *Precarious Life* to meditate on mourning and grief, building on her Antigone book to elaborate further on "who counts"—detainees in Guantánamo, Palestinian refugees, people with AIDS. Who is reduced to "bare life"? And there is an interesting intersection between Agamben and Rancière on the question of "the people." Agamben has a long section on "the people," who are both the whole of the state, and the poor, those who for Rancière have no part; he cites Badiou on the set as defined mathematically, in his discussion of the state of exception: *"The exception is what cannot be included in the whole of which it is a member and cannot be a member of the whole in which it is always already included,"* a "limit figure" (25). Agamben, like Badiou, condemns humanitarianism, claiming that it reduces those in refugee camps to bare life and keeps them there, attending only to their bare life needs.

Agamben is a philosopher building a synthesis, or a new line, between Foucault and deconstruction, and in some sense seeing Heidegger's *Dasein* as a resistant and attractive figure, in its facticity, not divided between *zoe* and *bios*. He rather arbitrarily selects interesting examples of what he's concerned with, in chronological order—to move inexorably toward the Nazi concentration camp, thereby critiquing Foucault implicitly, who uses the Panopticon of Bentham as the exemplary space, presaging the spectatorship of modernity. Agamben sees rather the power over life and death in the death camps of the Nazis as the paradigmatic space and activity of the modern state, one that has not been overcome;

in practices of medicine, abortion, and euthanasia, the scientist and the doctor approach the power of the sovereign in the new environment of biopolitics.

Agamben's characterization is difficult to sustain as a description of the classical city, where the *oikos* is the site of bare life, *zoe,* and the *polis* the site of *bios*. How can they be distinguished, and how does gender figure in this analysis? Many feminists have worked on the division between *oikos* and *polis*—as he notes, the two cannot really be kept apart. And he acknowledges further that the world has changed since the classical ages of Athens and Rome: "Today it is not the city but rather the camp that is the fundamental biopolitical paradigm of the West" (181). "We no longer know anything of the classical distinction between *zoe* and *bios,* between private life and political existence, between man as a simple living being at home in the house and man's political existence in the city. This is why the restoration of classical political categories proposed by Leo Strauss and, in a different sense, by Hannah Arendt can have only a critical sense. There is no return from the camps to classical politics" (188). Though Agamben seems to want to argue for some new kind of politics, never specified, his work is relevant to questions of prisoners, the tortured, refugees, the stateless, Darfur, the de-naturalization and denationalization of persons by states, the turning of them into "bare life," imperative questions concerning who is worthy and who unworthy of life in the present world (187–188). The author ends in *aporia,* calling for more research (188), insisting pessimistically on the difference between the classical city of the Greeks, the *polis,* and the world of the present. The classical city is merely the first layer in Agamben's archaeology of the present, a moment that cannot be returned to. The monstrous events of the recent past and present reveal us all to be in a camp, *homines sacri,* with little hope for healing the fracture between *zoe* and *bios,* their union an object of nostalgic impossibility as we gaze toward the classical age.

The last text I'll address is *Empire,* by Michael Hardt and Antonio Negri, as optimistic in its way as Agamben's is pessimistic in his.[25] Subject to passionate debate upon publication, the text argues that we find ourselves now in a new historical situation, not postcolonial, not within first, second, and third worlds, but rather in "Empire," which replaces the old imperialist situation of the colonialist nation-states and their colonies and former colonies. Therefore, politics must be reconceived, not as national liberation movements, for example, but taking into account the global, postmodern empire. In the authors' view, the sovereignty of nation-states has declined, but not sovereignty itself, which is now located in a more abstract, fluid transnational domain. "Sovereignty has taken a new form, composed of a series of national and supernational organisms united under a single logic of rule. This new global form of sovereignty is what we call Empire" (xii). They see the history of the United States, and its constitution's form, as relying on an "imperial," rather than imperialist, example, "inspired by the ancient imperial model" (xiv). They trace the development of sovereignty and its entry into postmodern Empire. Empire's sovereignty is administered differently from that of the nation-states and their imperialist phases, and the authors recount the ways this sovereignty is maintained, in a constant state of crisis and response that constitutes Empire. Crucial to their argument is the identification of "counter-Empire," the poor, the laboring classes, the proletariat, also a transnational element, sometimes called "the multitude," which flows across borders and which they identify as the force that will lead "through" Empire to something new.[26]

Theirs is a particularly frustrating and fascinating use of ancient history and ancient historiography. The authors call upon the ancient historians—for example, Thucydides, Livy, and Tacitus—who, in their view "all teach us (along with Machiavelli commenting on their work)" that "Empire is formed not on the basis of force itself but on the basis of the capacity to present force as being in the service of right and peace" (15). Ancient empire, Athenian and Roman, lies as a shadow, an almost invisible paradigm, behind their analysis of the present and future. And their utopian solution relies heavily on an analogy between the present and high and late imperial Rome. They cite Augustine, inverting his distinction between the city of God and another, calling rather for an "earthly city" that will realize their utopianism. They may have been influenced by the great book of Jerome Carcopino, *Daily Life in Ancient Rome,* written in the fascist period by a fascist classical historian, which covertly promises an end to troubled times by pointing allegorically to the arrival of Christianity in the Roman Empire as a light that dispels darkness. Hardt and Negri themselves use this analogy, turning it in a progressive direction:

> Allow us, in conclusion [to the introduction], one final analogy that refers to the birth of Christianity in Europe and its expansion during the decline of the Roman Empire. In this process an enormous potential of subjectivity

was constructed and consolidated in terms of the prophecy of a world to come, a chiliastic project. This new subjectivity offered an absolute alternative to the spirit of imperial right— . . . Empire was accepted as the "maturity of the times" and the unity of the entire known civilization, but it was challenged in its totality by a completely different ethical and ontological axis. In the same way today, given that the limits and unresolvable problems of the new imperial right are fixed, theory and practice can go beyond them, finding once again an ontological basis of antagonism—within Empire, but also against and beyond Empire, at the same level of totality. (21)

The authors end the book with an invocation of the spirit of Saint Francis: "There is an ancient legend that might serve to illuminate the future life of communist militancy: that of Saint Francis of Assisi" (413). This is a paradigm that evokes Badiou's Saint Paul. They rise rhetorically to a level of hortatory and ecstatic prose:

Once again in postmodernity we find ourselves in Francis's situation, posing against the misery of power the joy of being. This is a revolution that no power will control—because biopower and communism, cooperation and revolution remain together, in love, simplicity, and also innocence. This is the irrepressible lightness and joy of being communist. (413)

Negri and Hardt incorporate the work of the ancient historians themselves to analyze Empire in the present. Polybius, the Greek historian of the formation of the Roman Empire, figures prominently, especially in his analysis of the structure of the Roman Empire, to which he attributes its great success:

For Polybius, the Roman Empire represented the pinnacle of political development because it brought together the three "good" forms of power—monarchy, aristocracy, and democracy, embodied in the persons of the Emperor, the Senate, and the popular comitia. The Empire prevented these good forms from descending into the vicious cycle of corruption in which monarchy becomes tyranny, aristocracy becomes oligarchy, and democracy becomes ochlocracy or anarchy. (314)

Although there are clearly problems of anachronism here, since the role of emperor did not exist in the time of Polybius, who witnessed and testified only to the formation of the empire during the time of the Roman Republic, Hardt and Negri point to a tripartite structure that came to define the later Roman empire and that is implicit in Polybius' celebration of the beginnings of empire. Modern political theory, following Polybius through Machiavelli, produced not a tripartite but rather a "trifunctional model of constitutional construction" (315). Hardt and Negri see a structure more like Polybius' in postmodern empire. "In certain respects the original ancient Polybian model of the constitution of Empire is closer to our reality than the modern liberal tradition's transformation of it" (316). But rather than the wholesome harmony described by Polybius, "one could even argue that our experience of the constitution (in formation) of Empire is really the development and coexistence of the 'bad' forms of government rather than the 'good' forms, as the tradition pretends" (316). Monarchy appears as a global police force (later identified with the United States), aristocracy as transnational finance ("a parasitical oligarchy"), and democracy "as a set of superstitions and fundamentalisms, betraying a spirit that is conservative when not downright reactionary" (316). In their view, however, these functions are not separated in postmodernity, but appear as hybridizations. The authors continually use the ancients, especially Polybius, to orient their analysis of Empire in the twenty-first century. Unlike other twentieth- and twenty-first-century theorists, like Heidegger, Derrida, and Badiou, they tend to neglect Plato, who first discussed the corruption of the various forms of polity, and avoid Aristotle, relying instead on the ancient historians of the empires centered in Athens and Rome.

Classical scholars of the Roman Empire turn to Polybius as a source of factual detail concerning the rise of Rome, placing less emphasis on his political theory; political theorists tend not to be classicists and to focus on his structural model as a source for early modern political theory, without considering in great detail its accuracy concerning Rome itself. But Hardt and Negri's interpretation of the classical text is crucially linked to this broader argument, forming an invisible but powerful articulation for the analysis, both of Empire and of counter-Empire.

The authors are ecstatic and often vague, willing to deconstruct but not satisfied with deconstruction, impatient with orthodox Stalinist Marxism, but communists after all, perhaps in a Franciscan sense. Deleuze and Guattari are the crucial authors here, especially in *Anti-Oedipus,* a source not only for a critical methodology but also for their literary style, which tends toward the exclamatory and generalizing and ecstatic, going back to Nietzsche before Deleuze and Guattari, looking for the "rhizomatic and undulatory" rather than the arboreal, finding the potential for resistance among the "deterritorialized" and exploited precisely because of that very deterritorialization.

The pessimism and dark view of the future found in Agamben's work are countered by Negri and Hardt's invocation of the joy of the new multitude. They conclude their reading of the new empire by invoking not only Augustine and the Christianization of the Roman Empire, but also the very language of the Romans to describe their own utopian vision for the future: "Against the divine city, the earthly city must demonstrate its power as an apparatus of the mythology of reason that organizes the biopolitical reality of the multitude. The name that we want to use to refer to the multitude in its political autonomy and its productive activity is the Latin term *posse*—power as a verb, as activity" (407). Hardt and Negri see the present Empire in the old, and Polybius' insights as valuable in analyzing the structure of the contemporary imperial order. And they use the allegory of the rise and conquest of the Roman Empire by Christianity to inspire hope in the multitudes currently being deterritorialized and reterritorialized by imperial capitalism, in the name of a multitudinous emancipation.

Each of the contemporary theorists discussed here mines classical antiquity for purposes of her own. Judith Butler reads Antigone as exemplary figure, bracketing literary and historical questions to set Antigone in the context of Hegelian and Lacanian discussions, to elaborate, within queer theory, an exploration of melancholy and grief, based on Antigone as a model, someone who speaks without permission. Jacques Rancière, relying on the history of the *demos,* the people of the Athenian democracy, names the part that has no part, seeing its speech as politics, against the police and policing, which are everything else. Alain Badiou, using an individual—the figure of Saint Paul—as example, interprets him as the militant produced by an event and carrying forward a truth, in all its historical specificity, with an allegorical reading that sees Paul as the ancient world's Lenin, the model revolutionary. Giorgio Agamben goes to Aristotle to find naked, bare, mere life, the life that human beings and animals share. Seeing postmodernity as the site where bare life becomes the life of everyone, he records the transition into modernity as biopolitics rules and the death camps of the Nazis become the paradigm of postmodern sovereignty. For Michael Hardt and Antonio Negri the Roman Empire serves as a model for contemporary postmodern Empire, a model both for the

Polybian model of administration and for resistance and overcoming, just as Christianity became the source of the multitude's resistance and survival beyond the Roman period.

Each of these theorists authorizes, justifies, grounds his or her work with these readings of antiquity, finding beginnings, origin, examples, negative and positive, in ancient texts. If some of these writers find resistance and opposition inscribed cryptically into the ancient records of Greece and Rome, and draw those out for purposes of theory, they are swimming against the current of the preservation of ancient society by the tradition, which has consistently privileged élite statements, antidemocratic political theory, and horror at the resistance by the *demos* and slaves to imperial power. Yet the ancient formulations have a kind of weight that is appropriated by those who theorize from within it, seeing them either as original and therefore formative for Western civilization or as offering an opportunity for critique, adjustment, and correction of our course, by going back to these origins.

Some see the ancient Greek city as a point of origin for the political tradition of Western civilization, the site of the invention of democracy and of the discourse concerning politics that becomes political theory and political philosophy. Looking at the assumptions and practices of these beginnings offers insights into the development of the tradition. Just as Emile Benveniste locates the source of Aristotle's categories in the linguistic forms of ancient Greece and identifies their subterranean shaping of the subsequent history of philosophy, so the ancient city was the first paradigm for all later thinking about political life. Examination of this moment in the history of the West reveals structures, justifications, remedies that form the tradition, and features that may have been lost as empires rose and fell, sovereigns came and went, political forms evolved into unrecognizable entities. So the archaeology of political theory offers the possibility of the recuperation of lost truths, or lost possibilities, to those who see much needing change in the contemporary world. The investigation into the errors of the classical Greek past, moments at which radical possibilities were not pursued, where resistance was crushed out, suggests the hope that a return to these beginnings with different intentions could rescue us from what has become an increasingly unjust, stratified, imperialist world, one that has been led astray, its injustices amplified by the evolution of a mistaken original practice of governance.

Other motives for the return to the classics include an appropriation of the prestige of a once exclusive body of knowledge, the Greek that

Virginia Woolf complained she had not been taught, the Greek and Latin that was once the carefully guarded terrain of male scholars of prestigious universities. In the case of some European scholars, trained in the classical languages and in ancient history as a matter of course, before entering such disciplines as philology and philosophy, the terrain of the classics is familiar ground. Familiar to all readers, especially, who share that training and that set of references, so that questions of a more abstract nature can be explored with the confidence that all those to whom the text is addressed share a common vocabulary and set of examples, or that in the case of a historical argument, the readers of an argument can follow the allusions and register the specificity of the writer's references.

Some of the claims of these writers may seem absurd to those schooled in the discipline of classics; they may seem remote from the evidence valued by the scholarly tradition, to come from remote edges of the central debates of historical scholarship, to distort or misread or exploit the ancient sources. Yet one virtue they share is clarity about their interest in changing the present, a consciousness of the stakes in writing that is sometimes mystified or denied in what some historians claim are empiricist, positivist, unbiased historical practices. Much of the most exciting work in the field of historical studies in recent times has allowed for the view that all scholarly work is interested, has a perspective, that the very subjects we choose to study speak to the concerns we have about the present and future.

And thus another, further, question arises: For whom do we write? In all the discussions of these writers who use Greek and Roman antiquity for thinking about transformation, revolution, the future, how much do their assumptions limit their theories to so-called Western civilization? If they take for granted a common vocabulary, matrix, set of narratives, based in ancient Greek and Roman societies, and limit their rhetorical range to Europe—although the ancient Mediterranean world of classical and Hellenistic Greece included not just Europe, but also northern Africa, Southwest Asia, and Asia Minor, with connections that stretched far beyond these margins—then does this affect these theorists' ability to theorize in the context of globalization and world civilizations? Are there forms of naturalization of ancient assumptions, reifications of local institutions like democracy, vestiges, traces of ethnocentrism, conscious or not, that mark their visions of the future? And if so, does this limit their value? Does the division of social reality into *oikos* and *polis*, public and private, ground and found the work of Giorgio Agamben, for example, in ways that inhibit its translation into the world of the Confucian diaspora?

Yet if Judith Butler sees herself, or a model, some tragic yet fruitful example in Antigone, she is not alone in finding a rhetorical purchase in this figure from Greek antiquity. Rather than dissecting these theorists' work with an eye to philological or historical error, we can see them as other nodes in a great network of engagement with antiquity. Antigone has acquired a burden of meaning; she can be read only through the elaborate, rich, palimpsestic layerings of many commentaries that make her a powerful subject for contemporary resistance. Like other figures from classical antiquity, from Spartacus and Saint Paul to the *homo sacer* of ancient Roman law, ancient subjects, ancient institutions, narratives, historical texts, even the conservative and reactionary formulations of ancient political theory endure, persist, leap out and open up possibilities of deliberation and a shared matrix of great rhetorical power for these potentially revolutionary thinkers of our present and future. These are all classical studies.

NOTES

1. Prologue

1. See, for example, G. Nagy, "Patroklos, Concepts of Afterlife, and the Indic Triple Fire," in *Greek Mythology and Poetics* (Ithaca, N.Y.: Cornell University Press, 1990), 85–121, and this volume as a whole, on the relationship between Indo-European forms and Hellenization.

2. M. L. West, *The East Face of Helicon: West Asiatic Elements in Greek Poetry and Myth* (Oxford: Clarendon Press, 1997).

3. Walter Burkert, *Babylon Memphis Persepolis: Eastern Contexts of Greek Culture* (Cambridge, Mass.: Harvard University Press, 2005), 123–124.

4. See P. duBois, "The Tyranny of Germany over Greece," in *The Soul of Tragedy, Essays on Athenian Tragedy*, ed. V. Pedrick and S. Oberhelman (Chicago: University of Chicago Press, 2008), 291–306.

5. See, for example, Charles Segal's *Tragedy and Civilization: An Interpretation of Sophocles* (Cambridge, Mass.: Harvard University Press, 1981).

6. duBois, "The Tyranny of Germany over Greece," 291–306.

7. Charles Segal, "Classics, Ecumenicism, and Greek Tragedy," *Transactions of the American Philological Association* 125 (1995), 1–26; passage cited, 1.

8. For a valuable survey of the history of *Rezeptionsgeschichte* and its translation into Anglophone scholarship, see Lorna Hardwick, *Reception Studies, New Surveys in the Classics no. 33, Greece & Rome* (Oxford: Oxford University Press, 2003). Hardwick points out that reception studies reveal aspects of the receiving society but "also focus critical attention back towards the ancient source and sometimes frame new questions or retrieve aspects of the source which have been marginalized or forgotten" (4). See also Charles Martindale and Richard F. Thomas, *Classics and the Uses of Reception* (Oxford: Blackwell, 2006).

9. Miriam Leonard, *Athens in Paris: Ancient Greece and the Political in Post-War French Thought* (Oxford: Oxford University Press, 2005), 230.

10. Barbara Goff and Michael Simpson, *Crossroads in the Black Aegean: Oedipus, Antigone, and Dramas of the African Diaspora* (Oxford: Oxford University Press, 2007).

11. On *The Island,* see Rush Rehm, "'If You Are a Woman': Theatrical Womanizing in Sophocles' *Antigone* and Fugard, Kani, and Ntshona's *The Island,*" in *Classics in Post-Colonial Worlds,* ed. L. Hardwick and C. Gillespie (Oxford: Oxford University Press, 2007), 211–227; and Goff and Simpson, *Crossroads,* 271–320.

12. There are various strains in contemporary classical studies, including work focused on traditionally philological issues, and others that stress a new historical "cultural poetics," or psychoanalysis, or a cultural studies or even postcolonial studies. See, for example, Leslie Kurke, *Coins, Bodies, Games, and Gold: The Politics of Meaning in Archaic Greece* (Princeton, N.J.: Princeton University Press, 1999); Victoria Wohl, *Love Among the Ruins: The Erotics of Democracy in Classical Athens* (Princeton, N.J.: Princeton University Press, 2002); Hardwick and Gillespie, *Classics in Post-Colonial Worlds.*

13. Dipesh Chakrabarty, *Provincializing Europe: Postcolonial Thought and Historical Difference* (Princeton, N.J.: Princeton University Press, 2000).

14. Michael Hardt and Antonio Negri, *Multitude: War and Democracy in the Age of Empire* (New York: Penguin, 2004), 313.

15. See Homi Bhabha, *The Location of Culture* (London: Routledge, 1994), 5: "The very concepts of homogenous national culture, the consensual or contiguous transmission of historical traditions, or 'organic' ethnic communities—*as the grounds of cultural comparativism*—are in a profound process of redefinition."

16. Michael Isikoff and David Corn, *Hubris: The Inside Story of Spin, Scandal, and the Selling of the Iraq War* (New York: Crown Publishers, 2006).

17. See P. duBois, *Trojan Horses: Saving the Classics from Conservatives* (New York: NYU Press, 2001).

18. Lee Pearcy, *Grammar of Our Civility* (Waco, Tex.: Baylor University Press, 2005).

19. I use the *Longman Anthology of World Literature,* edited by David Damrosch (New York: Longman, 2008).

20. See Bruce Trigger, *Understanding Early Civilizations: A Comparative Study* (Cambridge: Cambridge University Press, 2007).

21. G. E. R. Lloyd, *The Ambitions of Curiosity: Understanding the World in Ancient Greece and China* (Cambridge: Cambridge University Press, 2002), 19. See also Geoffrey Lloyd, "Literacy in Greek and Chinese Science: Some Comparative Issues," in *Written Texts and the Rise of Literate Culture in Ancient Greece,* ed. Harvey Yunis (Cambridge: Cambridge University Press, 2003), 122–138. "The intense Chinese respect for the canonical texts of past wisdom did not preclude disagreement, but the sense of loyalty within the lineage was, in general, far greater than what obtained in Greek philosophical groups such as the Academy or medical groups such as the Herophilean school. (Perhaps the Epicureans were an exception.) Brought up in a culture of debate and probably owing more of their instruc-

tion to the oral mode, Greek pupils were not above challenging, and even refuting, their teachers in ways that cannot be paralleled in our Chinese evidence whether from the Warring States or from the Han periods" (138).

22. Sima Qian, *Records of the Grand Historian: Qin Dynasty,* trans. Burton Watson (Hong Kong and New York: Columbia University Press, 1993), 232–233.

23. François Jullien, *Detour and Access: Strategies of Meaning in China and Greece,* trans. S. Hawkes (New York: Zone Boos, 2000 [1995]). See also Lisa Raphals, *Knowing Words: Wisdom and Cunning in the Classical Traditions of China and Greece* (Ithaca, N.Y.: Cornell University Press, 1992).

24. Marcel Detienne, ed., *Tracés de fondation* (Louvain: Peeters, 1990).

25. Charles Malamoud, "Sans lieu ni date. Note sur l'absence de fondation dans l'Inde Védique," in *Tracés de fondation,* ed. Marcel Detienne (Louvain: Peeters, 1990), 183–191.

26. See, for example, the groundbreaking work by Carol Dougherty, *The Poetics of Colonization: From City to Text in Archaic Greece* (Oxford: Oxford University Press, 1993).

27. Jean-Pierre Vernant, with Jacques Gernet, "Social History and the Evolution of Ideas in China and Greece from the Sixth to the Second Centuries B.C.," in *Myth and Society in Ancient Greece,* trans. Janet Lloyd (New York: Zone Books, 1990 [1974]), 94.

28. Louis Gernet, *The Anthropology of Ancient Greece,* trans. J. Hamilton and B. Nagy (Baltimore: Johns Hopkins University Press, 1981 [1968]), viii.

29. For a philosophical meditation on "thinking the world," or *mondialisation,* see Jean-Luc Nancy, *The Creation of the World, or Globalization,* trans. F. Raffoul and D. Pettigrew (Albany: State University of New York Press, 2007 [2002]).

30. K. Ross, "The World Literature and Cultural Studies Program," *Critical Inquiry* 19 (1993), 666–676; passage quoted, 670.

31. Shigeshisa Kuriyama, *The Expressiveness of the Body and the Divergence of Greek and Chinese Medicine* (New York: Zone Books, 2002), 12.

32. See duBois, *Trojan Horses.*

33. Gilles Deleuze and Félix Guattari, *A Thousand Plateaus: Capitalism and Schizophrenia,* trans. B. Massumi (Minneapolis: University of Minnesota Press, 1987 [1980]), 21.

34. S. Nimis, "Fussnoten: Das Fundament der Wissenschaft," *Arethusa* 17 (1984), 105–134; passage cited 130. I discuss these matters more fully in "The Tyranny of Germany over Greece," in *The Soul of Tragedy: Essays on Athenian Drama,* ed. V. Pedrick and S. Oberhelman (Chicago: University of Chicago Press, 2005), 291–306.

35. See Nicole Loraux, *The Mourning Voice: An Essay on Greek Tragedy,* trans. E. T. Rawlings (Ithaca, N.Y.: Cornell University Press, 2002).

36. See, for example, Sean Gurd, "On Text-Critical Melancholy," *Representations* 88 (2004), 81–101: "While restoring a definitive original has always been textual criticism's defining problem or ideal, its objects of study are those partial and

imperfect solutions produced by previous editors" (85). See also S. Gurd, "Cicero and Editorial Revision," *Classical Antiquity* 26 (2007), 49–80; and Hans Ulrich Gumbrecht, *The Powers of Philology: Dynamics of Textual Scholarship* (Urbana and Chicago: University of Illinois Press, 2003), especially chapter 1, "Identifying Fragments," 9–23.

37. Greg Forter and Paul Allen Miller, eds., *Desire of the Analysts: Psychoanalysis and Cultural Criticism* (Albany: State University of New York Press, 2008), 9.

38. On these questions, see P. duBois, *Sowing the Body* (Chicago: University of Chicago Press, 1988).

39. Jean-Pierre Vernant, "Oedipus without the Complex," in Jean-Pierre Vernant and Pierre Vidal-Naquet, *Myth and Tragedy in Ancient Greece,* trans. J. Lloyd (New York: Zone Books, 1990 [1972]), 85–111. But see Nicole Loraux's critique of Vernant's project of "othering" the Greeks: Nicole Loraux, "*Back to the Greeks?* Chronique d'une expédition lointaine en terre commune," in *Une école pour les sciences sociales: De la VIième section à l'Ecole des Hautes Etudes en Sciences Sociales,* ed. Jacques Revel and Nathan Wachtel (Paris: Editions du CERF, 1996), 275–294.

40. Shoshana Felman, ed., *Literature and Psychoanalysis: The Question of Reading: Otherwise* (Baltimore: Johns Hopkins University Press, 1982).

41. Ellen Oliensis, "Freud's *Aeneid,*" *Vergilius* 47 (2001), 39–63; passage cited, 45. On psychoanalytic interpretation as a model for reading, see Francesco Orlando, *Toward a Freudian Theory of Literature,* trans. Charmaine Lee (Baltimore: Johns Hopkins University Press, 1978); Michael Riffaterre, "The Intertextual Unconscious," *Critical Inquiry* 13 (1987), 371–385; Jonathan Culler, "Textual Unconscious and the Literary Unconscious," *Style* 18 (1984), 369–376; Elizabeth Wright, *Psychoanalytic Criticism: A Reappraisal* (Cambridge: Polity Press, 1998); James Porter and M. Buchan, eds., *Before Subjectivity: Lacan and the Classics,* spec. issue of *Helios* 31 (2004).

42. On this question, see Thomas Habinek, *The World of Roman Song: From Ritualized Speech to Social Order* (Baltimore: Johns Hopkins Press, 2005), which brilliantly discusses ritual; "song," defined very capaciously; and questions of embodiment and cultural hierarchy in an immense variety of materials drawn from "what is customarily, if anachronistically, referred to as 'Latin literature' " (2).

43. On the phenomenology of hearing, and listening, especially to music, see Jean-Luc Nancy, *Listening,* trans. Charlotte Mandell (New York: Fordham University Press, 2007 [2002]).

44. See Jacques Derrida, *Resistances: De la psychanalyse* (Paris: Galilee, 1996). A reading, a listening attuned to resistances and counter-transferences, seems to me a more productive deployment of psychoanalysis in the present, in relation to classical antiquity, than projecting a modern psyche onto ancient persons, characters in texts, or social allegories.

45. James Clifford, responding cautiously to the utopian tone of some writing on cosmopolitanism, offers a sobering corrective that nonetheless points to a continuing

history of fluid objects of study: "People have, for many centuries, constructed their sense of belonging, their notions of home, of spiritual and bodily power and freedom, along a continuum of sociospatial attachments. These extend from local valleys and neighborhoods to denser urban sites of encounter and relative anonymity, from national communities tied to a territory to affiliations across borders and oceans. In these diverse contact zones, peoples sustain critical, non-absolutist strategies for survival and action in a world where space is always already invaded. These competences can be redeemed under a sign of hope as 'discrepant cosmopolitanisms.' But it is a chastened hope associated more with survival and the ability to articulate locally meaningful, relational futures than with transformation at a systemic level" (367).

Pheng Cheah points to the mixed possibilities in such tendencies: "Diaspora studies has become such a fashionable topic that in the past decade or so there has being growing support within the staid field of China studies for the suggestion that the study of Chinese culture ought to shift its focus from mainland China in favor of a broader, more cosmopolitan definition of 'Chineseness'" (121). Cheah also discusses the celebration of "chauvinistic Confucianism claimed by East Asian states as the animating ethos of the East Asian economic model" (120).

46. James Clifford, "Mixed Feelings," in *Cosmopolitics: Thinking and Feeling beyond the Nation,* ed. Pheng Cheah and Bruce Robbins (Minneapolis: University of Minnesota Press, 1998), 362–370; passage cited 363.

47. On the ahistorical use of psychoanalytic theory to interpret ancient psyches and ancient texts, see duBois, *Sowing the Body.*

48. See P. duBois, *Centaurs and Amazons* (Ann Arbor: University of Michigan Press, 1982). On the paradoxical intensification of identities in the contexts of dislocation and distance from the "homeland," see R. McElreath, R. Boyd, and P. Richerson, "Shared Norms and the Evolution of Ethnic Markers," *Current Anthropology* 44 (2003), 122–129.

49. See duBois, "The Tyranny of Germany over Greece," 291–306.

50. Thomas Scanlon in a personal communication.

2. Spartacus

1. Martin Winkler, ed., *Spartacus: Film and History* (Malden, Mass.: Blackwell, 2007); Brent Shaw, ed., *Spartacus and the Slave Wars: A Brief History with Documents* (Boston: Bedford / St. Martin's, 2001).

2. For an overview of the complex history of representations of Spartacus, see Lorna Hardwick, *Reception Studies, New Surveys in the Classics no. 33, Greece & Rome* (Oxford: Oxford University Press, 2003), 37–43.

3. See Arnaldo Momigliano, *The Development of Greek Biography* (Cambridge, Mass.: Harvard University Press, 1993).

4. Plutarch, *The Lives of the Noble Grecians and Romans—The Dryden Translation,* ed. and rev. Arthur Hugh Clough (New York: Modern Library, 2000).

5. See P. E. Easterling, "From Repertoire to Canon," in *The Cambridge Companion to Greek Tragedy*, ed. P. E. Easterling (Cambridge: Cambridge University Press, 1997), 211–227, with bibliography; Easterling notes that the fact that the story of Crassus' head "is most unlikely to be a true story only enhances its significance: it brings out yet again the sense in which drama and life are felt to interconnect" (221).

6. Shaw, *Spartacus*, 132

7. Shaw, *Spartacus*, 78.

8. Shaw, *Spartacus*, 113.

9. Homi Bhabha, "Of Mimicry and Man," in *The Location of Culture* (London and New York: Routledge, 1994), 85–92; passage cited, 86.

10. James Scott, *Domination and the Arts of Resistance: Hidden Transcripts* (New Haven, Conn.: Yale University Press, 1990).

11. Shaw, *Spartacus*, 84.

12. See Keith Bradley, *Slavery and Rebellion in the Roman World, 140 B.C.–70 B.C.* (Bloomington: Indiana University Press, 1989); on Spartacus, 83–101. He concludes, "It becomes impossible to view the Spartacan movement as being in any way dominated by abstract or ideological imperatives: freedom from slavery was the intent of the fugitives; the slavery system itself remained unaffected" (101).

13. Alain Badiou, *Logics of Worlds: Being and Event 2*, trans. Alberto Toscano (London and New York: Continuum, 2009 [2006]). See also Badiou, *Being and Event*, trans. Oliver Feltham (London and New York: Continuum, 2005).

14. Marx to Engels, London, February 27, 1861, Karl Marx–Friedrich Engels: *Werke* (Berlin, 1964), 30:160, cited in Brent Shaw, *Spartacus and the Slave Wars* (Boston: Bedford/St. Martin's, 2001), 14–15.

15. "The official notion that the 'Spartakus uprising' in January 1918 was caused or inspired by its leaders—Rosa Luxemburg, Liebknecht, Jogiches—is a myth." Hannah Arendt, "Rosa Luxemburg: 1871–1919," in *Men in Dark Times* (San Diego, Calif.: Harcourt Brace Jovanovich, 1968 [1955]), 33–56; passage cited, 46.

16. Helmut Trotnow, *Karl Liebknecht (1871–1919): A Political Biography* (Hamden, Conn.: Archon Books, 1984), 170.

17. W. Z. Rubinsohn, *Spartacus' Uprising and Soviet Historical Writing*, trans. J. G. Griffith (Oxford: Oxbow Books, 1987 [1983]), 1.

18. Yuri Grigorovich and V. V. Vanslov, *The Authorized Bolshoi Ballet Book of Spartacus* (Neptune City, N.J.: T. F. H. Publications, 1990), 21.

19. Grigorovich and Vanslov, *Authorized Bolshoi Ballet Book of Spartacus*, 23.

20. T. Wiedemann, *Slavery* (Oxford: Clarendon Press, 1987), 47.

21. Arthur Koestler, *The Gladiators*, trans. Edith Simon (New York: Macmillan, 1939), 295–296.

22. Maria Wyke, *Projecting the Past: Ancient Rome, Cinema and History* (New York and London: Routledge, 1997).

23. William Fitzgerald, "Oppositions, Anxieties, and Ambiguities in the Toga Movie," in *Imperial Projections: Ancient Rome in Modern Popular Culture*, ed.

Sandra R. Joshel, Margaret Malamud, and Donald T. McGuire Jr. (Baltimore: Johns Hopkins University Press), 23–49.

24. Martin Winkler, "The Holy Cause of Freedom: American Ideals in *Spartacus*," in Winkler, *Spartacus: Film and History,* 154–188; passage cited, 157–158.

25. Kirk Douglas, *The Ragman's Son* (New York: Simon and Schuster, 1988), 304. On the involvement of Dalton Trumbo, the blacklisted screenwriter, in the production of *Spartacus,* see Bruce Cook, *Dalton Trumbo* (New York: Charles Scribner's Sons, 1977), 270–278.

26. Vito Russo discusses the scene in *The Celluloid Closet: Homosexuality in the Movies* (New York: Harper and Row, 1981), 119–120.

27. *Le Devoir de Violence* (Paris, 1968); Yambo Ouologuem, *Bound to Violence,* trans. Ralph Manheim (London, 1968). The novel is discussed by Kwame Anthony Appiah in "Is the Post- in Postmodernism the Post- in Postcolonial?" *Critical Inquiry* 17 (Winter 1991), 336–357.

28. On this episode, William Bennett, and the homoeroticism of the Spartan army, see P. duBois, *Trojan Horses: Saving the Classics from Conservatives* (New York: New York University Press, 2001).

3. Sappho between Africa and Asia

1. M. L. West, *Indo-European Poetry and Myth* (Oxford: Oxford University Press, 2007). West compares the Rig Veda 1.81.5, "none like thee Indra, has ever been born nor ever will be," to Sappho fr. 56, "nor do I think that there will ever (again) be any girl of such musical skill born to the light of day" (104).

2. M. L. West, *The East Face of Helicon: West Asiatic Elements in Greek Poetry and Myth* (Oxford: Clarendon Press of Oxford University Press, 1997), 526–531.

3. W. K. Simpson, ed., *The Literature of Ancient Egypt: An Anthology of Stories, Instructions, and Poetry,* trans. W. K. Simpson, R. O. Faulkner, et al. (New Haven, Conn.: Yale University Press, 1972). On the relations between Egypt and the Greeks, see Phiroze Vasunia, *The Gift of the Nile: Hellenizing Egypt from Aeschylus to Alexander* (Berkeley: University of California Press, 2001).

4. Alexander Jones, ed., *Jerusalem Bible* (New York: Doubleday, 1966).

5. Fragment 105A, *If Not, Winter: Fragments of Sappho,* trans. Anne Carson (New York: Knopf, 2002).

6. Michel Foucault, "Different Spaces," in *Aesthetics, Method, and Epistemology,* ed. J. D. Faubion, trans. R. Hurley and others, *Essential Works of Foucault, 1954–1984* (New York: New Press, 1998), 175–185. The flying carpet, *le tapis volant,* is mentioned only in Foucault's own oral presentation of this text, in French, at http://www.foucault.info/documents/heteroTopia/foucault.heteroTopia.fr.html.

7. Louis Marin, *Utopics: Spatial Play,* trans. R. A. Vollrath (Atlantic Highlands, N.J.: Humanities Press, 1984 [1973]).

8. On Sappho in Longinus, see Neil Hertz, "A Reading of Longinus," in *The End of the Line: Essays on Psychoanalysis and the Sublime* (New York: Columbia University Press, 1985), 1–20; on Sappho, 4–8.

9. *If Not, Winter: Fragments of Sappho*, trans. Anne Carson (New York: Knopf, 2002).

10. *If Not, Winter*, fragment two. See also P. duBois, *Sappho Is Burning* (Chicago: University of Chicago Press, 1995).

11. Lennard Davis, *Enforcing Normalcy: Disability, Deafness, and the Body* (London: Verso, 1995), 126.

12. Kenneth Clark, *The Nude: A Study in Ideal Form* (Princeton, N.J.: Princeton University Press, 1956).

13. On empire and ruins, see the classic nineteenth-century text *The Ruins, or, Meditation on the Revolutions of Empires: and the Law of Nature* of Constantin François de Chasseboeuf de Volney.

14. Dominic Montserrat, "Unidentified Human Remains: Mummies and the Erotics of Biography," in Dominic Montserrat, ed., *Changing Bodies, Changing Meanings: Studies on the Human Body in Antiquity* (London: Routledge, 1998), 162–197; passage cited 163–164.

15. For an exemplary discussion of Sappho, see G. Nagy's "Phaethon, Sappho's Phaon, and the White Rock of Leukas: 'Reading' the Symbols of Greek Lyric," in *Greek Mythology and Poetics* (Ithaca, N.Y.: Cornell University Press, 2000), 223–262, in which Nagy foresees the emergence of this aging presence before the full fragment was discovered. On Eos as the mother of Phaethon, see 242ff.

16. *Times Literary Supplement* 5334 (June 24, 2005), 8.

17. R. B. Onians, *The Origins of European Thought about the Body, the Mind, the Soul, the World, Time, and Fate* (Cambridge: Cambridge University Press, 1988).

18. Gilles Deleuze and Félix Guattari, *Kafka: Toward a Minor Literature* (Minneapolis: University of Minnesota Press, 1986 [1975]), 13.

19. *Greek Lyric Poetry*, trans. M. L. West (Oxford: Oxford University Press, 1993).

20. See West, *Indo-European Poetry and Myth*, on the Spartan Aotis in Alkman's first Partheneion: "Here then is a dawn goddess celebrated on the occasion of what is presumably an annual festival" (226).

21. *The Homeric Hymns*, trans. A. Athanassakis (Baltimore: Johns Hopkins University Press, 1976).

22. For a discussion of questions of meter and the epithet used of Eos, see Nagy, *Greek Mythology and Poetics*, 246–249.

23. West, *Indo-European Poetry*, 225.

24. Nagy, "Phaethon," 250–251.

25. West, *Indo-European Poetry*, 221–222.

26. FGrH 4 F 140.

27. *The Collected Dialogues of Plato*, ed. E. Hamilton and H. Cairns (Princeton, N.J.: Princeton University Press, 1961), 259bc.

28. Jacques Derrida discusses these myths in "Plato's Pharmacy," *Dissemination,* trans. Barbara Johnson (Chicago: University of Chicago Press, 1981 [1972]), 61–171.

29. Jesper Svenbro, *Phrasikleia: An Anthropology of Reading in Ancient Greece,* trans. J. Lloyd (Ithaca, N.Y.: Cornell University Press, 1993), 46.

30. Sophocles, "Ajax," trans. J. Moore, in *The Complete Greek Tragedies,* ed. D. Grene and R. Lattimore, vol. 2 (Chicago: University of Chicago Press, 1992).

31. Onians, *Origins,* 401, 430.

32. Onians, *Origins,* 430 n. 2.

33. On the warrior Memnon, see François Lissarrague, *L'autre guerrier: Archers, peltastes, cavaliers dans l'imagerie attique* (Paris: La Découverte; Rome: Ecole française de Rome, 1990).

34. John Boardman, *The Archaeology of Nostalgia: How the Greeks Re-created Their Mythical Past* (London: Thames and Hudson, 2002), 122–123.

4. The Tattoos of Epimenides

1. P. duBois, *Sappho Is Burning* (Chicago: University of Chicago Press, 1995).

2. See Marcel Detienne, *The Masters of Truth in Archaic Greece,* trans. Janet Lloyd (New York: Zone Books, 1996 [1967]); on Epimenides, 123–134: "Between Epimendes [*sic*] of Crete and Parmenides of Elea, between the ecstatic magus and the philosopher of Being, the gap seems unbridgeable" (130). On the incantatory quality of Sappho's lyrics, see Charles Segal, "Eros and Incantation: Sappho and Oral Poetry," *Arethusa* 7 (1974), 139–160.

3. See the work of Peter Kingsley on magic and shamans in the ancient world: *Ancient Philosophy, Mystery and Magic* (New York: Oxford University Press, 1997).

4. Rosemarie Garland Thomson, ed., *Freakery: Cultural Spectacles of the Extraordinary Body* (New York: New York University Press, 1996), 5.

5. Leonard Cassuto, "'What an object he would have made of me!': Tattooing and the Racial Freak in Melville's *Typee,*" in Thomson, *Freakery,* 234–247; passage quoted, 244.

6. Michel Foucault, *Abnormal: Lectures at the College de France, 1974–1975,* ed. Valerio Marchetti and Antonella Salomoni, trans. Graham Burchell (New York: Picador, 2003 [1999]).

7. John J. Winkler, *The Constraints of Desire: The Anthropology of Sex and Gender in Ancient Greece* (New York and London: Routledge, 1990).

8. Plato uses the phrase *teras legeis kai thaumaston* (Hippias Major 283c).

9. Aristotle, *Minor Works,* trans. W. S. Hett (Cambridge, Mass.: Harvard University Press, 1936).

10. See Christopher Faraone, *Ancient Greek Love Magic* (Cambridge, Mass.: Harvard University Press, 1999); C. Faraone and D. Obbink, *Magika Hiera: Ancient Greek Magic and Religion* (New York: Oxford University Press, 1991).

11. Diogenes Laërtius, *Lives of Eminent Philosophers,* vol. 1, trans. R. D. Hicks (Cambridge, Mass.: Harvard University Press, 1925).

12. E. R. Dodds, *The Greeks and the Irrational* (Berkeley: University of California Press, 1966 [1951]), 142.

13. Marcel Detienne, *Les maîtres de verité dans la Grèce archaïque*, 2nd ed. (Paris: Francois Maspero, 1973 [1st ed., 1967]).

14. Herodotus, *The Histories*, trans. Robin Waterfield (Oxford: Oxford University Press, 1998), 1.31.

15. The Curetes were the divine male warrior youths of Crete associated with the birth of Zeus; they danced around his cave on Mount Ida, which may be the site of Epimenides' long sleep, and clashed their shields together to drown out the baby's crying or to distract his malevolent father, Kronos. Their armed dance was said to promote the fertility of flocks and fields. Bronze shields of the eighth to the sixth centuries B.C.E. were discovered in excavation of the Idaean cave, and it may be that initiation rites for Cretan boys were performed there in the time of Epimenides; the dancers were said to have acted out the birth and death of Zeus. The Corybantes also danced around the infant Zeus and also attended the child Dionysus and danced in the cult of Cybele.

16. Robert Parker, *Miasma: Purification and Pollution in Early Greek Religion* (Oxford: Clarendon Press, 1983), 211. See also Plutarch, *Life of Solon*, 12.8–12.9.

17. Robert Parker, *Athenian Religion: A History* (Oxford: Clarendon Press, 1996), 50.

18. Plutarch, *The Lives of the Noble Grecians and Romans*, trans. J. Dryden, rev. A. H. Clough (New York: Modern Library, no date), 103. All references to Plutarch's *Lives* refer to this edition unless otherwise noted.

19. Plato, *The Collected Dialogues*, ed. E. Hamilton and H. Cairns (Princeton, N.J.: Princeton University Press, 1961), Laws 642de.

20. Thomas McEvilley, *The Shape of Ancient Thought: Comparative Studies in Greek and Indian Philosophies* (New York: Allworth Press, 2002), xxxi. See especially his first chapter, 1–22.

21. Richard Martin, "The Seven Sages as Performers of Wisdom," in *Cultural Poetics in Archaic Greece: Cult, Performance, Politics,* ed. Carol Dougherty and Leslie Kurke (Cambridge: Cambridge University Press, 1993), 108–128. See also J. Mitchiner, *Traditions of the Seven Rsis* (Delhi: Motilal Banarsidass, 1982); E. Reiner, "The Etiological Myth of the 'Seven Sages,'" *Orientalia* 30 (1961), 1–11; A. Oikonomides, "The Lost Delphic Inscription with the Commandments of the Seven and P. Univ. Athen. 2782," *ZPE* 37 (1980), 179–183; A. Oikonomides, "Records of the 'Commandments of the Seven Wise Men' in the 3rd c. B.C.," *Classical Bulletin* 63 (1987), 67–76.

22. On Ai Khanum and Hellenism, see Grant Parker, "Creating Alexander's Legacy in India," in *Memory as History: The Legacy of Alexander in Asia,* ed. H. P. Ray and D. T. Potts (New Delhi: Aryan Books International, 2007), 112.

23. D. Fehling, *Die sieben Weisen und die fruhgriechische Chronologie: Eine traditionsgeschichtliche Studie* (Bern: P. Lang, 1985), 9–19.

24. Martin, "Seven Sages."

25. Martin says of Mitchiner that "he speculates (269) that the Indus Valley civilization acted as a conduit for a prehistoric notion of Seven Sages to enter Indic culture from Mesopotamia" ("The Seven Sages," 127, n. 47).

26. Jesper Svenbro, *Phrasikleia: An Anthropology of Reading in Ancient Greece,* trans. Janet Lloyd (Ithaca, N.Y.: Cornell University Press, 1993 [1988]).

27. Jane Kaplan, ed., *Written on the Body: The Tattoo in European and American History* (Princeton, N.J.: Princeton University Press, 2000).

28. Xenophon, *The Persian Expedition,* trans. Rex Warner (London: Penguin, 1972).

29. See P. duBois, *Slaves and Other Objects* (Chicago: University of Chicago Press, 2003), 106–109; C. P. Jones, "Stigma and Tattoo," in Kaplan, *Written on the Body,* 1–16, and "*Stigma:* Tattooing and Branding in Graeco-Roman Antiquity," *Journal of Roman Studies* 72 (1987), 139–155. Jones argues that human beings were tattooed, while branding was reserved for animals; he also discusses the stigmata of Paul on p. 10 of "Stigma and Tattoo," arguing that Paul's use of the term *stigmata* was metaphorical, referring to his own "bruises and welts," and that as a slave of Christ, "Paul may have been led to the metaphor by the practice of religious tattooing, of the sort found at the sanctuary of Atargatis in Syria."

30. Aristotle, *Generation of Animals,* trans. A. L. Peck (Cambridge, Mass.: Harvard University Press, 1953), 721b32.

5. Slaves in the Tragic City

1. Michel Foucault, "On the Genealogy of Ethics: An Overview of Work in Progress," *The Foucault Reader,* ed. Paul Rabinow (New York: Pantheon, 1984), 349–350: "Among the cultural inventions of mankind there is a treasury of devices, techniques, ideas, procedures, and so on, that cannot exactly be reactivated, but at least constitute, or help to constitute, a certain point of view which can be very useful as a tool for analyzing what's going on now—and to change it."

2. Barbara Goff and Michael Simpson, *Crossroads in the Black Aegean: Oedipus, Antigone, and Dramas of the African Diaspora* (Oxford: Oxford University Press, 2007).

3. On the criminal justice system in America as an inheritor of slavery, see Loïc Wacquant, "From Slavery to Mass Incarceration: Rethinking the 'Race Question' in the U.S.," *New Left Review* n.s. 13 (2002), 41–60.

4. On these questions, see Page duBois, *Trojan Horses: Saving the Classics from Conservatives* (New York: NYU Press, 2001).

5. Euripides, *The Bacchae,* trans. W. Arrowsmith, in *The Complete Greek Tragedies,* vol. 4, ed. D. Grene and R. Lattimore (Chicago: University of Chicago Press, 1992), 545.

6. Aeschylus, *Suppliant Women,* trans. Seth G. Benardete, in *The Complete Greek Tragedies,* ed. D. Grene and R. Lattimore, vol. 1 (Chicago: University of Chicago Press, 1992), 543–553.

7. See Nicole Loraux, "Herakles: The Super-Male and the Feminine," in Nicole Loraux, *The Experiences of Tiresias: The Feminine and the Greek Man,* trans. Paula Wissig (Princeton, N.J.: Princeton University Press, 1995), 116–139.

8. Friedrich Nietzsche, *The Birth of Tragedy from the Spirit of Music,* in *Basic Writings of Nietzsche,* trans. W. Kaufmann (New York: Modern Library, 2000 [1872]), 37. On this text, see James Porter, *The Invention of Dionysus: An Essay on the Birth of Tragedy* (Stanford, Calif.: Stanford University Press, 2000).

9. John Jones, *On Aristotle and Greek Tragedy* (New York: Oxford University Press, 1962), 11. Although this book has been superseded by later treatments of Aristotle, it has the great merit of attempting to historicize Aristotle's analysis, rather than considering it the final word on tragedy.

10. Perry Anderson, *Passages from Antiquity to Feudalism* (London: NLB, 1974), 44, and further: "The Macedonian royal state, precisely because it was morphologically much more primitive than the city-states of the South, was not subject to their impasse and so proved able to overleap their limits in the new epoch of their decline" (45).

11. Jean-Pierre Vernant, "Tensions and Ambiguities in Greek Tragedy," in J.-P. Vernant and Pierre Vidal-Naquet, *Myth and Tragedy in Ancient Greece,* trans. Janet Lloyd (New York: Zone, 1990), 29–48; passage cited, 29.

12. Jean-Pierre Vernant, "The Historical Moment of Tragedy in Greece," in Vernant and Vidal-Naquet, *Myth and Tragedy,* 23. See Miriam Leonard on Vernant's arguments and their influence on the Parisian understanding of the Greeks in postwar France. On the mutual implication of historical and tragic writings, see C. C. Chiasson, "Herodotus' Use of Attic Tragedy in the Lydian *Logos,*" *Classical Antiquity* 22 (2003), 5–35. P. E. Easterling argues that fourth-century tragedy merits attention and should not be ignored simply because none is extant; see "'The End of an Era?' Tragedy in the Early Fourth Century," in *Tragedy, Comedy, and the Polis: Papers from the Greek Drama Conference, Nottingham, 18–20 July 1990,* ed. A. H. Sommerstein, S. Halliwell, J. Henderson, and B. Zimmermann (Bari, Italy: Levante, 1993), 559–569.

13. See P. duBois, "Ancient Tragedy and the Metaphor of Katharsis," *theatre journal,* special issue on tragedy, ed. David Román, 54, no. 1 (2002), 19–24.

14. Edith Hall takes a more positive view of Aristotle's distance from Athens in "Is there a *Polis* in Aristotle's *Poetics?*" in *Tragedy and the Tragic: Greek Theatre and Beyond,* ed. M. S. Silk (Oxford: Clarendon, 1996), 304–305: "The *Poetics'* near-total displacement of the *polis* from tragedy seems to me to be an astonishingly original innovation, which adumbrates the incipient and future status of tragedy as an international art-form."

15. See Martha Nussbaum, *The Therapy of Desire: Theory and Practice in Hellenistic Ethics* (Princeton, N.J.: Princeton University Press, 1994).

16. Simon Goldhill, "The Audience of Athenian Tragedy," in *The Cambridge Companion to Greek Tragedy,* ed. P. E. Easterling (Cambridge: Cambridge University Press, 1997), 56; see also Simon Goldhill, "The Great Dionysia and Civic Ideology," in *Nothing to Do with Dionysos? Athenian Drama in its Social Context,* ed. J. J. Winkler and F. Zeitlin (Princeton, N.J.: Princeton University Press, 1990), 97–129.

17. Vernant, "Tensions and Ambiguities," 33.

18. Jones, *On Aristotle,* 13. See also the valuable collection of essays edited by Amelie Oksenberg Rorty, *Essays on Aristotle's Poetics* (Princeton, N.J.: Princeton University Press, 1992), which for the most part, excepting J.-P. Vernant's assembled remarks, treat the *Poetics* as an abstractly philosophical text and do not historicize Aristotle's relationship to the tragedy of the fifth century or the distance between fourth-century culture, soon to be Hellenistic, and the culture of the fifth-century democracy. See also the important work of Stephen Halliwell, *The Poetics of Aristotle: Translation and Commentary* (Chapel Hill: University of North Carolina Press, 1987), and *Aristotle's Poetics* (Chapel Hill: University of North Carolina Press, 1986).

19. Aristotle, *The Poetics,* trans. W. H. Fyfe, rev. ed. (London: Heinemann [Loeb], 1932), 1449b.

20. On tragic pleasure, see F. Decreus, "About Western Man and the 'Gap' That Is Constantly Threatening Him. Or How to Deal with the Tragic When Staging Greek Tragedies Today?" *Euphrosyne* n.s. 31 (2003), 61–82.

21. Michelle Gellrich, *Tragedy and Theory: The Problem of Conflict since Aristotle* (Princeton, N.J.: Princeton University Press, 1988), 46.

22. G. F. Hegel, *Phenomenology of Spirit,* trans. A. V. Miller (Oxford: Clarendon Press, 1977), 275.

23. G. F. Hegel, *Aesthetics,* trans. T. M. Knox (Oxford: Clarendon Press, 1975), 1160–1161. On Hegel's admiration for Sophocles' *Antigone,* see pages 1217–1218: "This sort of development is most complete when the individuals who are at variance appear each of them in their concrete existence as a totality, so that in themselves they are in the power of what they are fighting . . . For example, Antigone lives under the political authority of Creon . . . [T]he *Antigone* seems to me to be the most magnificent and satisfying work of art of this kind."

24. On Freud and the Greeks, see Jacques Le Rider, *Freud, de l'Acropole au Sinaï. Le retour à l'antique des Modernes viennois* (Paris: Presses Universitaires de France, 2002). Le Rider argues that Freud, in his interpretation of Oedipus Rex, conceived himself as an "anti-Nietzsche," unveiling the implicit and hidden Christian assumptions of Nietzsche (157).

25. Sigmund Freud, *The Interpretation of Dreams,* trans. J. Strachey (New York: Basic Books, 1965), 294.

26. For a critique of psychoanalytic interpretations of *Oedipus Rex,* see Jean-Pierre Vernant, "Oedipus without the Complex," in *Myth and Tragedy,* 85–111. See also E. R. Dodds, "On Misunderstanding the *Oedipus Rex,*" *Greece and Rome* 13 (1966), 37–49.

27. See also Theodor Adorno, *Problems of Moral Philosophy,* ed. T. Schroder, trans. R. Livingstone (Stanford, Calif.: Stanford University Press, 2000), 112: "At the very outset of the bourgeois age, a play was written in which the category of the bourgeois individual, the autonomous, independent individual, can be said to have appeared for the first time. I am thinking of Shakespeare's *Hamlet.*"

28. *The Seminar of Jacques Lacan, Book 7: Ethics of Psychoanalysis 1959–1960,* ed. Jacques-Alain Miller, trans. Dennis Porter (New York: Norton, 1992), 247. Later, he identifies Antigone as "the real hero" (258). Of the chorus he says only, "In my view, the Chorus are people who are moved . . . The emotional commentary is done for you" (252).

29. Judith Butler, *Antigone's Claim* (Stanford, Calif.: Stanford University Press).

30. Terry Eagleton, *Sweet Violence: The Idea of the Tragic* (Oxford: Blackwell, 2003), 288–289. The expulsion and destruction of the most high, the powerful, who abuse their power, fall from view, and the urging of sacrifice by the low, echo one somewhat masochistic tendency in Christianity.

31. Eagleton, *Sweet Violence,* 289

32. Gellrich, *Tragedy and Theory,* 10–11.

33. On the chorus, see John Gould, "Tragedy and Collective Experience," in *Tragedy and the Tragic: Greek Theatre and Beyond,* ed. M. S. Silk (Oxford: Clarendon Press, 1996), 217–243, and Simon Goldhill's response in the same volume, 244–256.

34. Euripides, *Hecuba,* trans. W. Arrowsmith, in *The Complete Greek Tragedies,* vol. 3 (Chicago: University of Chicago Press, 1992), 905–941. Martha Nussbaum, who discusses this play in *The Fragility of Goodness: Luck and Ethics in Greek Tragedy and Philosophy* (Cambridge: Cambridge University Press, 1986), typically does not consider the chorus. For a rich, illuminating reading of this tragedy as a whole, see Froma Zeitlin, "Euripides' *Hekabe* and the Somatics of Dionysiac Drama," *Ramus* 20 (1991), 53–94.

35. Aeschylus, *The Libation Bearers,* trans. R. Lattimore, in *The Complete Greek Tragedies,* vol. 1, ed. D. Grene and R. Lattimore (Chicago: University of Chicago Press, 1992).

36. Euripides, *The Phoenician Women,* trans. E. Wyckoff, in *The Complete Greek Tragedies,* vol. 4, ed. R. Lattimore and D. Grene (Chicago: University of Chicago Press, 1992), 203–205.

37. On slavery in ancient Greece, on slaves' ubiquity and invisibility, and on the impact of American slavery on classical studies in the United States, see Page duBois, *Slaves and Other Objects* (Chicago: University of Chicago Press, 2003).

38. Sophocles, *The Women of Trachis,* trans. M. Jameson, in *The Complete Greek Tragedies,* vol. 2, ed. R. Lattimore and D. Grene (Chicago: University of Chicago Press, 1992), 531–540.

39. Robert Goheen, *The Imagery of Sophocles' Antigone: A Study of Poetic Language and Structure* (Princeton, N.J.: Princeton University Press, 1951), 28.

40. Thucydides, *The Peloponnesian War,* trans. S. Lattimore (Indianapolis: Hackett, 1998), 5.32. Thucydides cites other such brutal acts of war: 1.114; 2.27; 5.3, 5.32, 5:116.

41. Xenophon, *A History of My Times,* trans. Rex Warner (London: Penguin, 1966), 2.2.3.

42. Nicole Loraux, *La voix endeuillée: Essai sur la tragédie grecque* (Paris: Gallimard, 1999): "I would like to engage myself in studying from now on what in Athenian tragedy, under the generic figure of mourning, resists the ascendancy, omnipresent in Athens, of the political" (my translation) (27).

43. Vernant, "Tensions and Ambiguities," 33–34.

44. Charles Segal, "Greek Tragedy: Writing, Truth, and the Representation of the Self," in *Interpreting Greek Tragedy: Myth, Poetry, Text* (Ithaca, N.Y.: Cornell University Press, 1986), 99–100.

45. See Bruno Snell, *The Discovery of the Mind,* trans. T. G. Rosenmeyer (Oxford: Oxford University Press, 1953); on democratic ideology, see Page duBois, *Centaurs and Amazons: Women and the Prehistory of the Great Chain of Being* (Ann Arbor: University of Michigan Press, 1982).

46. Pierre Vidal-Naquet, "The Place and Status of Foreigners in Greek Tragedy," in *Greek Tragedy and the Historian,* ed. C. Pelling (Oxford: Clarendon Press, 1997), 109–119.

47. Edith Hall, "The Sociology of Athenian Tragedy," in *The Cambridge Companion to Greek Tragedy,* ed. P. E. Easterling (Cambridge: Cambridge University Press, 1997), 95.

48. Mark Griffith, "Brilliant Dynasts: Power and Politics in the *Oresteia,*" *Classical Antiquity* 14 (1995), 62–129, and "The King and Eye: The Rule of the Father in Greek Tragedy," *Proceedings of the Cambridge Philological Society* 44 (1998), 20–84. For an argument against an ahistorical application of psychoanalytic theory to Greek antiquity, now increasingly fashionable, see Page duBois, *Sowing the Body: Psychoanalysis and Ancient Representations of Women* (Chicago: University of Chicago Press, 1988).

6. Alexandrias

1. Arrian 3:1, in *Alexander the Great: Selections from Arrian, Diodorus, Plutarch, and Quintus Curtius,* ed. James Romm, trans. Pamela Mensch and James Romm (Indianapolis: Hackett, 2005), 71–72. Plutarch tells another version of this story, in which birds devour the barley-meal used to mark out the boundaries of the

new city, and the seers convince him that rather than being a bad omen for the city, it presaged abundant resources that would feed "men of every nation" *(pantodapon anthropon)* (*Life of Alexander* 26.10) (J. R. Hamilton, *Plutarch, Alexander: A Commentary* (Oxford: Clarendon Press, 1969), 68.

2. P. M. Fraser, *Cities of Alexander the Great* (Oxford: Clarendon, 1996), 240–243; Fraser argues that much of the evidence concerning these foundations is fictional. He includes in an appendix an account of the pilgrimage of the Chinese Buddhist Hsuan-Tsang (629–644 C.E.), sometimes used as a source for the historical geography of these cities.

3. See Peter Parsons, "Identities in Diversity," *Images and Ideologies: Self-definition in the Hellenistic World,* ed. A. Bulloch, E. S. Gruen, A. A. Long, and Andrew Stewart (Berkeley and Los Angeles: University of California Press, 1993), 152–170.

4. Richard Armstrong, *A Compulsion for Antiquity: Freud and the Ancient World* (Ithaca, N.Y.: Cornell University Press, 2005), 107.

5. Dan Selden, "Alibis," *Classical Antiquity* 17 (1998), 290–412; passage quoted, 297–298.

6. Parsons, "Identities in Diversity," 169.

7. M. Rostovtzeff, *The Social and Economic History of the Hellenistic World,* vol. 2 (Oxford: Clarendon, 1941), 806.

8. Peter Green, *Alexander to Actium: The Historical Evolution of the Hellenistic Age* (Berkeley: University of California Press, 1990), 390.

9. On revolts, see Ricardo Martinez Lacy, *Rebeliones populares en la Grecia helenistica* (Mexico: Universidad Autonoma de Mexico, 1995).

10. Herodas, *The Mimes and Fragments,* ed. A. D. Knox, notes by Walter Headlam (London: Bristol Classical Press, 2001), 84; Headlam adds, "To conceal his barbarian origin he has adopted a distinguished Greek name" (85). Battarus' male ancestors in fact bore effeminate "flower-names," characteristically applied to courtesans (l.76, note p. 98).

11. See Gerhard Thür, *Beweisführung vor den Schwurgeritchtshöfen Athens: Die Proklesis zur Basanos* (Vienna: Verlag der Österreichische Akademie der Wissenschaften, 1977); P. duBois, *Torture and Truth* (New York and London: Routledge, 1990); M. Gagarin, "The Torture of Slaves in Athenian Law," *Classical Philology* 91, no. 1 (1996), 1–8; Gerhard Thür, "The Role of the Witness in Athenian Law," in *The Cambridge Companion to Ancient Greek Law,* ed. Michael Gagarin and David Cohen (Cambridge: Cambridge University Press, 2005), 146–169.

12. Theophrastus, *Characters,* Herodas, *Mimes, Sophron and Other Mime Fragments,* ed. and trans. J. Rusten and I. C. Cunningham (Cambridge, Mass.: Harvard University Press, 2002), 358–359.

13. Simon Goldhill, "The Naïve and Knowing Eye: Ecphrasis and the Culture of Viewing in the Hellenistic World," in *Art and Text in Ancient Greek Culture,* ed. S. Goldhill and Robin Osborne (Cambridge: Cambridge University Press, 1994),

197–223: "This discussion can be seen as the first step towards the necessary rewriting of the history of ecphrasis not merely as the history of a rhetorical topos but as *the history of the formations of a viewing subject*" (223). Goldhill discusses several Hellenistic epigrams: "In each poem what is dramatized is the moment of looking *as* interpreting, reading. Seeing meaning" (204). "My opening three epigrams . . . discuss the process of interpretation as it is performed" (205). They "represent not merely a work of art but also *the poet as seeing subject*. The self-conscious and self-reflexive dramatization of viewing—seeing oneself seeing—is a fundamental element of Hellenistic ecphrasis which is regularly ignored by the general heading 'description.' Hellenistic culture is where 'art history' as a discipline first develops" (205). "Thirdly, this dramatization of response is implicitly and explicitly value-laden and directive" (205–206). "The mass of epigrams—a major part of Hellenistic cultural activity—create and police the position of the Hellenistic viewing subject" (206). He adds, fourth and fifth, that these are poets' tombs, and that there is a connection between philosophy and literature in the Hellenistic period (206–210). He discusses the concept of phantasia and argues for "a shared educational and intellectual background between different writers: I am suggesting that these epigrams are to be appreciated as the products of *sophoi* in the context of contemporary *sophia*" (210). When discussing Theocritus' Idyll 15, he remarks on the women's use of "the privileged terms of Hellenistic evaluative discourse" (218), but admits the possibilities of irony: "There is . . . a direction in the poem towards the evaluation of the singer's song, but it is a direction framed by the poet's ironic distance from the speakers of the evaluation" (218). "This text dramatises the response of figures framed as *other*, different from the Hellenistic poet—an ironic strategy of distancing which turns back on the reader the requirement of evaluative response" (223).

14. On the text, see, in addition to Headlam, Herodas, *Mimiambi,* ed. I. C. Cunningham (Oxford: Clarendon Press, 1971).

15. See P. duBois, *History, Rhetorical Description, and the Epic* (Cambridge: Boydell and Brewer, 1982).

16. On the poem, see Richard Hunter, *Theocritus and the Archaeology of Greek Poetry* (Cambridge: Cambridge University Press, 1996), 110–138. He points out that the Idylls are "in touch" with the Syracusan tradition of mime, which we know through the fragments of Sophron, and also with "wider performance traditions of a 'popular' kind" (7–8). Theocritus' Idyll 4 was, according to a scholiast, modeled on Sophron's "The Women at the Isthmian Festival" (118). He notes, concerning the Doric poems, that they were, according to Ruijgh, "in fact composed in the language of an *émigré* Cyrenean elite living in Alexandria; this language was basically Cyrenean Doric, tempered by an admixture of forms influenced by the Attic *koine*" (37). C. J. Ruijgh, "Le Dorien de Théocrite: Dialecte cyrénéen d'Alexandrie et d'Egypte," *Mnemosyne* 37 (1984), 56–88.

17. Selden, "Alibis."

18. Joan B. Burton, *Theocritus' Urban Mimes: Mobility, Gender, and Patronage* (Berkeley and Los Angeles: University of California Press, 1995), 145.

19. A. A. Long, *Hellenistic Philosophy: Stoics, Epicureans, Sceptics,* 2nd ed. (Berkeley: University of California Press, 1986), 98. See also Thomas Gelzer, "Transformations," in *Images and Ideologies: Self-Definition in the Hellenistic World,* ed. A. Bulloch, E. S. Gruen, A. A. Long, and Andrew Stewart (Berkeley and Los Angeles: University of California Press, 1993), 130–151; on Hellenistic poets: "Their aesthetic curiosity and their judgments on matters of taste are directed not only to poetry but also to art (painting, sculpture, handcrafts), and their ekphraseis and epigrams show that they are familiar with the art theories of their time. A key word in their evaluation of the new poetry is *leptotes,* which means 'finesse' or 'connoisseurship' but also denotes something funny, something playful in rubbing shoulders with the Old Masters" (145).

20. In *Theocritus' Urban Mimes* (note 19), Joan Burton offers a more generous interpretation of Praxinoa's and Gorgo's reactions to the Adonia, connecting them with Theocritus' appeal to Arsinoë, sponsor of the festival: "Arsinoë's Adonia offered Theocritus a special, court-sponsored excuse to explore a public suspension of traditional patriarchal values: to look at how carnivals, even those connected with courts, can offer forums for inverting hierarchies (e.g., male over female), dissolving boundaries (e.g., insider over outsider), and deconstructing assumptions of power (e.g., the bystander's over the Syracusan women). But *Idyll* 15 also shows how festivals can enable a hegemony to reset social boundaries to encompass and contain what used to be marginal (women immigrants)" (147). Burton also points to the homoerotic dimension of the representation of Adonis, who is associated with Ganymede and the Erotes in the ekphrasis (86). Dan Selden (note 4) argues for a very different interpretation of Callimachus, one that emphasizes his humor: "The much misunderstood humor in Callimachus has less to do . . . with the subversive laughter of Mikhail Bakhtin than with what Baudelaire calls *le comique absolu,* the demystified ironic consciousness that knows itself to be inauthentic, but is not for that reason any more inartificial" (411).

21. W. J. T. Mitchell, Mitchell, "Ekphrasis and the Other," *South Atlantic Quarterly* 91 (1992), 695–719.

22. See Graham Shipley, *The Greek World after Alexander, 323–30 BC* (London and New York: Routledge, 2000), 188, and Michael Grant, *From Alexander to Cleopatra: The Hellenistic World* (New York: Scribner, 1982).

23. Peter Weiss, *The Aesthetics of Resistance,* vol. 1, trans. Joachim Neugroschel (Durham, N.C.: Duke University Press, 2005 [1975]), 3–4. The novel recounts the story of Aristonicus (41ff.).

24. Walter Benjamin, "Theses on the Philosophy of History," in *Illuminations,* trans. Harry Zohn, ed. Hannah Arendt (New York: Schocken Books, 1969), 256.

25. Shipley, *Greek World after Alexander,* 305; map, 306.

26. Robert E. Fisher, *Buddhist Art and Architecture* (London: Thames and Hudson, 1993), 46; on Gandharan architecture: "The blending of Western classi-

cal motifs with a number of regional elements created a distinctive style, well illustrated in the Gandharan stupa . . . Gandharan examples consisted of . . . classical pilasters with Corinthian capitals, topped with a strongly vertical tower of umbrellas. Excavated monasteries, such as Takht-i-bahi near Peshawar, reveal this mixture of styles that formed a regional architectural programme, one widely dispersed throughout the western Himalaya region and into Central Asia. Buddhist temples and Hindu shrines of the eighth to tenth centuries in Kashmir continued this formula, extending the life of Gandharan architectural styles on the subcontinent" (53–54).

27. On Buddhism in the present, see Richard S. Cohen, *Beyond Enlightenment: Buddhism, Religion, Modernity* (London and New York: Routledge, 2006).

28. Thomas McEvilley, *The Shape of Ancient Thought: Comparative Studies in Greek and Indian Philosophies* (New York: Allworth Press and the School of Visual Arts, 2002), 17: "Menander, the probable conqueror of Pataliputra, seems to have been a Buddhist, and his name belongs in the list of important royal patrons of Buddhism along with Asoka and Kanishka" (375).

29. "The Questions of King Menander: 'The Simile of the Chariot,' " in *Sources of the Indian Tradition,* 2nd ed., vol. 1, ed. and rev. Ainslie T. Embree (New York: Columbia University Press, 1988), 105–106.

30. T. McEvilley, *Shape of Ancient Thought,* discusses the status of the text, p. 376.

31. *Buddhist Scriptures,* trans. E. Conze (London: Penguin, 1959), 146.

32. See the translation of the Letter of Aristeas in J. H. Charlesworth, ed., *Old Testament Pseudepigrapha,* vol. 2 (Garden City, N.Y.: Doubleday, 1985).

33. Although Nagasena is traditionally considered to be Indian, McEvilley, *Shape of Ancient Thought,* argues that he may have been a Greek student of the Greek monk Dharmaraksita (378).

34. W. W. Tarn, *The Greeks in Bactria and India* (Cambridge: Cambridge University Press, 1951); see also George Woodcock, *The Greeks in India* (London: Faber and Faber, 1966).

35. A. A. Long and D. N. Sedley, *The Hellenistic Philosophers,* vol. 1, *Translations of the Principal Sources, with Philosophical Commentary* (Cambridge: Cambridge University Press, 1987), 172–173.

36. The "ship of Theseus paradox" persists into the present; see M. Rea, "The Problem of Material Constitution," *Philosophical Review* 104 (1995), 525–552.

37. On these questions, see further: Madeleine Hallade, *The Gandhara Style and the Evolution of Buddhist Art,* trans. D. Imber (New York: H. N. Abrams, 1968), and, by the same author, *Gandharan Art of North India and the Graeco-Buddhist Tradition in India, Persia, and Central Asia,* trans. D. Imber (New York: H.N. Abrams, 1968). See also the volume edited by Pia Brancaccio and Kurt Behrendt, *Gandharan Buddhism: Archaeology, Art, Texts* (Vancouver: University of British Columbia Press, 2006), especially John M. Rosenfield, "Some Debating Points on Gandharan Buddhism and Kusana History," 9–39.

7. Histories of the Impossible

1. This chapter was inspired by the memory of George Walsh, in admiration for his readings, attuned as they are to the unexpected that has become naturalized, domesticated, and familiar. I would like to thank Jonathan Hall, Shadi Bartsch, and the members of the George Walsh Memorial Lecture Committee at the University of Chicago for inviting me to deliver the memorial lecture, a version of which was published in *Classical Philology*.

2. M. I. Finley, "Utopianism Ancient and Modern," in *The Use and Abuse of History* (London: Chatto and Windus, 1975), 178–192; passage quoted, 188. See also Claude Mosse, "Les utopias égalitaires à l'époque hellénistique," *Revue historique* 241 (1969), 297–308.

3. See Peter Green, who, in *Alexander to Actium: The Historical Evolution of the Hellenistic Age* (Berkeley: University of California Press, 1990), dismisses the resistant impulses of the Hellenistic age as "fugal myths": "Only in dreams or fantasy do we find such principles as the abolition of slavery" (394). See also Daniel Ogden, ed., *The Hellenistic World: New Perspectives* (London: Duckworth, 2002).

4. Michel-Rolph Trouillot, *Silencing the Past: Power and the Production of History* (Boston: Beacon Press, 1995); passage quoted, 26.

5. See, for example, George Walsh, "Surprised by Self: Audible Thought in Hellenistic Poetry," *CP* 85 (1990), 1–21.

6. Walter Benjamin, "On the Concept of History," in *Selected Writings*, vol. 4, 1938–1940, trans. E. Jephcott and others, ed. H. Eiland and M. S. Jennings (Cambridge, Mass.: Belknap Press of Harvard University Press, 2003), 391.

7. See Fredric Jameson, *The Political Unconscious: Narrative as a Socially Symbolic Act* (Ithaca, N.Y.: Cornell University Press, 1981).

8. Louis Marin, *Utopics: The Semiological Play of Textual Spaces*, trans. R. A. Voollrath (Atlantic Highlands, N.J.: Humanities Press, 1984), 11.

9. Philip E. Slater, *The Glory of Hera: Greek Mythology and the Greek Family* (Boston: Beacon Press, 1968). This book was written long ago, but it still provides an example of a certain strain of psychoanalytic criticism of antiquity; Deleuze and Guattari's "schizoanalysis," in which whole swathes of European history are diagnosed with psychoanalytic disorders, shares attributes of this technique. But as Ellen Oliensis has said in her much more subtle and convincing use of psychoanalysis, "I do not seek to cure the Aeneid."

10. Strabo, *The Geography*, trans. H. L. Jones (Cambridge, Mass.: Harvard University Press [Loeb Classical Library], 1989).

11. Joseph Fontenrose, "The Crucified Daphidas," *TAPA* 91 (1960), 93–99, 99n41.

12. L. Robert, *Etudes anatoliennes: recherches sur les inscriptions grecques de l'Asie Mineure* (Amsterdam: A. M. Hakkert, 1970), 389, note.

13. See Ricardo Martinez Lacy, *Rebeliones populares en la Grecia helenistica* (Mexico City: Universidad Autonoma de Mexico, 1995).

14. Polybius, *The Rise of the Roman Empire,* trans. Ian Scott Kilvert, selected by F. W. Walbank (London: Penguin, 1979), 41.

15. Athenaeus, *The Deipnosophists,* trans. C. B. Gulick (Cambridge, Mass.: Harvard University Press [Loeb Classical Library], 1929).

16. #144 "Offer of Reward for Escaped Slaves" UPZ 1 121 (text and German translation in *C. Ptol. Sklav.* 81), in *The Hellenistic Period: Historical Sources in Translation,* 2nd ed., ed. R. S. Bagnall and Peter Derow (Oxford: Blackwell, 2004), 238.

17. See Lucian of Samosata, *De Dea Syria,* ed. Jane L. Lightfoot (Oxford: Oxford University Press, 2003).

18. Erica Reiner, "Runaway—Seize Him," in *Assyria and Beyond: Studies Presented to Mogens Trolle Larsen,* ed. J. G. Dercksen (Leuven: Peeters, Nederlands Instituut voor het Nabije Oosten, 2004), 475–482. I am indebted to the late Professor Reiner. See also P. duBois, *Slaves and Other Objects* (Chicago: University of Chicago Press, 2003), sections "The Tattooed Slave" and "The Tattooed Orator" (3–6).

19. Doyne Dawson, *Cities of the Gods: Communist Utopias in Greek Thought* (New York and Oxford: Oxford University Press, 1992): "The little-known revolt of Aristonicus included mass emancipation of slaves and expansion of citizen bodies. We are also told his followers were called *Heliopolitai,* 'citizens of the sun' (Strabo 14.1.38). All this has inspired speculation that Aristonicus' revolt, uniquely among Greek reform movements, tried to appeal to slaves and may have tried to put into practice the utopian communism of Iambulus' novel . . . Aristonicus' emancipation of slaves could have been a traditional war measure; his Heliopolis could have been a new city he meant to found for his freedmen, also in the tradition of Hellenistic monarchs, and the name may have signified nothing but the protection of the sun god. This is not to deny that there was an atmosphere of extreme radicalism about this movement" (254n32).

20. For a detailed discussion of these reports, see Esther V. Hansen, *The Attalids of Pergamum,* 2nd ed. (Ithaca, N.Y.: Cornell University Press, 1971).

21. Strabo, *The Geography,* trans. H. L. Jones, vol. 6 (Cambridge, Mass.: Harvard University Press, 1929).

22. See Hansen, *Attalids of Pergamum,* 15–18; on Aristonicus, 150–160.

23. For the lively debate on the import of the Aristonicus revolt, see G. Cardinali, "La morte di Attalo III e la rivolta d'Aristonico," *Saggi di Storia Antica e di Archeologia offerti a G. Beloch* (Rome: Loescher, 1910), 269–320; D. R. Dudley, "Blossius of Cumae," *Journal of Roman Studies* 31 (1941), 94–99: "For the slaves and poor of all the Orient the Sun-cult promised freedom and a better world: Aristonicus and Eunus were the messianic rulers whose task was to bring this world into being for their followers" (99); T. W. Africa, "Aristonicus, Blossius and the City of the Sun," *International Review of Social History* 6 (1961), 110–120; J. D. Dumont, "A propos d'Aristonicos," *Eirene* 5 (1966), 189–196, who argues for a similar pattern of freeing slaves under other rulers, as a tactic of war (194): further,

he argues: "This military deployment of the slaves of the adversary . . . who counts on the slave as the virtual enemy of his owner . . . expresses a fundamental opposition." (196); Franco Carrata Thomes, *La rivolta di Aristonico e le origini della provincia romana d'Asia* (Turin: G. Giappichelli, 1968); V. Vavrinek, *La révolte d'Aristonicos* (Prague: Rozpravy Ceskoslovenske Akademie Ved 1957), no. 2, and "Aristonicus of Pergamum: Pretender to the Throne or Leader of a Slave Revolt?" *Eirene* 13 (1975), 109–129. In *La révolte,* Vavrinek argues for "a struggle between slaves and slavers" (193).

24. Louis and Jeanne Robert, *Claros I: Décrets Hellénistiques,* fasc. 1 (Paris: Editions Recherche sur les Civilisations, 1989).

25. OGI 338 (D. Magie, *Roman Rule in Asia Minor* 2 [Princeton, N.J.: Princeton University Press, 1950–1951], 1040); Robert Sherk, ed. and trans., *Rome and the Greek East to the Death of Augustus* (Cambridge: Cambridge University Press, 1984), 40. See also #39, a stele from Pergamum (OGIS 338): "Decree of Pergamum on citizenship after the death of Attalus III, 133 BC, passed by the Pergamenes 'to stall further defection to his [Aristonicus'] cause' "; "the text continues . . . depriving certain others who had left the city or who may hereafter leave it of their civic rights."

26. The Roberts refer to other such nominations: "Pour le tour avec un génitif local, *epi poleos, epi Khou, epi Hromes*"; cf. L. R. [Louis Robert], *Revue des Etudes Anciennes* 1960, 328, n. 3.

27. *Diodorus of Sicily,* 12 vols., trans. C. H. Oldfather, Charles L. Sherman (Cambridge, Mass.: Harvard University Press [Loeb Classical Library], 1952–1954), 2.58.1.

28. Aristotle, *Politics,* trans. H. Rackham (Cambridge, Mass.: Harvard University Press [Loeb Classical Library], 1944). On the question of the state, see Ranajit Guha, *History at the Limit of World-History* (New York: Columbia University Press, 2002), 7–47.

29. Aristotle, *The Organon I: The Categories, On Interpretation,* trans. H. P. Cooke; *Prior Analytics,* trans. Hugh Tredennick (Cambridge, Mass.: Harvard University Press [Loeb Classical Library], 1938), 7a35–7b.

30. Dawson, *Cities of the Gods.* See also John Ferguson, *Utopias of the Classical World* (London: Thames and Hudson, 1975), especially "Blossius, Tiberius Gracchus and Aristonicus," 138–145.

31. Dawson, *Cities of the Gods,* 175.

32. Plutarch, "On the Fortune of Alexander," 329ab, cited in Dawson, *Cities of the Gods,* 170.

33. Dawson, *Cities of the Gods,* 178.

34. Emile Benveniste, "Cities and Communities," in *Indo-European Language and Society,* trans. E. Palmer (London: Faber and Faber, 1973), 295–304: "It follows that the connexion established in Latin between *civis* and *civitas* is the exact reverse of that shown in Greek between *polis* 'city' and *polites* 'citizen' " (299). See also Emile Benveniste, "Civilization: A Contribution to the History of the Word,"

in *Problems in General Linguistics,* trans. M. E. Meek (Coral Gables, Fla.: University of Miami Press, 1971), 289–296.

35. See W. W. Tarn, "Alexander the Great and the Unity of Mankind," *Proceedings of the British Academy* 19 (1933), 123–166, and *Alexander the Great* (Boston: Beacon, 1956 [1948]); passage cited, 147–148.

36. See, for a start, E. Badian, *The Deification of Alexander the Great: Protocol of the Twenty-First Colloquy, 7 March 1976* (Berkeley, Calif.: Center for Hermeneutical Studies in Hellenistic and Modern Culture, 1976); for a sober assessment, see Paul Cartledge, *Alexander the Great: The Hunt for a New Past* (Woodstock, N.Y.: Overlook Press, 2004).

37. Mikhail Rostovtzeff, *The Social and Economic History of the Hellenistic World,* vol. 2 (Oxford: Clarendon, 1941): "The failure of Aristonicus in his naval adventure and the hostility of the cities transformed a war of independence . . . into a war of the 'oppressed' against the oppressors, a war of the country against the city, of slaves and serfs against their masters" (807–808). On slave rebellions in the West, see Keith R. Bradley, *Slavery and Rebellion in the Roman World, 140 B.C.–70 B.C.* (Bloomington: Indiana University Press, 1998).

38. Trouillot, *Silencing,* 151.

39. Niall Ferguson, *Empire: The Rise and Demise of the British World Order and the Lessons for Global Power* (New York: Basic Books, 2003); see also Michael Hardt and Antonio Negri, *Empire* (Cambridge, Mass.: Harvard University Press, 2000). Hardt and Negri use the work of Polybius on the Roman Empire to frame their analysis of the current world order (314–316).

40. Fredric Jameson, "The Politics of Utopia," *New Left Review* 25 n.s. (2004), 35–54; passage cited, 37.

41. See Karl Raaflaub, *The Discovery of Freedom in Ancient Greece* (Chicago: University of Chicago Press, 2004 [1985]).

42. In *Provincializing Europe: Postcolonial Thought and Historical Difference* (Princeton, N.J.: Princeton University Press, 2000), Dipesh Chakrabarty says of his project: "Since 'Europe' cannot after all be provincialized within the institutional site of the university whose knowledge protocols will always take us back to the terrain where all contours follow that of my hyperreal Europe—the project of provincializing Europe must realize within itself its own impossibility" (45), although he disavows his former "politics of despair" (45–46).

8. Jesus and Other Jews

1. Daniel Boyarin, *Dying for God: Martyrdom and the Making of Christianity and Judaism* (Stanford, Calif.: Stanford University Press, 1999), 8.

2. See, for example, Virginia Burrus, *Saving Shame: Martyrs, Saints, and Other Abject Subjects* (Philadelphia: University of Pennsylvania Press, 2008).

3. *The New Oxford Annotated Bible: New Revised Standard Edition with the Apocrypha,* 3rd ed., ed. Michael D. Coogan (Oxford: Oxford University Press,

2007), 4 Maccabees 8.12–14. (All citations from the Hebrew Bible and the New Testament refer to this edition.)

4. See P. duBois, *Slaves and Other Objects* (Chicago: University of Chicago Press, 2003).

5. duBois, *Slaves and Other Objects*.

6. On the Maccabean rebellion, see Josephus, *The Jewish War*, trans. G. A. Williamson, rev. E. Mary Smallwood (London: Penguin, 1981): "Antiochus . . . tried to force the Jews to break their ancient Law by leaving their babies uncircumcised and sacrificing swine on the altar." Bacchides is sent to enforce these requirements and tortures the citizens. "Matthias, son of Asamonaeus, a priest from the village of Modein, raised a tiny force consisting of his five sons and himself, and killed Bacchides with cleavers" (33). For debates on the origins of redemptive martyrdom, see Jan Willem van Henten, *The Maccabean Martyrs as Saviours of the Jewish People: A Study of 2 and 4 Maccabees* (Leiden: E. J. Brill, 1997); and on recognition and reward after death, G. Bowersock, *Martyrdom and Rome* (Cambridge: Cambridge University Press, 1995).

7. Dayna Kalleres, "Imagining Martyrdom in Antioch during Theodosian Peace," in *Ancient Christian Martyrdom in Context*, ed. Anders Klostergaard Petersen and Jakob Engberg, vol. 5 of Early Christianity in the Context of Antiquity, ed. Jörg Ulrich, David Brakke, and Anders-Christian Jacobsen (Frankfurt: Peter Lang, forthcoming 2009).

8. Boyarin, *Dying for God*. Boyarin discusses the martyrdom of the Maccabees in a chapter entitled "Whose Martyrdom Is This, Anyway?" 93–126.

9. See Virginia Burrus, "Torture and Travail: Producing the Christian Martyr," in *Feminist Companion to Patristic Literature*, ed. A. J. Levine and M. M. Robbins (London: T&T Clark International, 2008), 56–71.

10. David Brion Davis, *The Problem of Slavery in Western Culture* (Ithaca, N.Y.: Cornell University Press, 1969), 64; Davis cites Exodus 2.23, 6.6, 13.3–4.

11. On Paul, see Daniel Boyarin, *A Radical Jew: Paul and the Politics of Identity* (Berkeley: University of California Press, 1994), with bibliography; see especially chapter 2, "What Was Wrong with Judaism: The Cultural Politics of Pauline Scholarship," 39–57, written, of course, before the attention paid to Paul by Badiou, Agamben, Žižek, and others.

12. Giorgio Agamben, *The Time That Remains: A Commentary on the Letter to the Romans*, trans. P. Dailey (Stanford, Calif.: Stanford University Press, 2005 [2000]), 12.

13. For a clear and persuasive historical account of this great shift, see Brent Shaw, "Body/Power/Identity: Passions of the Martyrs," *Journal of Early Christian Studies* 4 (1996), 269–312; he points to "a total inversion of the dominant male discourse on the body, the selective appropriation of its values, and the elevation of 'feminine' bodily powers as the primary modes of identification and resistance" (312); for recent theoretical work on Judaism and Christianity, see, for example,

Slavoj Žižek, *The Puppet and the Dwarf: The Perverse Core of Christianity* (Cambridge, Mass.: MIT Press, 2003); Slavoj Žižek, Eric L. Santner, and Kenneth Reinhard, *The Neighbor: Three Inquiries in Political Theology* (Chicago: University of Chicago Press, 2005).

14. On Apollonius of Tyana, see Glenn Most, *Doubting Thomas* (Cambridge, Mass.: Harvard University Press, 2005), 112–113: "The holy man Apollonius is being mourned by his followers Damis and Demetrius, who are unaware that he has been transported miraculously from the scene of his trial at the Emperor's palace to a temple of the nymphs at Dicaearchia" (112). Most cites this as an example of "transference," not in the psychoanalytic sense, but rather of "motifs" from the story of Thomas to that of Apollonius.

15. Morton Smith, *Jesus the Magician: Charlatan or Son of God?* (San Francisco: Harper and Row, 1978).

16. Walter Burkert, *Babylon Memphis Persepolis: Eastern Contexts of Greek Culture* (Cambridge, Mass.: Harvard University Press, 2004), 107–109.

17. Erich Auerbach, *Mimesis: The Representation of Reality in Western Literature,* trans. Willard R. Trask (Princeton, N.J.: Princeton University Press, 1968).

18. Dirk Obbink, "Dionysus Poured Out: Ancient and Modern Theories of Sacrifice and Cultural Formation," in *Masks of Dionysus,* ed. T. H. Carpenter and C. Faraone (Ithaca, N.Y.: Cornell University Press, 1993), 79.

19. Walter Burkert, *Greek Religion,* trans. J. Raffan (Cambridge, Mass.: Harvard University Press, 1985), 163.

20. But see Susan Guettel Cole, "Voices from beyond the Grave: Dionysus and the Dead," in *Masks of Dionysus,* ed. T. H. Carpenter and C. Faraone (Ithaca, N.Y.: Cornell University Press, 1993), 276–295. Cole concludes, "In the tomb inscriptions of the late Hellenistic and Roman imperial periods, Dionysus is not a savior who promises to his worshipers regeneration, but with the stories of his own rebirth and rejuvenation, he is one who makes this life more sweet and the next one, perhaps, only a little less harsh" (295).

21. Albert Henrichs, "Human and Divine in Dionysus," in *Masks of Dionysus,* ed. T. H. Carpenter and C. Faraone (Ithaca, N.Y.: Cornell University Press, 1993), 18. See also A. Henrichs, "Between Country and City: Cultic Dimensions of Dionysos in Athens and Attica," in *Cabinet of the Muses: Essays on Classical and Comparative Literature in Honor of Thomas G. Rosenmeyer,* ed. M. Griffith and D. Mastronarde (Atlanta, Ga.: Scholars Press, 1990), 257–277.

22. *The Bacchae,* trans. William Arrowsmith, in *The Complete Greek Tragedies,* vol. 4, ed. D. Grene and R. Lattimore (Chicago: University of Chicago Press, 1992), 552.

23. Smith, *Jesus the Magician,* 26, 92ff.

24. Michael Jameson, "The Asexuality of Dionysus," in *Masks of Dionysus,* ed. T. H. Carpenter and C. Faraone (Ithaca, N.Y.: Cornell University Press, 1993), 44–64.

25. Smith, *Jesus the Magician,* 33.

26. For conflicting conclusions on the authenticity of the "other," "secret" gospel of Mark, see Scott G. Brown, *Mark's Other Gospel: Rethinking Morton Smith's Controversial Discovery* (Waterloo, Ontario: Wilfrid Laurier University Press, 2005), and Peter Jeffery, *The Secret Gospel of Mark Unveiled: Imagined Rituals of Sex, Death and Madness in a Biblical Forgery* (New Haven, Conn.: Yale University Press, 2006).

27. Morton Smith, *Clement of Alexandria and a Secret Gospel of Mark* (Cambridge, Mass.: Harvard University Press, 1973), 447. On the wearing of linen in Bacchic rites, see Herodotus, *Histories,* 2.81.

28. On all these questions, see Theodore Jennings Jr., *The Man Jesus Loved* (Cleveland, Ohio: Pilgrim Press, 2003).

29. Carolyn Bynum, *Holy Feast and Holy Fast: The Religious Significance of Food to Medieval Women* (Berkeley: University of California Press, 1988). Bynum has several images suggestive of Dionysus transformed: plate 5 shows Christ in the wine press, his blood pouring out as wine; plate 4 a grapevine growing from Christ's left foot; plates 26 and 27 show blood from the wound in Christ's side spurting into the eucharistic chalice.

30. On the dangers associated with improper ingestion of the body of Jesus, see Dale B. Martin, *The Corinthian Body* (New Haven, Conn.: Yale University Press, 1995), 190–197.

31. Thomas F. Mathews, *The Clash of Gods: A Reinterpretation of Early Christian Art,* rev. ed. (Princeton, N.J.: Princeton University Press, 1999), 16.

32. For more detail, see P. duBois, *Sowing the Body: Psychoanalysis and Ancient Representations of Women* (Chicago: University of Chicago Press, 1988), especially "The Platonic Appropriation of Reproduction," 169–183.

33. For a fascinating reorientation of the seminal work of Auerbach, see James Porter, "Erich Auerbach and the Judaizing of Philology," *Critical Inquiry* 35 (2008), 115–147.

34. As the merest tip of the iceberg, see Elizabeth Clark, *Women in the Early Church* (Wilmington, Del.: Michael Glazier, 1983); Virginia Burrus, *The Making of a Heretic: Gender, Authority, and the Priscillianist Controversy* (Berkeley: University of California Press, 1995); Kate Cooper, *The Virgin and the Bride* (Cambridge, Mass.: Harvard University Press, 1996); Brent Shaw, "Body/Power/Identity: Passions of the Martyrs," *Journal of Early Christian Studies* 4 (1996), 269–312; *New Testament Masculinities,* ed. Stephen Moore and Janice Capel Anderson (Atlanta, Ga.: Society of Biblical Literature, 2003); Peter Brown, *The Body and Society: Men, Women, and Sexual Renunciation in Early Christianity* (New York: Columbia University Press, 1988).

35. This section of the chapter draws from a paper delivered at a panel on rhetoric at the Society of Biblical Literature in 2007.

36. Kathryn Gutzwiller, *The New Posidippus: A Hellenistic Poetry Book* (Oxford: Oxford University Press, 2008), #134 [GPAsclep. 37, AP 12. 17].

37. Lynn Huber, *"Like a Bride Adorned": Reading Metaphor in John's Apocalypse* (New York: T&T Clark International, 2008).
38. See D. Halperin, *One Hundred Years of Homosexuality* (New York and London: Routledge, 1989).
39. Michel Foucault, *The History of Sexuality,* vol. 3, *The Care of the Self,* trans. R. Hurley (New York: Vintage, 1988).
40. Suetonius, *Lives of the Caesars,* 2 vols., trans. J. C. Rolf (Cambridge, Mass.: Harvard University Press [Loeb Classical Library]), 1951).

9. The Persistence of Oedipus

1. Alain Robbe-Grillet, *The Erasers,* trans. Richard Howard (New York: Grove Press, 1964), 200 (*Les Gommes* [Paris: Editions de Minuit, 1953], 208). An earlier version of this chapter appeared in "Crime Fictions," *Yale French Studies* 108 (2005), edited by Andrea Goulet and Susanna Lee, 102–115; I thank Susanna Lee for editorial advice.
2. P. duBois, *Sowing the Body: Psychoanalysis and Ancient Representations of Women* (Chicago: University of Chicago Press, 1988).
3. Richard H. Armstrong, *A Compulsion for Antiquity: Freud and the Ancient World* (Ithaca, N.Y.: Cornell University Press, 2005), 96.
4. On the centrality of Sophocles, and even Oedipus, to discussion of "the tragic" in eighteenth- and nineteenth-century German philosophy, see Philippe Lacoue-Labarthe, "Oedipus as Figure," *Radical Philosophy* 118 (2003), 7–17.
5. Miriam Leonard, *Athens in Paris: Ancient Greece and the Political in Post-War French Thought* (Oxford: Oxford University Press, 2005).
6. See Peter Rudnytsky, *Freud and Oedipus* (New York: Columbia University Press, 1987).
7. Leonard, *Athens,* 220.
8. Jacques Lacan, *The Ego in Freud's Theory and in the Technique of Psychoanalysis* (New York: Norton, 1988).
9. Slavoj Žižek, "Two Ways to Avoid the Real of Desire," in *Looking Awry: An Introduction to Jacques Lacan through Popular Culture* (Cambridge, Mass.: MIT Press, 1991), 48–66.
10. Geraldine Pederson-Krag, "Detective Stories and the Primal Scene," reprinted in *The Poetics of Murder,* ed. Glenn W. Most and William W. Stowe (San Diego, Calif.: Harcourt Brace Jovanovich, 1988 [1949]), 14–20. See also Peter Brooks, *Reading for the Plot* (New York: Vintage, 1985); Shoshana Felman, "Beyond Oedipus: The Specimen Story of Psychoanalysis," in *Lacan and Narration: The Psychoanalytic Difference in Narrative Theory,* ed. R. C. Davis (Baltimore: Johns Hopkins University Press, 1983), 1021–1053; Cynthia Chase, "Oedipal Textuality: Reading Freud's Reading of *Oedipus,*" in *Decomposing Figures: Rhetorical Readings in the Romantic Tradition* (Baltimore: Johns Hopkins University Press, 1986), 175–195.

11. Geoffrey Hartman, "Literature High and Low: The Case of the Mystery Story," in *The Poetics of Murder,* ed. Glenn W. Most and William W. Stowe (San Diego, Calif.: Harcourt Brace Jovanovich, 1988), 210–229; passage cited, 228.

12. Glenn Most, "The Hippocratic Smile: John Le Carré and the Tradition of the Detective Novel," in Most and Stowe, *Poetics of Murder,* 341–365; passage cited, 348.

13. Claude Lévi-Strauss, "The Structural Study of Myth," in *Structural Anthropology,* trans. C. Jacobsen and B. Schoepf (New York: Doubleday/Anchor, 1967), 206–233.

14. Claude Lévi-Strauss, *The Jealous Potter,* trans. Benedicte Chorier (Chicago: University of Chicago Press, 1988).

15. Graham Law discusses the dichotomy between popular and serious fiction in an important article, "Il s'agissait peut-être d'un roman policier: Leblanc, Macdonald, and Robbe-Grillet," *Comparative Literature* 40 (1988), 335–357. He argues that critics must attend to narrative complexity and formal issues when assessing the engagement of late modernist and postmodern fiction with popular narrative forms. See also Alain-Michel Boyer, "Du double à la doublure: l'image du détective dans les premiers romans de Robbe-Grillet," *L'Esprit Créateur* 26 (1986), 60–70. On the detective novel, see Tzvetan Todorov, "Typologie du roman policier," in *Poétique de la prose* (Paris: Seuil, 1971), 55–65. Todorov points to the two stories possible here, the drama in which the criminal is the hero, and the inquiry in which the hero is the detective.

16. Bruce Morrissette, *Les Romans de Robbe-Grillet* (Paris: Editions de Minuit, 1963), especially "Oedipe ou le cercle fermé: *Les Gommes,* 1953," 37–75. See also "Games and Game Structure in Robbe-Grillet," *Yale French Studies* 41 (1968), 159–167. In *The Nouveau Roman and the Poetics of Fiction* (Cambridge: Cambridge University Press, 1980), Ann Jefferson argues that "the highly teleological construction of the Greek tragedy is used by Robbe-Grillet's novel to draw attention to the fact that what lies at the centre is always an artifice, an invention" (23). See also Olga Bernal, *Alain Robbe-Grillet: Le roman de l'absence* (Paris: Gallimard, 1964), who sees the references to Oedipus as an ostentatious trap into which the reader must be careful not to fall; and K. Smith, "The Flaw in the Case against Tragedy—A Re-evaluation of Robbe-Grillet's Views on Tragic Experience," *Aumla, Journal of the Australasian Universities Language and Literature Association* 85 (1996), 83–91: "Intermittent shadows cast by the ancient myth help dramatise the insecurities generated by the absence of intelligibility that is one of the grounds of modern tragedy" (84).

17. Robbe-Grillet, *The Erasers,* 125.

18. Corinthe recurs in Robbe-Grillet's texts: For example, Henri de Corinthe is named as a friend of the author's father in his autobiographical writings.

19. Kristin Ross, *Fast Cars, Clean Bodies: Decolonization and the Reordering of French Culture* (Cambridge, Mass.: MIT Press, 1995), 75.

20. Sigmund Freud, *The Interpretation of Dreams,* trans. James Strachey (New York: Basic Books, 1965), 296.

21. Jean Bellemin-Noel, "Une écriture freudienne?" *Critique* 651–652 (2001), 619–629; passage cited, 619.

22. See Page duBois, "Toppling the Hero: Polyphony in the Tragic City," *New Literary History,* forthcoming; and "Ancient Tragedy and the Metaphor of Katharsis," *Theatre Journal* 54 (2002), 19–24.

23. Robbe-Grillet, *The Erasers,* 244.

24. See Pierre Assouline, *Simenon: A Biography,* trans. Jon Rothschild (New York: Knopf, 1997). Assouline recounts Simenon's writing of seventeen anti-Semitic articles for the *Gazette de Liege,* "Lé peril juif," cribbed from the Protocols of the Elders of Zion; Simenon later recalled having been "assigned" to write "two or three" (28). During the occupation, in charge of Belgian refugees, Simenon complained, "They were almost exclusively stateless Israelites" (176). Simenon, who lived in a chateau in the Vendée during the first years of the Occupation, was later himself accused of being Jewish, "Simon alias Simenon," and had to provide documents proving his Aryan purity (202–204).

25. Georges Simenon, *Maigret and the Man on the Bench,* trans. E. Ellenbogen (San Diego, Calif.: Harcourt Brace, 1975), 4–5 (*Maigret et l'homme du banc* [Paris: Presses de la cité, 1953]).

26. The journal *Critique* devoted a special issue to Robbe-Grillet to mark the novel's publication: *Critique* 651–652 (August–September 2001) includes essays by Tom Bishop, "Topologie d'une reprise ou le retour de Robbe-Grillet," 595–604 ("Far from concealing his game, Robbe-Grillet joyously underlines the Oedipal aspect of *La Reprise.*" [599]); Guy Scarpetta, "Représentation de la perversion et perversion de la représentation," 630–639; and on the Grail legend in Robbe-Grillet's work, Torfi H. Tulinius, "Le premier romancier et le dernier," 640–651.

27. Alain Robbe-Grillet, *Repetition,* trans. Richard Howard (New York: Grove Press, 2003), 78 (*La Reprise* [Paris: Minuit, 2001], 111). On the novel, see the volume of *Critique* noted above, and J. Waters, "The Author Is Dead, Long Live the Author: Authorship and Mortality in the Last Works of Duras and Robbe-Grillet," *Nottingham French Studies* 41 (2002), 98–105.

10. Twenty-first-Century High Theory and the Classics

1. I discovered Paul Allen Miller's *Postmodern Spiritual Practices: The Construction of the Subject and the Reception of Plato in Lacan, Derrida, and Foucault* (Columbus: Ohio State University Press, 2007) after I finished this chapter. Miller's book addresses similar but not identical issues and restricts his analysis to Plato, but it emphasizes, as I do here, the importance of ancient texts to poststructuralists.

2. See Ronald Weed, *Aristotle on Stasis: A Moral Psychology of Political Conflict* (Berlin: Logos Verlag, 2007).

3. J. Ober, *Athenian Legacies: Essays on the Politics of Going On Together* (Princeton, N.J.: Princeton University Press, 2005), 4. See also Arlene Saxonhouse, *Fear of Diversity: The Birth of Political Science in Ancient Greek Thought* (Chicago: University of Chicago Press, 1992).

4. Eric Havelock, *The Liberal Temper in Greek Politics* (New Haven, Conn.: Yale University Press, 1964), 376.

5. Miriam Leonard, *Athens in Paris: Ancient Greece and the Political in Post-War French Thought* (Oxford: Oxford University Press, 2005).

6. Judith Butler, *Antigone's Claim: Kinship between Life and Death* (New York: Columbia University Press, 2000).

7. On the history of readings of *Antigone,* see Leonard, *Athens in Paris,* 96–157.

8. Juliet Mitchell, *Psychoanalysis and Feminism* (New York: Pantheon, 1974).

9. Luce Irigaray, "The Eternal Irony of the Community," in *Speculum of the Other Woman,* trans. Gillian Gill (Ithaca, N.Y.: Cornell University Press, 1985); "The Universal as Mediation" and "The Female Gender," in *Sexes and Genealogies,* trans. G. Gill (New York: Columbia University Press, 1993); "An Ethics of Sexual Difference," in *An Ethics of Sexual Difference,* trans. Carolyn Burke and G. Gill (London: Athlone Press, 1993); and Jacques Lacan, *The Seminar of Jacques Lacan, Book VII: The Ethics of Psychoanalysis, 1959–60,* ed. J.-A. Miller, trans. Dennis Porter (New York: Norton, 1992), 243–290.

10. Butler, *Antigone's Claim,* 5.

11. Martin Heidegger, *Introduction to Metaphysics,* trans. G. Fried and R. Polt (New Haven, Conn.: Yale University Press, 2000), 156.

12. Thomas Elsaesser, "Antigone Agonistes: Urban Guerrilla or Guerilla Urbanism? The Red Army Faction, *Germany in Autumn* and *Death Game,*" in *Giving Ground: The Politics of Propinquity,* ed. J. Copjec and M. Sorkin (London: Verso, 1999), 267–302.

13. See Bonnie Honig's forthcoming book on mourning and Antigone.

14. Sophocles, *Antigone,* ed. Mark Griffith (Cambridge: Cambridge University Press, 1999).

15. On Thebes, see Froma Zeitlin, "Thebes: Theater of Self and Society," in *Nothing to Do with Dionysos? Athenian Drama in Its Social Context,* ed. J. J. Winkler and F. Zeitlin (Princeton, N.J.: Princeton University Press, 1990), 130–167.

16. Sophocles, *Antigone,* trans. D. Grene, in *The Complete Greek Tragedies,* vol. 2, ed. D. Grene and R. Lattimore (Chicago: University of Chicago Press, 1992), lines 760–779.

17. These lines are glossed by Heidegger in *Introduction to Metaphysics,* a lecture course given in 1935 but published later; he provides a second interpretation of Antigone in a 1942 lecture course, "Hölderlin's Hymn 'The Ister.'" *Introduction to Metaphysics,* trans. G. Fried and R. Polt (New Haven, Conn.: Yale University Press, 2000); *Hölderlin's Hymn to the Ister,* trans. W. McNeill and Julia Davis (Bloomington: Indiana University Press, 1996).

18. Jacques Rancière, *Disagreement: Politics and Philosophy*, trans. Julie Rose (Minneapolis: University of Minnesota Press, 1999 [1995]).

19. On Rancière's historical method, see Hayden White in his foreword to Rancière's *The Names of History: On the Poetics of Knowledge,* trans. Hassan Melehy (Minneapolis: University of Minnesota, 1994 [1992]), viii–ix.

20. Rancière, *Disagreement,* 7.

21. Among philosophers, there has recently been a flurry of interest in the figure of Paul; see Slavoj Žižek, *The Puppet and the Dwarf: The Perverse Core of Christianity* (Cambridge, Mass.: MIT Press, 2003), and Giorgio Agamben, *The Time That Remains: A Commentary on the Letter to the Romans,* trans. Patricia Daley (Stanford, Calif.: Stanford University Press, 2005 [2000]), as well as Badiou's work discussed here.

22. See Mary Beard, *The Roman Triumph* (Cambridge, Mass.: Harvard University Press, 2007), 43–45, figure 9.

23. Alain Badiou, *Saint Paul: The Foundation of Universalism,* trans. Ray Brassier (Stanford, Calif.: Stanford University Press, 2003 [1997]), 1.

24. Giorgio Agamben, *Homo Sacer: Sovereign Power and Bare Life,* trans. Daniel Heller-Roazen (Stanford, Calif.: Stanford University Press, 1998 [1995]).

25. Michael Hardt and Antonio Negri, *Empire* (Cambridge, Mass.: Harvard University Press, 2000). For some of the critical responses to this volume, see Paul A. Passavant and Jodi Dean, eds., *Empire's New Clothes: Reading Hardt and Negri* (New York and London: Routledge, 2004).

26. See the later book by Hardt and Negri, *Multitude: War and Democracy in the Age of Empire* (New York: Penguin, 2004); see also Negri and Hardt, *The Labor of Dionysus: A Critique of the State Form* (Minneapolis: University of Minnesota Press, 1994).

INDEX

Adonis, 100–101
Aeschylus, 75, 76, 84–85
Aesthetics of Resistance, 105–107
Africa, 3–4, 26, 37, 38, 93, 101–102
Agamben, Giorgio, 26, 135, 174, 190–192, 196, 199
Ai Khanum, 65–66, 108
Alexander, 77, 91, 92, 126
Alexandria, 7, 26, 91–113, 118; foundation, 91
Algeria, 165
Althusser, L., 128, 182
Amazons, 55
Anderson, P., 76
Antigone, 24, 80–81, 85–86, 158, 171, 175–182, 186, 199
Aphrodite, 5, 101
Apollonius of Tyana, 136, 137–138
Archilochus, 50
Arendt, Hannah, 192
Aristonicus, 32, 114–129
Aristophanes, 97, 132
Aristotle, 46, 54, 60, 69–70, 76–80, 122–123, 129, 144, 174, 182, 184, 190, 195, 196, 197
Armstrong, R., 92, 158
Artemis, 187
Asoka, 110
Athenaeus, 93, 117–118
Athens, 23, 42, 62–65, 72, 76–77, 85, 86, 111, 112, 125, 130, 132, 152–153, 181, 185, 190, 192

Auerbach, Erich, 138–139, 150
Augustine, 193, 196

Bactria, 108, 109, 110, 111
Badiou, Alain, 26, 174, 196; on Spartacus, 31–33; on Paul, 186–190, 191, 194
Beard, Mary, 2
Becoming-animal, 49–50
Bellerophon, 101
Benjamin, Walter, 107, 115
Benveniste, Emile, 125, 197
Berlin, 106, 171
Bhabha, H., 29, 130
Bhagavad-Gita, 10
Bible, Hebrew, 9, 10, 41, 134–135, 144, 145, 151; 4 Maccabees, 133–134
Bible, New Testament, 131, 135–136, 143; Revelation, 151–155
Boyarin, Daniel, 130–131
Bradley, K., 30
Buddhism, 26, 42, 108
Buddhist art, 109–110
Burkert, W., 2, 137–138, 141, 142
Butler, Judith, 9, 21, 26, 58, 81, 174, 186, 190, 191, 196; *Antigone's Claim,* 175–182, 199

Caracalla, 138
Carcopino, J., 193
Cassuto, L., 58

Castration, 11, 119, 145
Catharsis, 77–78
Chakrabarty, Dipesh, 5–7
Chandler, Raymond, 165, 166
China, 10–13, 14–15, 16, 17, 33, 65, 109–110
Cicadas, 49, 53, 55
Circumcision, 134, 135, 145
Classics, 1, 9–10, 16, 18, 19, 21, 25, 27, 56, 130–131, 174, 186, 198, 199
Clement of Alexandria, 146
Clifford, J., 23
Colette, 48
Comedy, 96–97
Confucius, 10
Contamination, 23–24
Crassus, 27–31, 37
Cynics, 124, 149

Daphitas, 116
Davis, David Brion, 134
Davis, Lennard, 45–47
Dawson, Doyne, 123–125
Deleuze, Gilles, and Félix Guattari, 4, 19–21, 195–196
Delphi, 157, 162,163
Democracy, 7, 17, 76, 85, 88, 127, 173, 181, 182, 185, 195, 196, 198
Democritus, 173, 174
Detienne, Marcel, 2, 12, 13, 101
Diaspora, 23, 40, 113
Dionysus, 28–30, 50, 74–75, 78, 82, 86, 134, 138, 139, 140–143, 148–149, 151, 181
Dodds, E. R., 61, 67
Douglass, Frederick, 131
Doulon polis, "city of slaves," 120, 127

Egypt, 16, 41, 47–48, 91, 92, 100, 134, 136, 137
Ekphrasis, 24, 45, 97–104, 151–152, 161–163
Empire, 8, 18, 123, 126, 188, 192–196
Eos, 51–53
Epimenides, 25–26, 57–71, 136
Espartaco, 1, 23, 27

Eunus, 28, 30
Euripides, 28, 74–75, 83–85, 141, 142, 148, 149
Europe, 6–7

Fast, Howard, 37
Finley, M., 25, 114, 120, 122
Fitzgerald, William, 36
Foucault, Michel, 4, 19, 21, 24, 41–42, 58–59, 154, 159, 182, 191
Francis of Assisi, 194
Freak, 60, 70
Freak show, 58, 68
Freud, S., 19, 22, 80, 92, 157, 164–165, 176

Gandhara, 109–110
Garland-Thomson, Rosemarie, 58
Gellrich, Michelle, 80, 83
Globalization, 1, 5, 19, 89, 126, 185
Goff, Barbara, and D. Simpson, 3, 72
Goheen, R., 85–86
Goldhill, Simon, 2, 78, 97–98
Griffith, M., 89, 180, 181
Félix Guattari. *See* Deleuze, Gilles, and Félix Guattari

Hall, Edith, 88–89
Hardt, Michael, and Antonio Negri, 6, 26, 174, 192–196
Hardwick, Lorna, 4
Hartman, Geoffrey, 160
Havelock, Eric, 173–174
Hegel, G. W. F., 80, 81, 127, 159, 175–177
Hegemony, 25, 76, 101, 113
Heidegger, M., 12, 178–179, 195
Heliopolis, 114, 127
Henrichs, A., 142
Hermon, 118, 120
Herodas, 94–97, 113
Herodotus, 10, 11, 23, 62, 68, 183
Heterotopia, 41–42, 56
Historians, Greek and Chinese, 10–11
Homer, 10, 52, 54, 102, 181
Homeric Hymns: to Hermes, 49; to Aphrodite, 51–52

Index

Homoeroticism, 143, 146–148, 152–155, 175
Huber, Lynn, 152–153, 155

Iamboulos, 105, 120, 121
Ikarios, 140
India, 5–7, 10, 13–14, 26, 65, 108–109, 138
Iraq war, 8
Irigaray, Luce, 179
Isis and Osiris, 91, 102, 141

Jameson, Fredric, 115, 127–129
Japan, 110
Jesus, 26, 35, 39, 81, 130–156; as magician, 136–137
Jones, John, 76, 79–80, 83
Judaism, 130–131, 187
Jullien, F., 11

Koestler, A., 35–36
Kuriyama, Shigeshisa, 17

Lacan, J., 19, 80–81, 88, 160, 176, 177
Leonard, Miriam, 3, 158–160
Levinas, E., 182
Lévi-Strauss, Claude, 160–161, 176
Lloyd, G. E. R., 10–11
Loraux, Nicole, 86–87
Luxemburg, Rosa, 33–34
Lyric poets, 50–51

Magic, 25, 57–58, 60–61, 70, 137–138, 149
Malamoud, C., 13–14
Mandela, Nelson, 4
Marin, Louis, 42, 115
Marseilles, 168
Martin, Richard, 65–67
Martyrs, 133–134
Marx, Karl, 33, 35, 182, 184, 186
Mathews, Thomas, 148–149
McEvilley, T., 65, 111–112
Medicine, Chinese and Greek, 16–17
Memnon, 53, 55
Mesopotamia, 10, 41, 66
Metaphor, 54, 144–145

Miller, P. A., 21
Mimes, 94–97, 111
Montserrat, Dominic, 47–48
Morrissette, Bruce, 161
Mourning, 86–87
Mummies, 47–48, 102

Nagasena, 24, 110–111
Nagy, Gregory, 2, 52
Nazis, 37, 112, 115, 166–167, 187, 191
Negri, Antonio. *See* Hardt, Michael, and Antonio Negri
Nero, 154–155
Nietzsche, F., 9, 22, 25, 75, 142

Ober, Josiah, 173
Oedipus, 7, 26, 80, 82, 157–166, 169–172
Oliensis, Ellen, 22
Onians, R. B., 50
Osiris. *See* Isis and Osiris
Ouologuem, Yambo, 37–38
Ouranopolis, 114, 117–118

Pantera, 143
Pasolini, Pier Paolo, 188
Paul, 137, 138, 145, 147–148, 186–190, 196, 199
Pearcy, L., 8–9, 17
Pederson-Krag, G., 60
Pergamum, 106, 116, 119, 121, 128
Persian, 39, 65, 75, 138
Pharmakos, 82, 83, 159
Plato, 10, 12, 24, 53, 64–65, 78, 110, 111, 115, 124, 125, 133, 149, 150, 159, 170, 173, 175, 182, 184, 195
Plutarch, 27–30, 64, 91, 111, 112, 124
Polybius, 117, 194–195, 196
Postcolonialism, 18–19, 23, 165
Proust, Marcel, 171
Psychoanalysis, 19, 21–23, 26, 58, 116, 157–158, 160, 165, 172, 184
Ptolemies, 92, 100, 102, 103, 113

Questions of King Milinda, 108, 110–111

Rancière, Jacques, 26, 174, 182–186, 189, 191
Reception, 3–4, 26
Religious studies, 130–131
Rhetoric, 25, 54, 144–145, 161–162, 181
Rhizome, 19–21, 25, 172, 195
Robbe-Grillet, Alain, 157–166, 169–172
Rome, 26, 27, 29, 34–35, 117, 118, 120, 125, 130, 138, 148, 153, 188, 190, 192, 193
Rostovtzeff, Mikhail, 93, 126
Rubinsohn, W. Z., 34

Sappho, 5, 7, 24, 25, 40–56, 101, 103, 175; fragment 94, 43; fragment 2. 44–45; fragment 58, 48–50
Sartre, Jean-Paul, 158–159
Scott, J., 29
Secret Gospel of Mark, 146
Segal, Charles, 2, 87–88, 180
Selden, D., 2, 92
Seven Sages, 65–67, 108, 138
Sima Qian, 11
Simenon, Georges, 160, 161, 166–169, 172
Simon Magus, 138
Simpson, D. *See* Goff, Barbara, and D. Simpson
Simpson, O. J., 73
Slater, Phillip, 115–116
Slaves, 7, 25, 26, 104, 107, 126, 128; revolts, 27–31, 93, 115, 185; tattooed, 69, 70, 118, 132; in tragedy, 75, 79, 83–86, 89; torture of, 94–95; in mimes, 94–96; in Theocritus, 99–100; city of, 120–122, 129; in New World, 131; clothing of, 132; in Rome, 132; in Hebrew Bible, 134–135; in Paul, 135, 189
Smith, Morton, 136–137, 142, 143, 146, 147
Socrates, 111–112, 139, 142, 149–150, 151, 159
Solon, 62, 64–65, 185
Sophocles, 54, 75, 80–81, 85–86, 166, 177, 180–181, 189
Soviet Union, 34–36, 126
Sparta, 38–39, 67, 76, 84, 123–124, 128, 173

Spartacist League, 34
Spartacus, 4, 27–39, 186, 199; ballet, 34–35; film, 37; novel, 37
Sphinx, 164, 170
Stoics, 120, 124–125, 127, 133, 149, 154
Strabo, 116–117, 119–120
Suetonius, 154–155
Svenbro, Jesper, 53–54, 67–69

Tattoos, 7, 24, 25, 58, 67–70, 95, 132; of Jesus, 136–137; of Paul, 137
Theban plays, 3
Theocritus, 98, 99–104
Theseus' ship, 112
Thrace, 1
300 (film), 38–39
Thucydides, 10, 11, 86, 178, 193
Tithonus, 40, 51–53
Torture, 94–95, 131–134, 165
Tragedy, 7, 26, 72–90, 180, 181
Trouillot, Michel-Rolph, 26, 32, 114–115, 125, 127
Troy, 83–84, 86

Utopia, 25, 42–43, 70, 106–107, 120, 123–125, 126, 127–129

Vasunia, Phiroze, 2
Vedas, 2, 13–14, 41, 49, 52, 56, 66–67, 91
Vernant, J.-P., 2, 14–15, 22, 25, 77, 78, 82, 87, 159, 181
Vine, 140, 141, 144–146

Wales, 111
Weiss, Peter, 105–107, 116
West, M. L., 2, 40–41, 49
White, Hayden, 184–185
Wilamowitz-Moellendorff, U. von, 20
Winkler, J., 59–60
Wohl, Victoria, 152–153
World literature, 15–16
Wyke, Maria, 36

Xenophon, 69, 86

Zeno, 124–125, 126